Praise for

NO RIGHT
TO REMAIN
SILENT

"A fine work. Roy is a good writer and a good person."
— *The Economist*

"In lucid and often engrossing prose, Roy paints a rich psychological portrait of a student from whom sadness emanated 'like the smell of smoke from a nicotine addict.'"
— *Chronicle of Higher Education*

"Written in the present tense and filled with a poet's mastery of tactile details, her description of these sessions [with Cho] is riveting, balancing sympathy for an anguished soul with horror over his presence. . . . Calm analysis only highlights the urgency of Roy's warning that fundamental problems in American culture need to be addressed lest similar tragedies recur."
— *Kirkus Reviews*

"The book raises important issues regarding the limits of privacy, where a family's duties end and a school's begin, and how likely it is that more rigorous attention could lead to unnecessary suspensions and expulsions."
— *Publishers Weekly*

ALSO BY LUCINDA ROY

FICTION
The Hotel Alleluia
Lady Moses

POETRY
The Humming Birds
Wailing the Dead to Sleep

NO RIGHT
TO REMAIN
SILENT

What We've Learned
from the Tragedy
at Virginia Tech

LUCINDA
ROY

THREE RIVERS PRESS
NEW YORK

Library of Congress Cataloging-in-Publication Data is
available upon request.

ISBN 978-0-307-58770-1

Printed in the United States of America

DESIGN BY BARBARA STURMAN

10 9 8 7 6 5 4 3 2 1

First Paperback Edition

For students and teachers everywhere
That they may learn together in peace

Acknowledgments

My thanks to CARE for helping me find ways to use funds from this book to assist families in Sierra Leone. My thanks also to educational and mental health nonprofit organizations in the United States for helping me find ways to support their endeavors.

My thanks to the faculty, staff, and students at Virginia Tech, who have been my friends and family for the past twenty-three years.

And thanks, as always, to Larry.

Contents

Prologue   1

PART ONE: HORROR STORY   11

1. April   13
2. A Boy Named Loser   30
3. Connecting the Dots   62
4. Prey   86
5. The Panel Review   96

PART TWO: BACKSTORY   113

6. The Setting   115
7. The First Amendment   141
8. Teachers and Students   167
9. Writers and Writing   191
10. Armed and Dangerous   213

PART THREE: DIALOGUE   241

11. Testimony   243
12. Translating Race   259
13. Parents and Children   275
14. The Anniversary   285

Epilogue   292
End Words: A Sestina   301
Recommended Texts and Resources   303
Notes   305
Index   317

You have the right to remain silent. Anything you say can
and will be used against you. . . .

—From the Miranda warning,
mandated by the United States Supreme Court
(Miranda v. Arizona), *1966*

Prologue

O N T H E morning of April 16, 2007, Seung-Hui Cho, wielding two semiautomatic handguns—a 9 mm Glock 19 and a .22-caliber Walther P22—killed thirty-two students and faculty members at Virginia Tech. His first two victims were shot in West Ambler Johnston Residence Hall at approximately 7:15 A.M. The two bodies were discovered by the Virginia Tech Police Department roughly nine minutes later. In the interval between the double homicide and the attack on Norris Hall, Cho went back to his dorm room in Harper Residence Hall to change clothes. At 9:01 A.M., from the downtown Blacksburg Post Office, he mailed a package to NBC and a letter to Virginia Tech's Department of English. Between 9:15 and 9:30 A.M., he chained shut three of the main doors to Norris Hall, attaching bomb threats to them. Cho then proceeded to the second floor where he opened fire. It was the second period of the day and classes had not been suspended, though an e-mail had been sent by the Virginia Tech administration at 9:26 A.M. notifying faculty, staff, and students that there had been a shooting in a dorm. The students who were killed or injured were in classes in Intermediate French, Elementary German, and Advanced Hydrology. A Solid Mechanics class, taught by seventy-six-year-old Holocaust survivor Professor Liviu Librescu, was also attacked, but most of the students escaped when Professor Librescu braced himself against the door and told students to jump out of the second-floor window. Students in a fifth class, Issues in Scientific Computing, successfully barricaded the door, preventing Cho from entering. In roughly eleven minutes, Cho fired approximately 174 rounds of ammunition, returning several times to classrooms he had already attacked. Courageous students and faculty did their best to escape from the barrage of bullets, some risking their own lives to try to save others, but Cho was determined to obliterate everyone he saw. During his murderous rampage in Norris Hall, student Seung-Hui Cho never uttered a word.

THAT MONDAY was one of the most bitterly cold and blustery April days we had seen in Blacksburg for some time. In the 2006–7 academic year, more than twenty-six thousand students had come to Virginia Polytechnic Institute and State University (known simply as "Virginia Tech") to learn. Surrounded by a breathtakingly beautiful 2,600-acre campus in rural southwestern Virginia, it seemed to be a place of abiding tranquillity. Students could learn and teachers could teach here in peace.

Eighteen months before the shootings, while serving as the chair of the English department at Virginia Tech, I worked one-on-one with Seung-Hui Cho after professor and poet Nikki Giovanni asked that he be removed from her class.* During that time, I tried to get him help. When I met with Cho in the fall of 2005, he seemed to acknowledge that he needed to seek assistance to deal with his de-

---

*Throughout this book, I have referred to Seung-Hui Cho using the designation his family requested when interviewed by the media. Rather than adopt the Korean form, which would place the last name, "Cho," in front of his other names, Cho's family elected to adopt the word order that is customary in the United States.

pression. Towards the end of that semester, he repeatedly contacted the Cook Counseling Center, which provides free, on-campus counseling services to students at Virginia Tech. According to *Mass Shootings at Virginia Tech: Report of the Review Panel* (hereinafter referred to as the Panel Report[1]), completed in August 2007 by a panel appointed by Governor Timothy M. Kaine, the response Seung-Hui Cho received was tragically inadequate. Even after he actively sought help, treatment was not administered by the Cook Counseling Center, nor did Cho receive follow-up treatment from on-campus or local counseling services following the order by a judge that he be treated on an outpatient basis. According to the Panel Report, there had been numerous "red flags," but none of them had resulted in a comprehensive evaluation or a coordinated response.

In the wake of the tragedy, the response from faculty, staff, and alumni was remarkable. The town of Blacksburg embraced the university community and helped many of us get through some of the toughest times we have ever known. This was coupled with a tremendous outpouring of sympathy from around the world.

But unfortunately, this story is not simply one of heroism, endurance, and sympathy. It is more complicated and more human than that. It is about what preceded and what followed the tragedy as much as it is about the tragedy itself. It is the story of a university hampered both by its own labyrinthine bureaucracy and by the dogged determination of its administration to protect itself. It is about a system of public education in dire need of reform—one which, in the case of Virginia Tech, resulted in conflicts of interest and a chronic inability to respond swiftly to crisis situations.

Seung-Hui Cho presents us with a series of difficult challenges. The sheer brutality of what occurred is overwhelming. This tragedy forces us to address some of the most pressing issues of our time: education, parenting, violence, youth subcultures, communication, censorship, mental health, gun control, and race. It is hardly surprising, therefore, that the debate has often been explosive. The story, hard as it is to tell, is as relevant to kindergarten through twelfth grade (K–12) as it is to higher education. Teachers at every level and parents of children at every age face similar challenges.

It is vital when we look at a tragedy like this that we rid ourselves of our assumptions and biases before we try to come up with solutions. We need to ask what actually happened. What do we know about Cho and about the culture at Virginia Tech? What do other school shootings teach us about students? What can we learn from teachers, parents, and students themselves? Knee-jerk reactions are not helpful, and silence is less helpful still. We need to be open to the idea that contradiction may lie at the heart of this issue, and that any solutions which do not take this into account will fail.

It is tempting to embark on a quest for the one thing that would have prevented this tragedy, to map the DNA of school shootings so we can avoid them in the future. But although the *how* (the easy interrogative) can be partially solved through investigation, the *why* (the resistant interrogative) is shrouded in mystery. Parts of this story are relatively easy to comprehend. The sequence of events, for example, can be followed through a linear timeline to its terrible culmination. At specific points in time, in specific places, the antagonist's descent into madness can be traced. So the story is the easy part, as telling as a bloody footprint: *He did this, then that, then this again.* We know the story because we witnessed it—part of it was captured on TV, part of it on a student's cell phone, part of it by Cho's own crazed rhetoric. But another aspect of the plot—the *why*—continues to foil us. We are plagued by the perpetrator's silence, for example, and the lack of real dialogue that preceded and followed the tragedy.

In middle school, Cho was diagnosed with *selective mutism,* an anxiety disorder that affects one's ability to speak in certain social situations. After the tragedy it seemed to me that his condition was contagious. It was as if a collective selective mutism had descended upon an administration determined to keep silent in the face of harsh criticism. Terrified of litigation, embroiled in a controversy about the infamous "two-hour delay" in notifying a campus, a president and his advisory team circled the wagons. No one was permitted to interrogate the specifics of the tragedy itself, and there was even resistance to attempts made by Governor Kaine's panel review board to find out what happened.

It is difficult for someone who loves Virginia Tech as I do and who has spent more than twenty years serving it to write about the tragedy and its aftermath effectively. Virginia Tech and Blacksburg have become my home; many of Tech's faculty and staff I think of as my family. The students inspire me, and the campus is one of the most beautiful I have ever seen. I would happily have spent the rest of my life here, but I realize that this book will, in all probability, oblige me to move on. I have had numerous ethical debates with myself about whether or not I should write it. But I have concluded that it is not right to remain silent when you witness something like this, not if you believe your account could help us avoid making similar errors in the future. I do not speak as someone who feels we did everything right at Virginia Tech; rather, I speak as someone who fully appreciates the terrible price we pay when things go wrong. I do not think that all such tragedies can be avoided, but some of them can, and some of them must be prevented if we wish to preserve our way of life.

I am a writer who teaches and a teacher who writes. I am a woman and a mother. I am biracial. My father was Jamaican and my mother was English, something that has helped me understand there are usually two sides to an issue, and each is worth listening to. I have taught in universities and secondary schools in England, Arkansas, Virginia, Massachusetts, and Sierra Leone, and have seen how people who appear to be very different are susceptible to the same kind of horror, and eager for the same type of joy. I have learned that, without open communication, we cannot begin to know each other. Our stories introduce us to each other; they are our penance and our salvation. This is why I have chosen to structure this narrative around the concept of the story, a story that needs to be spoken. I think of it as a "memoir-critique," a way of drawing upon personal experience in order to interrogate myself, others, and the culture that exists at Virginia Tech and elsewhere in education. It is not a perfect approach, but I am hoping it will be a useful one.

All over the United States, and in other countries around the world where the young have entered classrooms as executioners, there are mothers who pray that the term *lockdown* will never apply to their children's schools. There are teachers fearful that a particular child will be off his meds today, and that, as a result, he will be uncontrollable. There are administrators who are worried, too, but the specter of litigation haunts them, and the budget is a mess, and some of them haven't set foot in a classroom for years because they were hired to raise money and don't know much about young people or about learning—which terrifies them because what will they do if they have to confront a disturbed student, a process that is as unfamiliar to them as a space walk? Then there are the counselors, therapists, police officers, and psychologists who know as well as anyone that there are too many troubled young people being funneled through a mental health system that purports to treat them but that does not have the capacity to do so. They understand that something wild is growing in our midst, something untamed and eager, some brooding energy we are afraid to acknowledge.

In April 2007, Virginia Tech joined a terrible fraternity of schools and colleges attacked by shooters. Since 1966, when the University of Texas–Austin Tower massacre shook the nation, most of those who attack schools have been students determined to inflict the greatest pain on their own communities. Some of the killers, however, have been adults, as was the case in the 1996 Dunblane massacre in Scotland, the 2006 Amish school shooting in Lancaster County, Pennsylvania, and a number of other attacks here and elsewhere. The phenomenon of assaults on schools has become global. Since 1989, there have been attacks on schools and universities in the United States, Canada, Scotland, Finland, India, Argentina, Germany, Russia, Denmark, Yemen, the Philippines, and Australia, to name just a few. If we exclude countries mired in poverty or conflict—countries like Iraq and Afghanistan, where, regrettably, attacks on schools are a continuation of the bloody battles in the streets—the United States has the worst record in the world when it comes to school shootings. Most of the perpetrators in these attacks on schools have been male. Some have made a point of singling out female victims; others don't seem to care one way or the other.

There are some who continue to point to the relatively low rate of attacks and believe that those who suggest there are increasing numbers of severely disturbed students are being alarmist. Seung-Hui Cho, Eric Harris, Dylan Klebold, Kip Kinkel, and others, they point out, are anomalies. There is an effort to persuade us that these students appear out of nowhere, rather like F_5 tornadoes. It is true that, even though we lead the industrialized world when it comes to attacks on schools and colleges, student attacks on schools are still relatively rare, and massacres on the scale of the one that occurred in Blacksburg are almost unprecedented. It's also true, however, that a significant number of attacks are being foiled. Nor should we forget that some students who fantasize about attacking a school dream of killing hundreds rather than a handful. We have to admit that it is no longer unusual to hear reports of attacks on schools, and that only those with a high death and injury toll receive wide coverage. We have only to spend a few minutes online to be persuaded that Seung-Hui Cho was not as unique as we like to imagine. There we can find evidence that other young people are just as eager to kill as he was. After attacks on schools, the community is encouraged to believe that effective measures have been taken to safeguard students. But if some young people are regularly telling us online that they are eager to kill, why do we believe that they don't plan to act out their fantasies? Why do we assume that *all* of them are lying?

In spite of the title of this book, I am not suggesting that we dismantle the Constitution or trample people's civil rights. The Miranda warning is an essential part of the justice system and should not be revoked. But currently it is too easy to remain silent. It is what Cho did. It can be a way for us not to respond to urgent questions, a way to hand off problems to other people. The focus on an individual's privacy and confidentiality in higher education is sometimes so exclusive that it can exclude the welfare of everyone else. Often, people who report their concerns are ultimately left to deal with the issue themselves because, even when there are good people around trying their best to offer assistance, the legal, institutional, and personal ramifications associated with intervention are daunting.

Our education system is premised on the belief that students are willing to abide by the rules we establish and that they will seek help when they need it. Yet there are times when those who are mentally ill are not equipped to make a rational choice about such things as medication or counseling. At moments like these, who is morally obliged to intervene? The teacher, the parent, another student, a counselor, law enforcement? And what are the legal ramifications of intervention? In the United States, the legal options in the case of students who exhibit signs of being deeply troubled are less plentiful than we imagine. So we play a game of Russian roulette in education and in mental health, shuffling too many troubled young people through the system, convincing ourselves that no student would be crazy enough to load a gun and point it at someone's head.

Of course, the vast majority of students are good-natured young people who are eager to learn. This fact has inspired me to continue teaching for three decades. Teachers know how to communicate with young people who are responsive and engaged, and are frequently successful at reaching students who are plagued by conditions such as depression. These students are seeking comfort and support, and they welcome help when it is given. Some of the most gifted students I have had the privilege of working with have dealt heroically with mental illness and overcome significant obstacles to achieve success. They have taught me a great deal about courage. In our rush to address this issue, we have to make every attempt not to demonize the mentally ill and others who seem to be "different." For the sake of our children and students, however, we cannot ignore the challenges we face in education—not when there is evidence that a perfect storm is on the horizon, one which, as the tragedy at Virginia Tech demonstrates, we are sorely underprepared to face. It's time to heed the red warning flags waving madly in the wind.

Due to the broad range of issues that need to be addressed, and the fact that this account is grounded in a personal narrative, I have divided the book into three sections. The first section of the book focuses primarily on the tragedy—how it unfolded and its immediate aftermath. The second section is embedded primarily in the past and deals with the "backstory." The third and final section of the book is directed towards the future. It is an exploration of the kinds of dialogue in which we need to engage if we're going to address this issue in a comprehensive and effective fashion. Although I sometimes refer to research on school shootings, the majority of the book is a personal journey. It is my attempt to piece the shards together to try to find out if it is possible to learn from the fractured image that emerges.

For the most part, I have not written about the victims—the thirty-two killed, and the twenty-six or so who were injured.[2] This is not because I believe their stories are less worthy of telling. In fact, the opposite is true. But in a book that focuses on school shootings and troubled students written by someone who knew the shooter, it did not seem appropriate that the victims should have to dwell side by side with the person who murdered or injured them. I hope that by sharing this story I do not cause further distress for the victims and their families.

Causality is supposed to make the plot credible in a tragedy like this one. We are schooled to believe that an act of spontaneous evil is as unlikely as spontaneous combustion; we are trained to search for signs. The arc of the narrative becomes the slippery relationship between time and failure. If there is anything that a teacher is obliged to pass on to her students it is this: a sense of wonder and joy. Slowly, I am locating these again. I try to let my students know that the pen is mightier than the gun, and that life is more compelling than death.

In 2007, the story began like this:

Once there was a small town in Southwest Virginia, one of the most beautiful places in the world. Then, one day, a terrible thing happened. And afterwards we said to each other as people do, "How could this ugliness have happened here, to us?" knowing it would have been easier to bear had it happened elsewhere to other people. And the question spiraled out over the Appalachians; it barreled up the eastern seaboard. It leapt across the ocean to be asked in Tuusula, Finland, then migrated to the Midwest where it became an awful refrain at Northern Illinois before it leapt across the ocean again to Finland. And the lucky ones who weren't in that location said, "How could this ugliness have happened over there, to them?" But in their hearts even the lucky people knew that this unfortunate question belonged to them as well. Because what happened over there could happen anywhere. Because "we" are always "they" in the end.

But this was a large, uncomfortable thought which took up too much room in a world that was always chronically preoccupied. Better to remain silent, people whispered, afraid of attorneys, afraid of the media, afraid of jeopardizing the rights they treasured, afraid of what it would cost. So the thing floated in the air, an ugly hook of a question waiting for something to snag upon it. It hooked other questions so that soon there was a series of them hovering in the air above our heads. And people, when they looked up, saw a necklace of sorts, a noose.

Part One

HORROR STORY

1.

April

THERE IS a terrible moment in *The Collector of Treasures*, a volume of stories by the late Bessie Head, a biracial South African writer. The story is called "The Wind and a Boy." In it, Head writes of a grandmother called Sejosenye who is devastated when she learns of the death of her grandchild, Friedman. Friedman is the pride of Sejosenye's life, her reason for living. A policeman delivers the news of Friedman's death to her: The boy has been knocked off his bicycle by a truck and run over. It is the only time the policeman appears in the story. It is the grandmother's agonized response to the news that has always haunted me. "Can't you return those words back?" she asks him, as if death has no more permanence than an item purchased in a store. Her simple question reverberates with pain. The policeman—the figure of authority to whom Sejosenye appeals—is powerless to comply with her request, much as he may wish to return her beautiful grandson to her. Devastated by her loss, Sejosenye succumbs to death soon afterwards.

There was a terrible moment on CNN on April 16, 2007, when

Virginia Tech police chief Wendell Flinchum confirmed the rumors swirling around the campus. Reporters asked him to approximate how many had been killed: *More than twenty,* he said. The room full of reporters, accustomed though they were to bad news, gasped. I gasped, too. Everything refused to behave normally after that. I believe I sat perfectly still on the sofa for several seconds repeating what he'd said. *More than twenty? Impossible! Can't you return those words back?*

I wanted to rush out of my house and into the street—turn left at the end of the driveway then left again onto Countryside Court, the road that had seemed pretty to me before but which ends in a cul-de-sac (something I should have remembered)—turn right onto North Main and run for two solid miles until I hit the mall—turn right at the chapel where I was married to a VT alumnus thirteen years before—skirt the Drillfield and hurry up the wide stone steps of Burruss Hall and find Chief Flinchum to demand that he *return those words back* to where they came from because how would we bear it if he didn't? How would parents tearing down I-81 in a futile effort to arrive in time to save their children begin to comprehend what had happened? How would they survive without their beautiful sons and daughters who had come to Virginia Tech to learn *in safety* with us?

EARLIER THAT morning, I was sitting in my favorite chair, cradling my cup of tea. The tea was in a mug my husband, Larry, had ordered from some company online. A photo of my former executive assistant, Tammy Shepherd, and me had been glazed into the side. Tammy and I have our arms around each other's shoulders and we're grinning at the camera. We became friends during the four years when I served as chair of English. Tammy helped me wade through budget sheets and annual reports; she was a courageous ally when I was meeting with students who were in distress, insisting that she stay close by with her door open, even when I felt that it may be risky for her to do so. "You don't have a choice," she would tell me. "I'm staying."

I was thinking about that evening's class. That semester, I was teaching my graduate poetry workshop on Mondays from 6:00 P.M. to 8:45 P.M. It had turned out to be one of the most enjoyable and fulfilling classes I had ever taught. Although I was still codirecting the Creative Writing program, I had stepped down from the position of chair of Virginia Tech's English department nearly a year before. Now that I was no longer responsible for overseeing a department of fifty professors, more than fifty instructors, seven classified staff, and dozens of graduate students, I had more time to devote to teaching. We were approaching the end of the semester and I needed to make sure that my comments on the drafts of the student poems were helpful.

Outside the weather was unseasonable—blustery, positively mean. A biting wind whipped the field behind our house, and the grass writhed with such synchronized beauty that it looked as if the entire field were underwater. There were even a few snow flurries. The walk from the car park to Shanks Hall where I taught the graduate workshop would be very chilly. I needed to remember to retrieve my winter coat from the back of the closet.

I had risen early that morning with a sense of foreboding. I knew exactly where it came from: I had been consumed with thoughts about Sierra Leone where I had taught at the age of twenty-one. Larry and I had visited the country at the end of 2006, hoping to form partnerships between Sierra Leone and Virginia Tech. It had been something of a personal pilgrimage. I needed to find out if students I had taught, and a family with whom I had been close, had survived the horrifying civil war. The ghosts from that country—the murdered villagers, the amputees who hobbled through the streets begging for food—populated my nightmares. I refused to accept the fact that, in all likelihood, most of the students I had taught as a young woman had been killed or had died by now. It had been nearly thirty years since then, and I hadn't been much older than they were. The average life span in Sierra Leone even before the war was around forty years old.

In preparation for our trip back to West Africa, I had read first-hand accounts of the slaughter and amputations by rebels, and by children who had been forcibly conscripted into a juvenile army. The horror of what had transpired during a decadelong civil war made the infamous Children's Crusade seem like a day-care excursion. But when we arrived in Sierra Leone we were greeted by some remarkable news: The family I had been close to had survived. All their children, including the one named after me, had survived also. The family had lost one grandchild. And although it looked likely that many of my former students and their families had not survived the war, some were living safely in places like Guinea or Mali, and a few were said to be in the United States. I had celebrated with old friends and promised new friends we met that we would find a way to do something constructive to help with the rebuilding process. I had an obligation to give something back because it was in Sierra Leone that I learned, like so many of Bessie Head's female characters, to find abiding joy in simple things. My African students were the ones who had reminded me how precious education was, and how few people around the world had access to it. I had taught in Sierra Leone for two years as a volunteer in the United Kingdom's VSO program (Voluntary Service Overseas), the British equivalent of the Peace Corps. My Jamaican father had always told my English mother that Africa was home. He was right. In those two years in Sierra Leone I began to comprehend that lasting happiness could be wrung from very little.

Now that I was back in Blacksburg I had to work hard to keep my trip to Sierra Leone in the forefront of my imagination. The contrast between here and there was shocking, and the challenges posed by Sierra Leone's stuttering postwar economy were profound. It was difficult to know how best to partner with a country so impoverished that it lacked the most basic infrastructure. I had promised myself that I would find a way to do it, but I was concerned that I may have bitten off more than I could chew. The country was even less developed than it had been at the end of the seventies: a local currency that was almost worthless, no trustworthy banks or postal system, no credit cards (the banks in the country had been blacklisted because card numbers routed through the financial system were routinely stolen), appalling slums, a wounded populace, and a fragile government. And yet, in spite of all that, the resilience of the people was inspiring, and their friendliness touched me deeply. When I went back there, I had been welcomed like an old friend. Prior to our journey, Larry and I had joined forces with another professor at Virginia Tech, Ed Smith, who came from Sierra Leone. On a trip home himself, he had met us at Lunghi airport when we had visited. Having Ed as a guide made it a much more productive experience than it would otherwise have been. Upon our return to Blacksburg in January, I found solace in the serenity of the mountains and the peacefulness of the small college town. I had the luxury of recharging my batteries at Virginia Tech before returning refreshed to Sierra Leone for another visit.

I turned on CNN, something I have done habitually since 9/11. I was alone in the house. Larry, a computer systems network engineer and a classified staff person in the chemistry department at Virginia Tech, was working in the electronics shop in Davidson Hall. His office cubicle faces the Drillfield, the most recognizable feature of the Tech campus. He has a wonderful view out onto the center of campus at one side of the Drillfield, which functions as both hub and gathering place for students. The huge common area of grass and footpaths is where students throw Frisbees during the warmer months or hurry to class from their dorms located on the other side of the Drillfield from most of the classroom and administrative buildings. Burruss Hall dominates, with its castlelike appearance and its multicolored limestone facade, sitting majestically at the top of an imposing flight of stone steps. This is the seat of Virginia Tech's central administration—where the offices of the president, the provost, the treasurer, the vice presidents, the vice provosts, and other administrators are located.

Suddenly CNN was showing a map of Virginia. It took me a moment to realize that Blacksburg was being highlighted. Something was going on—a shooting incident on campus. Two people had been found dead.

The incident echoed a tragedy we had experienced eight months earlier. The previous August, on the first day of the fall semester, a gunman had been on the loose near campus. William Morva had shot and killed two people—hospital security guard Derrick McFarland on Sunday, August 20, and then, on Monday morning, Deputy Sheriff Eric Sutphin. He had also wounded another deputy sheriff. During that incident the administration had imposed a lockdown. It had been deemed too risky to do business as usual when no one knew exactly where the gunman was. Unaware that a gunman was on the loose, Larry and I had spent part of that August morning on an errand. We hadn't checked our e-mail and so had no idea what was going on. As we had driven along deserted streets we had congratulated ourselves for selecting a time when no one was out and about.

The double homicide committed by William Morva had shaken the close-knit community. Although a crime like this was not unprecedented, it involved a resident who had been educated locally. A lot of people knew the perpetrator, and many knew the victims, so the crime touched a personal chord in the community.

By April 2007, a mere eight months had passed since the Morva shootings; they were still fresh in everyone's mind. Some of those who knew Morva claimed that he hadn't shown any sign of aggressive behavior. Others felt differently, telling reporters that he had made them decidedly uncomfortable. The community responded to the tragedy in the way rural communities do when people in their midst have been harmed. There were benefits for the victims' families and memorial services. In smaller rural communities like Blacksburg and neighboring Christiansburg, each death is personal.

A gunman was on the loose again. It seemed as if we were about to relive what had become known as the "Morva incident." There were alarming reports coming into CNN of students hearing shots and seeing other students leaping from a classroom in Norris Hall. By now it was midmorning, the campus was in lockdown, and there were some horrifying rumors swirling around. Friends who monitored police channels were reporting a death toll that sounded too high to be credible. I reminded myself that people were prone to exaggeration during times of crisis. There had been bomb threats recently that had resulted in the closure of campus. The threats had been left in three different buildings but had turned out to be hoaxes. Maybe these incidents were related.

The first two victims—who had originally been characterized by reporters as victims of "domestic violence" or a "murder-suicide"— had been found in West Ambler Johnston, a residence hall on the other side of the Drillfield from Burruss. The Virginia Tech administration had inexplicably delayed notifying the campus by e-mail of the double homicide, and the fact that a gunman could potentially be on the loose. My heart went out to the families and friends of the two dead students.

I called the English department and spoke with Carolyn Rude, a close friend and the person who succeeded me as department chair in English. I also spoke with Tammy Shepherd, who was now serving as Carolyn's executive assistant. They were both on campus in Shanks and therefore in lockdown. I updated them about what I was hearing on the news. I flicked from CNN to WDBJ-7, the local channel out of Roanoke, which was doing a thorough job of covering the incident and already had reporters on the scene. I asked Tammy to find out if there were English classes being taught over in Norris

Hall. She checked the roster of classes. We were relieved to discover that there didn't seem to be any English faculty or TAs teaching in Norris that morning.

I called Larry. He was, as always, calm. "Don't go outside," I said to him needlessly. "They haven't found the shooter yet." Larry told me he could see the emergency personnel swarming towards Burruss. Ambulances and police cars were everywhere. "Stay away from the window!" I told him, furious that he was close enough to see anything.

The news was contradictory at first. In interviews with reporters, students spoke again of seeing people jumping from the windows of Norris Hall. The anchors on the local and national TV stations seemed to doubt these accounts, seemed to assume that the students were exaggerating. I can't recall the exact moment when I learned that this tragedy wasn't going to duplicate the one that had occurred in August, that it would be a grotesque enlargement of the homicides we'd seen then. But Virginia Tech police chief Wendell Flinchum wasn't the first to say the number twenty, just the first to confirm it. Hearing it from him was what made it real. Friends who had told it to friends who had recited the number to me over the phone could have been wrong. But now it was certain. The scale of the carnage was obscene.

I imagined how hard it must have been for Chief Flinchum to utter that phrase "more than twenty"—quite possibly harder to utter than any words he had uttered in his life. Wendell Flinchum had been promoted to the position of chief of the Virginia Tech Police Department (VTPD) just four months previously, in December 2006, having served in law enforcement for over twenty years. According to an article in the *Roanoke Times*,[1] Flinchum had beaten out ninety-three other applicants for the position. He was described by one colleague, Lieutenant Vince Houston, as having "unbelievable" decision-making skills. "Even in a rushed situation, you know he's always thinking the next step."

I watched Chief Flinchum as he tried to respond to the questions being hurled at him from reporters. I had no doubt that this tragedy would haunt him because it had happened on his watch. Some of those with guardianship responsibilities are able to shake these things off, move on. I felt instinctively that Chief Flinchum was *not* one of those men. The horror of this day would never really leave him. Like many others in the VTPD, he would have died to protect the students.

I continued to make calls to see if people who I thought could have been in Norris were safe, keeping conversations as brief as possible because signals were jammed due to the number of calls being made, and people were having trouble getting through to loved ones. I left a voicemail message for my brother and his family in Nottingham, England. I knew that this news, given the possible scale of the killings, would probably be broadcast in the United Kingdom. I didn't want my family to learn about the shootings from the television as I had. "We're fine," I lied to the machine. "Larry's in lockdown, but he's fine."

I waited for Larry to return. I yearned to hear the sound of the garage door because I knew it would be the most merciful sound I would hear all day. I paced back and forth waiting for his arrival, listening to fragments of news that seemed to come at me like bludgeons, the horror of the disclosure causing my head to ache the way it did after 9/11.

At last he arrived home. He was exiting the car when I rushed into the garage. "More than twenty," I said. He nodded. We held each other.

Throughout that day, the death toll rose. By the time the first responders had counted the dead in Norris Hall, the extent of the tragedy became clear. Not twenty, but more than thirty dead. The Virginia Tech president, Charles W. Steger, reserved and clearly shaken, was right to call it "a tragedy of monumental proportions."

It had taken law enforcement only three minutes to respond

after they received a 911 call from a student in Norris. Even though the three main doors had been chained shut, they quickly found an alternate entry and rushed into Norris Hall. And yet in spite of their swift response, there were dozens killed. The shooter had been ruthless, mowing down everyone in his path, turning classrooms into bloodbaths.

I continued watching TV, switching channels constantly, hoping to glean more information from the broadcasts. Anchors indicated with appalling insensitivity that the victim count would be a number for the record books, as if it were a worthy entry in *Guinness World Records*. There was some confusion about the title the gunman would claim. In those first few hours, it was already being billed as the largest death toll in an attack on a school in the United States until the Bath school disaster in Michigan in 1927 was found to have exceeded it. (The perpetrator in the Bath school disaster had utilized explosives as well as a rifle.) Later on, it became the largest mass murder by a single shooter. Each time I heard anchors and reporters talk about the record-breaking death toll I thought about those who were already titillated by violence and whose fantasies could now include a greater tally than before. The glorification of murder was in full swing. The final tally was thirty-three, including the gunman.

On CNN, a video from a student's cell phone was being played and replayed. The anchors exhorted us to listen carefully. If you did, you could hear the sound of a gun firing, like popcorn popping, a sound so innocent that it became even more sinister by contrast. The cell phone footage showed police surrounding the back of Norris Hall, approaching the building I had walked past a thousand times on my way to class or to a meeting. Law enforcement was breaking into the building from the other side. Usually it is pretty behind Norris—the landscaping crew takes great pride in the campus, especially in the buildings near the Drillfield. But today it looked like someone else's campus. It was like gazing down a well and seeing the image of a place you barely recognized trembling in the water below.

Outside there were flurries of snow. It was not spring in Blacksburg, but winter. The sky was grim. The biting, blustery wind was so strong, they said, that the medical helicopters couldn't land. It was as if nothing, not even the weather, would ever be merciful anymore.

Early that afternoon I had received a call from an editor at the *New York Times*. Would I write an op-ed about how the tragedy had affected the community? It would appear in the next morning's paper. I agreed to do it. Over the years, I have trained myself to write my way through suffering—not to escape it, but instead to attempt to decipher my experience. I hadn't begun to understand the implications of the war in Sierra Leone until I had written a novel about it.

I wrote the op-ed in a single sitting. It took about forty minutes. Then I spent the next couple of hours revising it. As I faxed it to the editor at the *New York Times* I remember thinking, "There, it's done now." Writing it down had forced me to admit the horror to myself. Now there would be time to mourn.

I assumed I would be spending a large part of the rest of my career helping Virginia Tech, its students, staff, and faculty, come to terms with what had happened. This was my community, and I knew and loved dozens of people in it. I was devastated but I wasn't afraid. In fact, thinking that there were things I could do to help with the recovery process was one of the few consolations I had. Virginia Tech would reach out to the families and friends of the victims. We would come together in our grief and comfort each other. Foolishly, now that the worst had happened, I thought I was prepared for what was still to come.

When police revealed that the shooter was an Asian English major, a faculty member suggested to me over the phone that it could have been Seung-Hui Cho. I assured him he was mistaken. I was almost certain that the student I had known as "Seung" had graduated. And besides, I told him, there were many Asian students on campus. I shoved his suggestion to the back of my mind.

But on the morning of April 17, Virginia Tech released his name.

A photo of Cho appeared on TV. And it was only then that I understood the depth of my own ignorance and felt the excruciating pain which comes with that realization.

The brooding young English major, the South Korean student who wanted to be a writer and whose presence seemed to mimic absence, was the one who had killed thirty-two people at Virginia Tech and then committed suicide. Something crumpled inside me. Now that I knew the identity of the shooter, sorrow was shot through with a new kind of anguish.

I had reported my concerns about this student to various units across campus, letting them know that he seemed depressed and angry. I had worked with him myself when it seemed there was no other viable alternative. I had struggled to get him into counseling. Eventually, if what he had told me was true—and now I had no reason to believe that it was—he had contacted the on-campus counseling center. But even if he had been telling me the truth and had sought help, it hadn't made a scrap of difference in the end.

In the first two days following the shootings, I began to learn that Seung-Hui Cho had produced writing more disturbing than the samples I had seen, and much of it had been written after I had stepped down from serving as chair. An example of a play he had written was posted on the Net by someone who had been in a playwriting class with him in the fall of 2006. Had Seung-Hui Cho modified his rhetoric when he had met with me? Why hadn't I realized that he could be the killer before it was officially confirmed that this was the case? I was known to be someone who could make her voice heard, someone people listened to, one of the most vocal people at Virginia Tech. But the efforts I had made had been futile. All those people dead.

I had been on research leave last semester. Had Seung-Hui Cho attempted to see me and found my office door closed? Had he looked for me again this semester, by which time I had mistakenly thought he had graduated? I was desperate for time to digest what had happened.

But there wasn't any time for reflection—no time to think before the next decision needed to be made. An e-mail had been sent to all Virginia Tech employees informing us that anyone who had information about the tragedy should contact the police. I conferred with Carolyn Rude, and we called faculty members in English who had taught Cho and advised them to call the police and let them know that they had taught him. I told them that any material they had about him should be handed over at once to authorities. I had material to hand over myself—e-mails I had written to various units around campus expressing my concern about him, copies of the work he'd shared with me, and the e-mails he himself had sent.

But before I had time to gather much of anything, the phone began to ring. Apart from the hours between 11:00 P.M. and 6:00 A.M., it didn't stop ringing for the next few days.

Reporters from newspapers, television, and radio all wanted to know whether or not it was true that I had tutored Seung-Hui Cho. I was fielding calls from across the United States, the United Kingdom, South Korea, and Canada. Could I confirm that I had warned the administration about him? When I asked them how they had found out about this they told me that my name and the details of my association with Cho had been given to them by a faculty member. I had thought that I had conveyed to those who knew about my contact with Seung-Hui Cho that questions from the media needed to be routed through University Relations, standard practice at the university. But I also realized that the pressure being placed on everyone by the media was intense. I reasoned it was quite possible that University Relations had routed them back to me.

I wasn't sure how to handle the media. I called the office of Larry Hincker, who was associate vice president for University Relations and the university spokesperson. I left an urgent message with his assistant asking for advice. I tried to imagine how I would feel if I had lost a son or daughter in the shootings. I had not been close to those who were killed, though I had, of course, known the person who had murdered them.

The thought of becoming known as Seung-Hui Cho's teacher weighed heavily on me, and I knew I would be obliged to carry this burden for the rest of my life. I would be questioned about it, forced to relive the association. But it seemed to me there was no choice. Having learned about Cho's furtiveness I was sick of secrets. There were those to whom I had appealed who had done their best to assist me. I would explain that their hands had been tied by privacy laws and by Virginia Tech's policies. I would not give out anyone else's name because I knew that would make them vulnerable. Had I known on April 17 as the phone rang off the hook and the reporters hammered on the door that my decision to answer questions would have so many lasting repercussions I would still have felt morally obliged to respond.

There was no word from Larry Hincker's office, and the reporters hadn't let up. I decided it was best to ask the media if they would leave if I responded to their questions all at once, talking with them as a group. I needed to get up to campus, and dodging their questions would mean I had to face them later. My husband ventured outside and asked them if they would be willing to abide by these terms, and they agreed. It didn't take long to speak with them, and those who were present honored our agreement.

Hastily, I put together a file of all the papers I could lay my hands on and hurried to Burruss Hall where the investigation was headquartered.

Larry and I drove to campus, which was heavily guarded. We were stopped by security, but when we said we were Tech employees and were going to hand things over to the police, we were permitted to drive around the Drillfield to Burruss Hall. At the doors of Burruss we were greeted again by security. We were ushered into the president's suite on the second floor where we ran into Provost Mark McNamee and his wife, Carole. Both were clearly devastated by what had happened. We embraced each other.

I noticed out of the corner of my eye that there was a young girl, who I assumed was a student, sitting on one of the sofas in the reception area. She was crying softly. Everyone, it seemed, was crying today. Before I could say anything to her, Larry and I were whisked off down a corridor. I was shown into a room I couldn't recall seeing before—probably someone's office—while Larry waited outside. I handed over my file to the officer. It consisted mostly of a series of e-mails written to people who worked in Student Affairs, the Cook Counseling Center, the College of Liberal Arts and Human Sciences, and the VTPD. I had included any work I could find by Seung-Hui Cho. Because my notes about the student had been copied to a number of people, I told the officer that this material would duplicate other material he would be receiving, or had already received, but I thought it wise to share it with him nevertheless.

The interview was very brief and, to my surprise, the officer didn't have any questions for me, though he did take the file. I asked him if I needed to speak with anyone else, and he said they would call me if they needed to talk to me. I met again with law enforcement on April 23 because I was concerned about a related security issue, but apart from a couple of other instances when I called the FBI to talk about concerns I had about the case, my interactions with them were over. Although it surprised me that they did not have more questions about Cho, I also understood that the FBI, the Bureau of Alcohol, Tobacco, Firearms and Explosives (ATF), and state and local police had thirty-two homicides and one suicide to investigate. The amount of work they would be doing to prepare the campus for the return of the students, faculty, and staff would be enormous. Before I left, I tried to impress upon the officer that I would be more than willing to assist with the investigation in any way possible.

I believe it was later that day when a friend told me that the student who had been crying in President Steger's reception area was blaming herself for what happened. Apparently she had been in a class with Cho and noticed his strange behavior but she hadn't reported it. From that moment on, every time I spoke about what had happened I tried to keep her in mind. She needed to understand that she was not to blame.

Soon afterwards, Nikki Giovanni, a university distinguished professor and faculty member in the English department, came forward and spoke to the media. Once she did, I acknowledged that she had been the professor who had reported her concerns to me about Seung-Hui Cho in October 2005. She had also shared with me a poem of his that she found particularly disturbing. I was grateful to her for stepping forward, and grateful, too, that she had voiced her concerns to me about Cho in the first place. If I hadn't been told that his writing and behavior were troubling, I may not even have realized he was an English major until after the shootings. We have about five hundred majors and around two hundred minors in English, and we serve many thousands of students in other majors. It would have been easy to miss him. Even though my efforts ended up being futile, the fact that Nikki had notified me about his work and behavior had at least given me the opportunity to reiterate my concerns about troubled students, and to try to get Cho into counseling.

It took many days before things calmed down enough for me to begin to take stock of what had happened; weeks before I realized how harsh the penalty would be for speaking out; months more before I had the strength to begin sifting through the horror story he crafted with himself in the starring role.

On April 20, Cho's sister, Sun-Kyung Cho, issued a statement, part of which is excerpted here:

> On behalf of our family, we are so deeply sorry for the devastation my brother has caused. No words can express our sad-

ness that 32 innocent people lost their lives this week in such a terrible, senseless tragedy. We are heartbroken.

We grieve alongside the families, the Virginia Tech community, our State of Virginia, and the rest of the nation. And the world . . .

We are humbled by this darkness. We feel hopeless, helpless and lost. This is someone that I grew up with and loved. Now I feel like I didn't know this person.

We have always been a close, peaceful and loving family. My brother was quiet and reserved, yet struggled to fit in. We never could have envisioned that he was capable of so much violence.

He has made the world weep.[2]

I think of Sun-Kyung and her family. Branded by Cho's actions, they cannot simply grieve; they have to assume the burden he has willed to them. Unable to compete with his Princeton-educated sister in life, Cho has triumphed over her in death. Sun-Kyung Cho will spend much of the rest of her life apologizing for something she did not do.

Her words are so full of anguish that they seem to tremble on the page. I cannot imagine how she will have the strength to carry her grief.

It is October 2005, eighteen months before the mass shootings at Virginia Tech.

The young man called Seung-Hui Cho enters my office in sunglasses and a cap. He sits down and speaks in the softest voice I have ever heard coming from a full-grown man; it is so soft in fact that I have to lean forward to hear him. He has already tried to persuade some of us in the English department that we have misunderstood him—that he isn't angry at all, that we overreacted to the disturbing poem he wrote, a poem he claims was meant to make us laugh.

T. S. Eliot was right: April is the cruelest month.

Bessie Head was right, too: Some things can never be taken back.

2.
A Boy Named Loser

IT COULD be hell trying to get help for a troubled student at Virginia Tech. I had tried to initiate a comprehensive assessment of another student whose work had been very disturbing in the spring of 2005. The entire process had proven to be a nightmare. It was particularly difficult to get help for a student if the primary cause for concern was something he or she had written. Few people in the various support services at Virginia Tech felt qualified to comment on it. I could see why this presented a dilemma: Creative writing and artistic license go hand in hand. What might seem provocative could simply be a testament to a student's vivid imagination. But experienced teachers tend to know when something just doesn't feel right. If there was also something troubling about a student's behavior, I felt that we needed to respond. And as soon as I read the poem that Seung-Hui Cho had written earlier for Nikki Giovanni's class, I realized why she had asked me to look at it. The tone was angry and accusatory, and it appeared to be directed at Nikki and her students.

I followed a series of protocols I had developed during my time as chair. I consulted with trusted colleagues in the department—in this case Professor Fred D'Aguiar, who was serving with me as co-director of Creative Writing, and Cheryl Ruggiero, an instructor who was serving as assistant chair in the Department of English. (Normally, I would also have consulted with Professor Nancy Metz, associate chair of English, but she was on research leave in the fall of 2005.) Fred, Cheryl, and I agreed that Nikki had been absolutely right to be concerned. Seung (the name he wished to go by) had read the poem aloud in class, and although his piece could perhaps be viewed as immature student venting, it could also be interpreted in a more threatening way. I wasn't at all surprised that Nikki's students had been alarmed by it.

On October 18, 2005, I alerted units that dealt with troubled students at Virginia Tech that we had a serious problem. It was the first in a series of e-mails I sent and phone calls I made about Seung. In one of the e-mail notes I characterized what had occurred in this way:

> In the poem he castigates all of the class, accusing them of genocide and cannibalism because they joked about eating snake and other animals. He says he is disgusted with them, and tells them they will all "burn in hell." He read the poem with dark glasses on. . . . His name is Seung-Hui Cho and I had him in my large lecture class last year. The students in Nikki's class have asked for assistance because they are intimidated by him. . . . Nikki no longer feels comfortable teaching the student, and the students have also requested relief. As I understand it . . . I can remove Seung from Nikki's class as long as I offer him a viable alternative. I will be suggesting that he take an Independent Study in lieu of the class, and that he work with either me or Fred D'Aguiar. Nikki, who is never rattled by anything, is genuinely concerned about this student's behavior.

All of those to whom I addressed e-mails were people who had proven to me in the past that they were concerned about student welfare. I was confident that they would do whatever they could to help us. But I also realized it was likely I would hit a brick wall because Virginia Tech's policies prohibited intervention unless a student had made an overt threat or seemed to be an "imminent danger" to himself or others.

I alerted several units at once: the division of Student Affairs, the Cook Counseling Center (CCC), the College of Liberal Arts and Human Sciences (CLAHS), and the Virginia Tech Police Department (VTPD).* It is not uncommon at any large institution for there to be a lack of communication between one unit and another, so I had learned to send out material to several places at once, in hopes that we would then all be on the same page. It wasn't a strategy that was always well received at Virginia Tech where reporting lines can be as rigidly adhered to as papal edicts. Because e-mails can be intercepted or misdirected, I was careful about what I wrote. I could be more frank about the situation in the follow-up phone calls.

I contacted the VTPD for two reasons. Initially when Nikki approached me, she had asked me to look over his work. Soon afterwards, however, she said she wanted him removed from her class. If Seung was as angry as his poem suggested, it was possible we would need to provide Nikki's classroom with security. But Seung agreed to meet with Fred and me instead, so the request for security for Nikki's class was canceled. The second reason I contacted the VTPD was because Nikki had told me Seung had used his cell phone to take photos of students in class—sometimes from under his desk—without asking their permission. I wanted to get advice from the campus police about how to handle this, and find out whether or not it was something we should pursue. The officer with whom I spoke was patient and helpful, but he felt obliged to point out that all students had cell phones, and that no laws had been broken.

---

*I am referring to these departments, colleges, and divisions as "units" because this is the term commonly applied to them at Virginia Tech. Some, like Student Affairs and CLAHS, are really "divisions" or "colleges" composed of multiple departments.

For the initial interview with Seung-Hui Cho, I asked Cheryl Ruggiero to join me in my office and requested that she take notes. Cheryl is a keen observer of human nature. She possesses a knack for sizing up a situation, and she is also a gifted teacher. I thought it better not to meet with Seung alone because of the tone of the e-mail he had sent me when I requested a meeting. His response had been worrying for a number of reasons, not least because it seemed to bear the hallmarks of someone in distress. He wrote that it was obvious he was in a lot of trouble, and that he would agree to "come and get yelled at or whatever you want to do to me." I had not specified why I needed to see him, and I had been surprised by this statement because it suggested that he expected to be verbally abused. I immediately wrote back reassuring him that I would never yell at a student and that I hoped our meeting would be productive.

I recalled seeing Seung's name before. He had been a student in the Intro to Poetry class I had taught in the spring of 2004. I remembered a couple of e-mails he had sent me. I also recalled snippets of his writing. Even though there had been more than 250 students in that class I had required all of the students to submit written responses which I had graded myself. I felt that reading their writing was the only way to know whether or not the students had understood the poetry. I remembered seeing Seung's handwriting because it was small and tight, and sometimes I had difficulty reading it. He came up to me sometimes after class worried about his grade. His language skills weren't good, he told me, would there be an allowance made for that? (I don't believe he used the word *allowance* but that's what he meant.) I said I'd work with him and also told him about the English department's Writing Center, a place where students who need help with writing can receive free tutoring. There are people here to help you, I assured him. At that time, he was majoring in Business Information Systems.

In the Intro to Poetry class, Seung had been an attentive student, as far as I could remember—someone who tried hard but who seemed excessively concerned about his grade. In March 2004, he had sent me an e-mail about a grade he had received on a test. He wanted to know if an F was zero or 59. He wrote, "That's a huge difference between 0 and 59 and I wanted to know where I stand now." I replied by e-mail, telling him that an F was 55 to 59 points, unless a student didn't hand in any work at all, in which case the F would be a zero.

Seung had e-mailed me again in November 2004 asking if I could recommend agents or publishers. He described his novel as "relatively short," about "a young couple going on their silly adventure, sort of like Tom Sawyer except that it's a bit silly in a lot of ways." His final sentence struck me as odd because he had expressed his misgivings about his work in such an explicit way, sounding both very young and very insecure: "I don't know if there's a market or an audience for my writing because it's really silly and pathetic depending on how you look at it, but that's what I'm trying to find out." He did not provide me with his name.

I replied to the anonymous note in a short, two-sentence e-mail: "Could you send me your name? You forgot to sign your note." I wasn't sure whether the student really had forgotten to sign it, but I thought it wise to suggest this as an option because the author seemed to be so sensitive. In response, I received an e-mail that consisted of two words: "Seung Cho." Again, it struck me as odd that he hadn't thought it necessary to preface his message in any way, assuming I would remember the original note.

I checked my class roster and student e-mails because his characterization of his own work in such a negative way had caused me concern. When I realized that he was the same person who had submitted a query about his grade and who had struggled with his English, I felt it would be wise to warn him that it could be very difficult to get published. When I replied, I recommended a book on agents and publishers, but I also advised him to study creative writing if he really wanted to write. I warned him that it was getting as difficult to find an agent as it was to find a publisher. I was concerned that he would submit a novel that was poorly written and be hurt if it were rejected.

Having contacted the various units around campus, it was time to meet with Seung and conduct an initial interview—a procedure I had instituted in English soon after I became chair so I could find out more about students who appeared to be disruptive, at risk, troubled, or even deeply disturbed. I use the term *deeply disturbed* to characterize writing and behavior that seemed to me to merit immediate intervention. The term *troubled* refers to students who seem to be in distress for one reason or another. Many "troubled" students are depressed, anxious about something, or overwhelmed by the pressures of academe. They are not potentially violent students, though, in my experiences, a small minority could wish to harm themselves. *At risk* is a broad term that is applied at some institutions to struggling minority students and those with low grade-point averages. It was not unusual to have a faculty member report that a student was in distress or at risk, but often these alerts were about students who seemed despondent, overwhelmed, or depressed. Angry and disruptive students were less common, though I had been asked by other faculty members to deal with them in the past, so it was not an unprecedented request by any means.

It seemed to me that we were experiencing an increase in the number of students who were suffering from depression or who were furious about something. Some came to the department seeking redress. Although the vast majority of students at Virginia Tech are responsive and polite to their professors, and are a joy to work with, it is not unusual for professors, instructors, and TAs to be confronted by students who feel entitled to higher grades than they have been awarded, or who are not averse to letting their teachers know that they have little respect for them or for the university.

In spite of the fact that I knew it would be very difficult to get help for a student unless he or she had made an explicit threat, I was grateful to the faculty members for their concern. Seeking help for a student was always risky because it usually meant that the student would know who had complained about him or her. Given how angry Seung appeared to be when he wrote the poem, it's quite possible that Nikki's prompt action safeguarded her entire class of undergraduates.

From the beginning of that initial interview on October 19, Cheryl and I realized that Seung was not simply a student who had issues with his poetry professor and his peers in the class. Shyness is common, but Seung was so silent it was alarming. After he had sat down on the sofa in my office, he remained almost completely motionless. At first I thought that he was rigid with fear, but there seemed to be more to it than that.

Seung entered wearing a baseball cap and reflective sunglasses. It took him roughly ten to twenty seconds to respond to questions—an extremely long span of time when you are attempting to converse with someone. Later, when I did an impression of the way he talked so that those with whom I spoke on the phone would understand how extreme his affect was, it was almost impossible to do it without shortening the length of time it took Seung to respond. If I didn't do that, it sounded as though I was exaggerating. The strange thing was that Seung didn't give the impression that he had failed to hear you. In fact, you knew that he had. His face—what you could see of it—registered his understanding, but the urge to reply seemed to be stifled somehow, or he stifled it himself, not willing to reveal anything about who he was.

During the admissions process, no one at Virginia Tech had been notified by Seung, his parents, or his high school that he suffered from *selective mutism*. This condition, previously known as "elective mutism"—a misleading term because it suggests that it is a choice rather than an anxiety disorder—is defined in the *Diagnostic and Statistical Manual of Mental Disorders* (DSM-IV-TR) as a constant failure to speak in specific social situations, despite being able to speak in other situations. (For example, many of those who suffer from this disorder can speak in the home but not at school.) Associated features include shyness and fear of social embarrassment. Those who suffer from selective mutism generally possess normal language skills. It is important to emphasize that this condition has *not* been linked to aggression or violence. Seung's family and school had not revealed his disability to Virginia Tech, nor did Seung himself disclose it, because they did not have to. It was considered a matter of personal privacy.

Over the years, I have adopted a strategy of asking all my students to fill out a questionnaire. One of the questions is this: *Do you have any disabilities which could affect your performance in class?* I then let the students know that the answers will remain confidential. I include this question because, while still a graduate student at the University of Arkansas in Fayetteville in the early 1980s, I taught a student who was struggling with her work. When I met with her she told me that she suffered from severe hearing loss. I asked her if she had informed her other teachers about it and she said that she had not. After this, I always gave students an opportunity to let me know if they needed special accommodation due to a disability. It never seemed to be enough just to mention this on the syllabus, so I devised a questionnaire I administered on the first day of classes. Often, students let me know they needed help. In Seung's case, I had no information from him to indicate that there could be a problem.

Although neither Cheryl nor I knew what to make of his behavior, we tried to make the atmosphere as comfortable as we could. We assumed that speech was very difficult for him and acted accordingly. I gave Seung plenty of time to respond, and we both did what we could to ease the tension in the room. When I asked about the complaint we had received, he said that photography was a "hobby" of his and that he took photos of lots of things. When we asked about the poem he wrote that seemed to be full of anger about his professor and classmates, he said it was a "satire." I tried to explain why unauthorized photos of students are inappropriate, and I asked him if he had written the poem because he was offended by something a classmate had said. In full sentences, which came out slowly and only after great hesitation, he was insistent that all he was doing was making fun of things.

At one point during the interview, I asked Seung to remove his sunglasses. I did so in a way that would allow him to refuse if he had to. I knew it wasn't the kind of thing I could demand of him when it was obvious that all forms of communication were painful. He may have felt exposed if he weren't able to take refuge behind his reflective sunglasses. I knew it was somewhat risky to ask him to remove them, but it was very difficult for me to converse with him when I couldn't see his eyes. I made the request as gently as I could. Very slowly, he removed his sunglasses. There was something about the way he did it that struck both Cheryl and me as being quite shocking—as if he had been asked to do something that violated who he was. I was immediately sorry that I asked him to do it, and I tried to let him know that. I asked him if it had been hard for him to remove them and he shook his head no. I asked him if something had happened to him in the past year because he didn't seem like the student I remembered from the class in the spring of 2004. He said no, nothing had happened. He had told us that he didn't want to lose the credits he needed to earn for the course, and I said I understood that. I asked him if he would be willing to work one-on-one with me and with Fred D'Aguiar. He said he would think about it. I could have insisted then and there that he do so, but I felt that it would not be a good idea. Students who are in distress can become desperate if they feel that they have run out of options.

During the interview, Seung confirmed that he was working on a novel. In my initial e-mail to him when I had asked him to come and see me, I had referred to his fiction writing. I referred to it again and suggested that he and I work on the novel together, if that would be helpful to him, that we didn't have to stick to poetry even though the independent study was meant to be a substitute for the poetry course with Professor Giovanni. He seemed momentarily excited by this idea. His body posture altered slightly, and I believe there was a slight change in his expression.

I asked him about his family and friends, and he said he had a sister, but he wasn't sure what she did for a living. Later, when Cheryl and I discussed our impressions of the meeting, we both agreed that this had been an odd response.

At one point, I asked him if he would be willing to see a counselor over in university counseling services. He said, "Sure." But his response seemed vacant and unenthusiastic—the kind of response someone gives you when they know it's what you want to hear. I said I would provide him with the names of counselors with whom he could work.

When I reread some lines out loud from the poem he wrote, he said he understood why some students would think he was angry. He seemed intent upon convincing us that he was not. I wanted to believe him, but I found it very difficult to do so. Reading the poem out loud had made it seem even angrier than it had seemed on the page.

Seung didn't register much emotion at all as he sat in front of us. He was strangely detached from his surroundings, and his manner seemed ingratiating when he spoke about needing credit for the class, but, at other times, it had an undertone of resentment.

When the interview ended, he got up and headed out. I was determined that he shouldn't leave empty-handed. He had seemed very distressed when he had sat in front of us, and I was genuinely concerned that he could be suicidal. I had worked with suicidal students before, and I had learned to be on the alert for things which could indicate that a student may be desperate. I kept one or two copies of my novels in my office. On occasion, I gave them to students who were trying to write fiction. I hurried after him with it. When I handed it to him I mumbled something about wanting to give him a novel because he wrote fiction, but that he shouldn't feel he had to read it. We stood facing each other in the third-floor corridor of

Shanks Hall for a moment. I shook his hand. He had put his sun-glasses on again, so it was impossible for me to be certain about this, but it appeared to me that he was crying.

I returned to my office. Cheryl and I agreed that we had never experienced anything quite like the interview we had just had with Seung-Hui Cho. There was no doubt in our minds that he was in trouble. He struck us as depressed, even though he denied that he was. Seung had left a sadness in his wake, an echo that seemed to linger after he had gone. As he sat in front of us his loneliness was so palpable it almost seemed as though I could reach out and touch it.

There was something else that bothered us. In this initial inter-view, Seung's voice had rarely been more than a whisper, yet he had apparently read his accusatory poem out loud to the entire class. It didn't make sense. He claimed he was shy, and his behavior when he met with Cheryl and me suggested that he certainly was. But there was a lot more to Seung-Hui Cho than simple shyness.

We were facing an enormous challenge. Seung had not admitted to anything. He was telling us he was fine, that his poem was satiri-cal. He was insisting that we had misinterpreted what he'd written and that he wasn't angry with anyone.

After the initial interview, I e-mailed a summary of my impres-sions of his behavior to contacts in all the aforementioned units on October 19. I elaborated on my concerns in follow-up phone calls. As I wrote at the time:

> Both Cheryl and I are genuinely concerned about him
> because he appeared to be very depressed—though of course
> only a professional could verify that. At one point, when I
> went into the corridor to give him a book, he was near to
> tears. He characterized his piece as a satire. He also said he
> understood why people assumed from the piece that he was
> angry with them. I strongly recommended that he see a
> counselor, and he didn't commit to that one way or the other.

I requested that he get permission from others before taking
their photos in class and he agreed to do so.

Those I contacted knew that I had been very vocal earlier that year
about Virginia Tech's inability to handle troubled students, but they
made it clear to me that I would not be able to compel Seung to see a
counselor. I was obliged to find him an "equivalent academic experience," i.e., transfer him to another class since the fall semester was
only about halfway through.

Without viable options, I volunteered to work with Seung myself. If he needed to receive counseling (and everyone seemed to
agree that he did), and if I was prohibited from requiring him to get
it, then someone had to try to persuade him to do so. Fred D'Aguiar
kindly agreed to meet with Seung also, and was able to do so once
later that semester. It was a gesture I deeply appreciated because I
was already working very long hours. I sent an e-mail to Nikki to
keep her apprised of the situation.

Cheryl and Tammy were adamant that they needed to be in their
offices when I met with troubled students so that I could call upon
them if necessary. They both insisted that they would be around
when I next met with Seung.

Because my concern about angry and troubled students had increased during the period when I served as chair, I had asked Dr.
Robert Miller, who was serving as director of the CCC at that time,
to come to the department during the annual staff retreat and speak
about how to handle students who are angry. We had seen a number
of instances where students showed up in administrative offices enraged about a grade or about the fact that they could not get into
classes they needed. One of the things we had done as a follow-up to
the session we had with Dr. Miller was to implement a code that
could be used to alert each other to the fact that we needed help. The
code we chose was "Ed Tucker," the name of a beloved professor

who had died not long before, and who would have rushed to our aid had we called upon him to do so. If any of us said, "I need to see Ed Tucker," it was the signal to call security.

Two days after our initial session with him, Seung sent me a long e-mail. He agreed to meet with Fred and me—something that relieved me greatly. (By then, Nikki had let me know that she did not want him to return to her class, so I would have had to remove him, even if he hadn't wanted to go.) Seung then launched into a long defense of the poem he had submitted to Nikki's class. He compared it to Jonathan Swift's "A Modest Proposal," the famous satire in which Irish infants are roasted and consumed by the English. A blistering commentary designed to shame the English into an understanding of their savage treatment of the Irish peasantry, it has become a standard text in English classes. He insisted that his work was satirical and that the class was overreacting. "[The poem] was supposed to be ha-ha," he said. "I had no anger when I wrote it." He repeated the word *sorry* three times at the end of the note. At times he went off on tangents before he wrenched himself back to his primary concern: the fact that he had been wrongfully accused. The e-mail was two single-spaced pages in length, and it had obviously taken him a long time to craft. It contrasted sharply with the silent person who had shown up for the initial interview. Again, the tone of the note worried me. I therefore forwarded it to the units I had first contacted. By this time I had agreed to meet with him one-on-one, but I was not comfortable with the arrangement, something I made abundantly clear when I spoke with a counselor at the CCC.

In one of the follow-up phone calls I made to support units after the initial interview with Seung, someone asked me if he seemed like someone who had been abused. I said that it seemed probable to me that he had been. But I also said it was impossible for me to know for certain and reiterated again why he needed to be evaluated by counseling services. I believe I was reluctant to commit to a single "diagnosis," not just because I was not trained in this area but also because it seemed to me that Seung-Hui Cho was many things in 2005, and most of these things were contradictory. When he looked at me sometimes it seemed as though there was a startling cruelty in his expression; at other times, however, he looked at me with a kind of gentleness. I realize that this suggestion of gentleness seems unlikely, even offensive given the horror of April, but it was there. I saw it. Sometimes I wish I hadn't.

I have experienced a lot in my life, including several robberies when I lived in Sierra Leone, one of which was carried out by intruders armed with machetes, but I didn't relish the idea of meeting one-on-one with students who could be unstable. It was a catch-22 situation: put Seung-Hui Cho in another class and lie awake at night worrying, or meet with him myself and lie awake at night worrying. I chose the latter.

One day, as I sat in my office in Shanks Hall thinking about having to meet with Seung, I was again struck by the absurdity of a policy that prohibited me from getting help for him and for other troubled students. In this case, we were obliged to teach Seung, judge whether or not he was unstable, and persuade him to go to counseling. Even though I knew I had exhausted all the possibilities, I decided to make a stab at persuading counseling services to evaluate him. I was hoping it would be possible for them to come over and meet Seung. It would only take a couple of minutes for them to recognize that there was an urgent problem.

I was put through to one of the counselors. I explained why the current policy placed students, faculty, and staff in jeopardy. I said it was ridiculous that Virginia Tech expected me and others to meet with students who had indicated through their work or their behavior that they had the potential to be violent. I wanted to require Seung to see a counselor. Weren't there times when students were unable to ask for help even though they might need it? I asked.

The counselor reiterated the rules, letting me know that intervention by counseling services in this case was impossible, that Virginia

Tech policies did not allow counseling services to treat students unless they went to the CCC voluntarily. I pleaded with her to come over to Shanks herself so that she could meet him with me and see why we were so concerned. She told me she had no intention of coming over to Shanks. I protested again, telling her I lacked the training to work with him and that the university had no right to expect me to do it. The argument did not sway her, however.

Though this refusal to intercede by counseling services had been delivered in a much harsher fashion than usual, the response did not surprise me. I reminded myself that people were as overworked in counseling services as we were in the English department. With only a handful of counselors for twenty-six thousand students, they were pushed to the limit. There was no avoiding it. I would have to convince Seung to see a counselor.

At least there was one consolation. If he did show up at the CCC, they would certainly take him seriously because he had been flagged. Several people over there, including Bob Miller—someone who had been helpful in the past—were aware of his writing and his behavior. There had only been one other occasion when I had been as insistent as this about needing help with a particular student, so counseling services would know that this was important. If Seung-Hui Cho called over to the CCC or stopped by for an appointment, I assumed he would be seen at once. All I had to do was persuade him that he needed help.

IT IS the fall of 2005 when Seung-Hui Cho enters my office in 303 Shanks Hall. Southwest Virginia is awash in orange and maroon. We Hokies claim that fall proves that God is a Hokie because the trees wear Virginia Tech's colors. It's hard to believe we're wrong when you look at the blazing orange and maroon leaves that adorn the trees in this part of Virginia in autumn. The season seems appropriate. I am winding down from serving as chair. Time to let go of things. I've been worrying too much about everything. Just seven short months to go before I'm done. One of the hardest tasks has been dealing with troubled students, and Seung-Hui Cho has proven to be one of the most challenging students I've faced in twenty-eight years of teaching. By this time, Seung has met once with me and the assistant chair, once with Fred D'Aguiar, and several times with me alone—though I can't recall the exact number of sessions we have had alone together; they all seem to run together. It is still apparent to me that he needs help. By the end of my sessions with him my energy is completely drained, and, sometimes, it is hard to know if we have made any real progress at all. He answers my questions in a whisper; it is so painful for him to speak that his responses seem to be a form of torture. I'm not yet convinced that he has called over to the on-campus counseling center. His responses to my questions about counseling have been vague, noncommittal. Even if he has called over, as he indicated he would in the initial interview, I won't be told about it. Faculty who refer students to counseling are usually not permitted to know whether a student has sought help.

As usual for our meeting today, Seung is wearing a baseball cap and sunglasses. When we had our first session together, I asked him how I should address him several times because I was aware of the Korean tradition of putting last names first. He told me he wanted to be called "Seung," not "Seung-Hui" or "Cho." He was insistent about it.

I rise when he enters. He seems tall to me, but then most people do because I'm only five-foot-two. I feel more in control of the situation when I'm standing up. It also means I can escape quickly if necessary. When he sits down I'm trapped. It's as though my office is a hammock, stretched downward in the center where he sits as heavy as lead. I would have to leap over him to get to an exit.

I have dealt with angry people many times in my life and I have learned to rely on my voice in tricky situations. My British accent and my language skills have served me well in the past. It's possible to deflect all sorts of things with wit and humor, to radically alter the mood in the room; it is possible to use your own voice to articulate something on behalf of someone else. I have no choice but to rely upon that skill now, though I am painfully aware of its limitations.

Each time he walks into my office, I am seized with the desire to fill the void he creates. There is something melodramatic about his entrance. He knows what impression he is creating and it seems to give him satisfaction. As a result, I talk a lot. It is partly nerves, but it's also because I want him to grow accustomed to my voice. Sometimes it's like talking to an inanimate object with limbs and an attitude. The core of his identity is impenetrable, his gaze strangely neutered, as if he has spent his entire life ridding it of expression.

At first, I don't think he's listening. But gradually I learn I am wrong—he has been paying very close attention from the beginning. I know this because, every so often, he will relay back to me things I told him, things he learned in the poetry class he took with me eighteen months ago. He remembers the poems we studied by Emily Dickinson, William Shakespeare, James Wright, Mary Oliver, and Robert Hayden. He remembers the poetic forms and techniques we talked about.

He aches to write fiction, but I know he is not ready to write the novel he seems to dream about because there is a part of him that appears to be profoundly immature. In the middle of his deliberate stillness there is an urgency that refuses to be patient. His egotism and insecurity create a dangerous combination because then he can ridicule everything that intimidates him. It is a character combination that is essentially dismissive of others. He is uncomfortable when challenged about his ideas, and yet he seems to yearn to be challenged, hoping that someone will topple the despair that colors what he sees.

Seung doesn't seem to be as resentful as he was when we had our very first meeting together—he doesn't shuffle in and sit down on the chair like someone who is daring you to find fault with him. His hands tremble once in a while even though he's used to me by now.

I'm nervous myself—I always am at the beginning of our sessions—but I need to focus on the student in front of me. I need to have my wits about me when I meet with him because the indicators he gives me about who he is are few and far between. I have spoken with him before about my own shyness—explained how I used to be physically sick before I had to make a presentation, told him about the stutter I have that can disappear for weeks, months even, then reappear when I least expect it to. His expression registers surprise at this disclosure—as if it hadn't occurred to him that I could suffer from a lack of confidence. When we speak about things like this, he will answer in full sentences, though still softly.

His sunglasses appear to be an important part of his identity, and now that I have come to understand this, I am even more careful when I ask him to remove them. I let him know that I would like to see his eyes but that we can still talk even if he doesn't comply. I am relieved when he does so without much hesitation or discomfort.

He still seems wary of me at times—as if he expects me to hurt him. Once in a while I see a flicker of what seems to be anger or resentment, but this passes quickly and has become rare. Sometimes, when we're writing together, he almost cowers in his chair; at other times, especially in the first few minutes of a session, he is utterly still and wears a sullen, defiant expression.

Mine is a corner office—one of the few perks I receive for serving as chair. It's fairly spacious as faculty offices go, measuring roughly fourteen by fourteen, but when Seung-Hui Cho enters, the room seems to shrink to the size of a cubicle, not because he is a particularly large person but because there is something about him that sucks up space and brings you into closer proximity with him. He has the capacity to drain energy from a room, calling attention to himself through his studied silence.

During the first session we had alone together there were few words. It was extremely difficult to know what to make of him, and I was not surprised that he was able to intimidate people. His silence seems, at times, to be cultivated—an affectation of sorts. Perhaps because of this it has the capacity to turn itself into its opposite, to become a kind of muffled scream.

If I were to paint a portrait of Seung-Hui Cho as he sits opposite me it would be not so much a portrait as a still life. At first glance, he would appear to be more absence than presence. The figure in the center of the canvas would seem to float in negative space. The face would be bereft of expression—just a pair of sunglasses fused to rock, the faces of those of us who happened to be caught in his sight distorted then reflected back at us. The presence wouldn't be mocking because mockery suggests some kind of ironic connection between subject and object, some kind of communion. Instead, the presence would be supremely, utterly indifferent, his gaze as "blank and pitiless" as the one described by Yeats in his haunting poem "The Second Coming." But here's the catch: Looking at the painting you would be filled with an indefinable sorrow because you would suspect that it was impossible for the subject to penetrate his own darkness.

At times it feels as if his silence is being used to intimidate. Then there are other times when it seems to be about something else. Silence is complicated and it can take many forms. It can be a testament to agony. The void it creates yearns to be filled with something human and humane—compassion, recognition, validation—the kinds of things we as parents and teachers are trained to offer. Though the people afflicted with this first type of silence may be full of self-loathing, though they may wish to tear at their own flesh, this type of silence isn't fueled by vengeance. But there is also another kind of silence—affliction's perverted first cousin. This other, more surreptitious form is the same brand of silence in the abusive father's pause before he beats his child; it's the form of silence that fury and indifference beget—a silence that refuses to interrogate itself because it is composed of absolutes. It is a particularly dangerous kind of silence because at its heart is a stunning lack of empathic imagination—the inability to see things from another person's point of view.

His solitariness troubles me deeply, as does the fact that he rarely laughs or even smiles. He doesn't appear to be able to locate a place of joy in himself or his surroundings, but I am convinced that his writing means a great deal to him, which is one of the reasons I am careful when I respond to it.

Seung is looking up at me—something he does now more often than before. I keep getting the sense that he wants to tell me something, but he seems to find it impossible to do so. We have only been able to meet occasionally because of my hectic schedule, so each session lasts at least an hour, sometimes an hour and a half—a long time to spend one-on-one with someone as hard to communicate with as he is. I try not to keep track of the time because it makes the minutes pass by even more slowly. A single minute can stretch out interminably when I am alone with him—multiply that by sixty or ninety and it helps to explain why I feel almost sick as the time for our session approaches.

It's not simply that Seung seems to be so depressed; it is his anger that troubles me, particularly when I am never sure how he will react to my suggestions that he seek counseling. I am aware of the fact that, in some cultures, admitting you need to see a counselor can be viewed as weakness and can therefore be offensive, especially to young men. But I keep suggesting this option because I am convinced that he needs help.

There are times when I feel that we may be getting somewhere, when he volunteers information, for example, or when he seems to be faintly amused by a joke or a story I have told him. But his problems seem so acute to me that it is almost impossible to tell for certain. Still, I feel as though we are making some progress today. He doesn't turn away as he used to, but sometimes he gives me a look so full of pain that I am not sure what to do with it.

I prepare for my sessions with Seung because I know he may be unwilling, or perhaps unable, to talk much. I try to coax him towards speech because it's obviously an excruciating process. I never criticize him for taking so long to respond to my questions because I fear it would cause him to clam up even more. The night before we meet, I review any work he has handed in, select poems I think we should look at together, try to see if I can build links between the work we read in the Intro to Poetry class and the poetry he is currently working on, and brainstorm about other issues we can discuss. There is one overarching goal I have that eclipses all the others: persuading him to go to counseling services. I pursue this theme doggedly—my constant refrain. I try talking with him about how helpful therapy can be. I try to tell him that all of us encounter difficulties that can make us feel hopeless. I talk about periods in my own life when I was lonely, homesick, or afraid.

One of the techniques I use to help students who have difficulty with writing is to cowrite work with them. Seung and I are writing a poem together, but it is a difficult process. I hope it will help me understand him better. The poem's title is "Seung," a title he chose, I believe—certainly one he agreed to.

I ask him to describe himself. After many long pauses and follow-up questions, he calls himself a "secret." In response to my question about what makes him who he is, he tells me he is covered, silent, waiting. I ask him what he is waiting for. He shrugs. "I don't know," he says. He tells me he's so focused that it hurts him. It is a spontaneous offering—a sentence unexpectedly given. I write it down, make it a line in the poem.

There is something about his attitude as we do this that makes me realize he has rarely worked collaboratively. He seems to be excited and nervous about the process, waiting for me to snag him somehow, criticize his use of English, mock his grammar. But I have tried to tell him that writing isn't about that—that grammar and perfect syntax aren't nearly as important as what is being said. He appears to be greatly relieved. After that, he has been willing—eager at times—to share his work.

Today he comes up with three adjectives when I ask him for

modifiers that apply to him: *unkempt, sad, solemn,* he says with great solemnity. The first and last of these surprise me, but the middle one has been patently obvious from the start. Sadness emanates from him like the smell of smoke from a nicotine addict. There is nothing unkempt about him, however. In fact, he is religiously neat when he visits my office, as if he believes that carelessness is a cardinal sin. That he thinks of himself as solemn is surprising to me because the word is weighty and suggestive. It's the kind of word you associate with religious ritual. He has indicated that he is religious. That was why the words of other students in Professor Giovanni's class offended him so much, he explains. He has a marked intolerance of difference even though he recognizes his own difference and seems to want others to be tolerant of it. He does not seem to feel there is anything paradoxical about this.

He takes off his baseball cap. There is still something disconcerting about seeing his face exposed. He looks like a little boy and a grown man at once. He has beautiful Korean features, but his expression seems to distort them somehow. I recall that, in the spring of 2004, when he was a student in my Intro to Poetry class, he didn't always hide behind sunglasses and a hat. I wonder what has happened to him since that time.

Seung's voice is still unnaturally quiet—almost sinister—though he speaks more often in full sentences and will occasionally elaborate on things. He tells me the story of a teacher he had in high school who he says was snorting coke. The poem he wrote about this is one we look at again. It is relentlessly accusatory. The girl in the poem is the person he cannot forgive. It's a poem about being mocked in class, and it seems to come from a place he usually keeps hidden. We talk about the girl in the poem—how she is portrayed. I tell him that it seems to me that he's turned her into a caricature, refused to see her as a person. I tell him that the teacher is drawn in such a way that he loses credibility. I try to talk with him about empathy, though it seems that his own pain is preventing him from acknowledging the pain of others. He agrees to rewrite his poem. Which brings us back to the recurring theme of our sessions.

I offer to go with him to counseling services. I tell him again that it's free to students and that counseling can help him. I tell him not to be afraid. I use those words now and he is not offended. Some weeks ago, however, when we met for the first time alone, he looked at me with such hatred that I thought he wanted to kill me. I wanted to get up and run as fast as I could, but I was the chair. I had no right to leave him there. I asked him if he was angry. He'd shaken his head no. I hadn't believed him because his body language seemed to counter his claim, just as it had when Cheryl and I had spoken to him during our first interview.

Even though he appears to be more at ease with me now, I glance at his backpack. When he enters, he has a way of slinging it off of his shoulder and planting it at his feet in a gesture that seems designed to intimidate, though perhaps this is because he rarely moves his body at all during our sessions, so any movement strikes me as worrisome. I have trained myself to glance down to see if there is anything odd-shaped in his backpack—anything that can conceivably hurt me. Although guns are banned on campus—a courageous move on the part of President Steger and the university spokesperson Larry Hincker, one that resulted in a torrent of hate mail from gun rights supporters—there isn't really anything to prevent students from bringing weapons to school. People wander in and out of buildings and security is lax. Tech is a land-grant university that prides itself on its open access—anyone can drop by at any time.

We are still working on the poem whose title is "Seung." I ask him what his favorite colors are.

"Olive," he says, "olive green, gray, and black."

He infers that he doesn't wish to stand out, that he likes to go by unnoticed—I don't recall his exact words. Olive seems like a strange choice to me until I remember that it is used for camouflage and so aligns itself with the word *secret*.

Sometimes he looks at me as though he is trying to focus through a migraine. He squints a little, seems to be in pain. We talk about other things. It seems to relieve the pressure on his face.

When the poem is finished I read it back to him. I read it slowly then ask if he wants to hear it again. He does. I read it one more time. It is only a few lines long—formed from his answers to my questions: *Who are you? What do people see when they look at you? What do you see? Why the dark glasses? What adjectives describe you? What are your favorite colors? What are you yearning for?*

He answers the last question because I have told him what I yearn for myself. I tell him about the dream I have of returning to Sierra Leone, that I had planned to go sooner but serving as chair has dominated my life for the past three years. I probably make my usual weak joke and say that I'm hoping to be promoted from "chair" to "table" one day. I tell him that it grieves me tremendously to have done so little to help the people of Sierra Leone because the suffering there is extreme. I feel I have let them down.

There are times when I think he will be offended by the questions I ask him because they are so direct, so I try to take my cues from his body language and expressions, such as they are. For some reason—perhaps because he trusts me more than he used to—he doesn't seem to mind. I realize that the fact that we are both immigrants is significant to him. We talk for some time about what it's like to be an outsider. He seems to be particularly animated when we discuss what it feels like to be lonely and a long way from home. I try to let him know that I believe he has potential because I believe he does, but I also try to impress upon him that writing takes a lot of hard work. I give him book recommendations. I tell him that there have been times in my life (when my mother died, for example) when I have been so full of sorrow that I have hardly been able to get out of bed. I tell him about my childhood, about my homesickness for England. I tell him I miss my mother, who died in 1992, robbing me of my best friend—how lonely I was when I first moved to the United States, but how much I have grown to love it here. I tell him that this kind of loneliness, this kind of yearning can pass.

I read him poetry. If memory serves, I read him a beautiful poem by Gwendolyn Brooks. It's called "To the Young Who Want to Die," and it exhorts young people not to give in to their own negative impulses. Green is their color, Brooks writes, they are "Spring." The poem is a glorious affirmation of life.

Seung nods when I ask if he is lonely, shakes his head when I ask if he has any friends. I go down the list.

"What about roommates?" I ask him.

He tells me a little about them.

"What about other students from Korea, do you know them?" I believe he nods.

"Do you hang out with them?"

He shakes his head.

"Why not?" I remember asking him.

"Nothing in common" is what I think he says, though I'm not sure if this is his exact response because he mumbles. He does indicate that it is hard for him to make friends.

Later, we talk about families. I tell him about mine, and he tells me a little about his. He says there are times when he finds it difficult to talk to them and that he doesn't speak with them much.

At one point I say that it seems as if he is someone who has been hurt very much by something or by someone. I do not use the word *abused*, though I am thinking it. He indicates that it's true—he has been hurt. Very much. It seems that he is about to cry, trying hard not to do so. The effort is excruciating to witness.

"Let me take you over to counseling now, Seung," I say. "They can help you."

I explain again why going to see a counselor takes courage—why it is often the thing that allows you to climb out of holes you may be living inside. It's something I've said to dozens of students over the years, some of whom have been suicidal. He nods, then tells me what I've been waiting to hear: He is seeing someone over there. He is seeing a counselor.

It's not clear whether or not he has seen one already or has simply made an appointment to do so, but I am so relieved that it's hard not to jump up and down with joy. He has refused to respond with any degree of enthusiasm to this question before, saying only that he'll think about it, or he avoids an intelligible response altogether.

But I am still not satisfied. Perhaps he is just so sick of my badgering him that he is making it all up. Even as I urge him to go over to counseling services I am worried that he will discover that I have already shared his work and my impressions of him with them. It could seem like a betrayal. I have to trust that the counselors will not disclose to him exactly what I have shared with them. I allow myself to think, perhaps, that his story will turn out better than I imagined, that depression will not make him suicidal, and that he will find a way to relate to other people at last.

We have gone over our allotted time and it is getting late. I have hours of work to do before I can crawl home at nine or ten at night. In response to my question, he confirms yet again that yes, he is going to counseling. He doesn't seem angry. I think I see a hint of determination in him. I tell him once more that, if he ever wants me to go with him, he can call or e-mail me. Tammy knows that he is my student, so his calls will be prioritized and put straight through to me.

Then he asks me out of the blue, "Will you read something if I give it to you?"

It's a difficult question to answer. I want to say no because I'm so bloody exhausted and so desperate to write and paint again that the last thing I want to do is read work by a troubled student who is now a burden I feel obliged to carry—worried that if I acquiesce it could mean that there will never be a time when I don't have to respond to him. But I have to say yes because of the way he asks, bracing himself for impact, like someone who expects to be hit. I have to tell him yes because, if you are the teacher of a troubled student once, to some extent, you always are. It's a pact you make with yourself. I will read his novel if he gets it to me in time.

We have finished now. I am reluctant to remind him that our time is up because it seems to me that he doesn't wish to leave, but I have mountains of work to do.

I realize that I won't have a copy of "Seung," the poem we have worked on together, unless I make one. I ask him if I can make a copy for myself.

"Sure," he says, sounding very American to my ears. He has attempted casualness before, but he can never quite pull it off.

I step out of my office, pass through Tammy's office, and go into the copy room. I make myself a copy and walk back. I hand him the original.

The semester is over. It is the last time I ever see Seung-Hui Cho.

SEUNG GAVE me the fragment of his novel framed by two poems at the end of the semester. It arrived after the deadline I had given him, but I wrote him saying I would still read and comment on it. I would have to do so over the December break. In January I re-turned it to him. I wrote a page of comments, placed it inside an envelope, and taped the envelope to my office door. I sent him an e-mail to let him know that I'd had a chance to read it and that I had written my comments on his copy. The novel disappeared from my door not long afterwards. I never heard directly from him again.

The novel, it emerged, had been rejected by a publisher.[1] It was framed by two poems, the first of which was entitled "a boy named LOSER" and was written in a complex, prescribed form known as a *sestina*.

Sestinas are composed of six six-line stanzas with the same six end-words repeated in a different order at the end of each line, fol-lowed by a final three-line stanza, or "envoy." In the envoy, all six end-words reappear, two per line. Each end-word, therefore, has to appear at least seven times. In Seung's poem, the word *loser* is repeated fourteen times and capitalized each time. His sestina was about someone trapped in a world where he cannot succeed. Because of this, he is forced to live in a dream world.

According to some poets, the sestina form has a magical quality. When you diagram the relationship between the end-words, the result is a hexagonal, star-shaped structure. In *The Discovery of Poetry*, Frances Mayes visually depicts the relationship between the lines of the sestina, in the process diagramming a beautiful, caged star. Like others before her, Mayes suggests that sestinas may have been used in the early twelfth century when the number six had mystical connotations.

Seung's sestina isn't a particularly accomplished use of the form; his poem tends towards mere repetition rather than accumulated meaning. In other words, the six end-words function as cul-de-sacs rather than resonant catalysts that force us to reassess their meaning each time they appear. Instead of the voice of the reflective poet, you hear the voice of the child banging on the table demanding to be heard, the voice of the lost boy who fears he is nothing but a "loser," has always feared it, but is desperate to be persuaded otherwise. The sestina may well have been written earlier for another class, or he may have written it when we looked at poetic form in Intro to Poetry. Either way, he positioned it in the manuscript to function as an introduction to his novel excerpt. He saw it as significant.

The six end-words he chose were *LOSER, house, dream, lives, life,* and *world.* The boy in the poem is disgusted with himself and his surroundings. He daydreams, regrets not having a life. An intense loneliness permeates the poem, but it is also similar to the kinds of poems young writers often produce in which they see themselves as isolated from the rest of humanity. One of the remarkable things about it, however, is how insistent his despair seems to be. The word *LOSER* takes over in the poem leaving little room for anything else. The final line would almost be funny if you didn't recognize the agony behind it. The sestina ends with the phrase *"My Gawd! What a LOSER!"* The phrase is italicized, as if someone else is uttering it, or to indicate that it needs to be said with particular emphasis. The spelling signals that the speaker is American. When I read it I recalled that there had been times when it seemed as though what he was saying about himself was what he had heard said about him over and over again. Rather than being an original utterance from his own mouth, his expressions of self-loathing seem to be a reconstitution of actual dialogue.

The fiction itself is, for the most part, adolescent and predictable. The story seems to be a kind of romance between two characters, but their names ("Spanky" is the male character, "Jelly" is the female one, characters who appear—I learned after the shootings—in his other writings) are vaguely troubling and suggestive. The relationship he depicts, however, is surprisingly tender at times—the kind of relationship a thirteen- or fourteen-year-old could have with someone he has a crush on. The girl adores the boy, but throughout the story you get the sense that this is fantasy, and that none of it is really happening.

Spanky takes pills so he can feel better and rid himself of a headache. At one point, Jelly almost bumps into the boy who is waiting outside for her as she leaves the room. It seems that the word Seung-Hui Cho was looking for when his characters collide with each other was "Whoa!"—the kind of thing you say when something surprises you. He had misspelled it, however, and the word Jelly utters instead is "Woe," W-o-e.

Jelly is a flirt who seems to be toying with him. Spanky is shy, moral to the point of priggishness, while Jelly is seductive. Even though, as she points out, they are both nineteen, Spanky suggests that they go to the playground to play. When they get there the girl sees him looking out over the landscape. The boy says it would be fun to spy on people, and the girl asks him if that's what he does in his spare time. He denies it and changes the subject. Later, she mockingly calls him a loser, though she doesn't seem to be serious. The entire novel excerpt has a fragile, dreamlike quality. You sense that nothing is real in this world, that, at any moment, it can disappear.

Towards the end of the excerpt, there is a description that is far more vivid than anything else in the story. The sun is shining down on the couple. They watch planes zipping through the sky, a blazing sun, and half-lit trees. Everything around them is pure—the light, the air, the flowers. There is an allusion to paradise, to a time before the Fall. For one paragraph, the two young people seem to have achieved a state of bliss. But the moment is fleeting. A cloud comes and the moment is gone. Soon afterwards the first chapter ends and another begins that reveals the truth: The boy in the story was only daydreaming. None of this is real. He has a crush on a girl in his class. He decides to write a poem about her. He calls it "Hair Poem."

I wrote my comments with care because I felt that Seung would not be able to take harsh criticism about his novel. I suggested he read Philip Roth, Salinger's *Catcher in the Rye,* Emily Brontë's *Wuthering Heights,* John Irving, Amy Tan. I didn't think that he would be offended by those writers' visions, and I hoped that he would relate to some of the themes in their work. Perhaps, if he read them, he would understand that there are ways to depict characters that allowed them to be more than projections. I asked him questions about the narrative arc of the story, if he decided to keep it in the form of a novel: *When will the pivotal events occur? What will be revealed/ disclosed/understood? Will the main characters come to know themselves and each other? What tone do you want to establish?* I ended by apologizing for taking some time to get to it. I was tempted to add something about counseling again but I decided against it because I was leaving the packet on my door in an envelope so he could pick it up. Besides, he'd told me repeatedly that he was going to counseling. I didn't want him to think I was accusing him of lying. I was worrying too much as usual. I had to let it go.

I stepped down from serving as chair in May 2006 and was on

leave in the fall of that year. I returned to campus in the spring of 2007, following a trip to Sierra Leone. I came back even more determined to help my former students and others in Sierra Leone who had been so brutalized by the civil war. It was good to be back in Blacksburg in January 2007. It was the antithesis of Freetown, which still, several years after the war had officially ended, seemed to smell of blood.

For some reason, I assumed that Seung-Hui Cho had graduated the previous December. I don't know why that is—perhaps he mentioned to me that he was planning on doing so.

After the shooting, I have sometimes wished that I had required Seung to continue meeting with me rather than simply suggesting that he do so. How would he have known that I didn't have the authority to do that? It's possible he would have shown up in spring 2006 if I had been insistent, but it's also quite possible that he could have felt targeted and resentful, and that I could therefore have placed faculty, students, and staff who work in Shanks Hall at risk. Perhaps there would still have been "a tragedy of monumental proportions" but in a different location.

At night when I lie awake replaying everything in my head, I think of the moment when I rushed after him after that initial interview and handed him my novel—how he seemed to flinch at first, until I explained that I was giving him a gift.

I remember taking his hand in mine to shake it. His hand had been artificially stiff, almost like that of a corpse, and it had been trembling.

Nearly a year and a half later, on the morning of April 16, having murdered two students more than two hours earlier, Seung-Hui Cho coolly fired approximately 174 rounds of ammunition in Norris Hall.

IT IS well known among poets that the best poetic form for obsessive-compulsive subjects is the sestina. You come back to the same six end-words at the end of every line. Even though it seems that, initially, you have confined yourself within a form that forces you back into a wall of six end-words, the trick is to make the form open itself up as a flower opens in sunlight, to move beyond those words into something sublime.

After April 16, these are my six end-words. All except one of them begin with *s*. The word that hurts the most ends with *s* instead: *Seung, sunglasses, sorrow, stone, silence,* and *guns.* They have built a hexagonal prison around me.

I realize that, to survive, I must choose another six end-words. After the catastrophe, I am trying to make my way towards these alternative words. But it is often dark, and the light they give is intermittent, and some routes are U-turns that lead me right back to where I started. Even so, these are the six I choose for my sestina: *students, teachers, beauty, voice, reconciliation,* and *peace*—words that must form the embedded, magical star of this tragic story.

3.

Connecting
the Dots

I N THE days that followed the tragedy, I began the agonizing process of trying to find out what had gone wrong. I needed to connect the dots, but this proved to be much more difficult to do than I had anticipated. The young man whom I had thought of as "Seung," but who was identified by the media as "Cho," and who became "Cho" to me, too, after the shootings, had told me he was going to counseling. Given the horrific attack he'd launched, it was likely he had lied to placate me. I didn't discover what had really happened at the end of the fall 2005 semester until June 2007, when I was interviewed by two of the panelists appointed by Governor Kaine. I learned during that interview that Cho had indeed contacted the Cook Counseling Center (CCC) in November and December of 2005. When the Panel Report was published, I could hardly believe what I read. Cho had contacted the CCC not once but *three* times. The following excerpts were some of the most heart-breaking of the entire report because they constituted a litany of missed opportunities.

NOVEMBER 30: Cho calls Cook Counseling Center and is triaged (i.e., given a preliminary screening) by phone at [*sic*] following his interaction with VTPD police.*

DECEMBER 12: Cho does not keep a 2:00 P.M. appointment at Cook Counseling Center but is triaged by them again by phone that afternoon.

DECEMBER 14: Cho then makes and keeps an appointment with the campus Cook Counseling Center.

DECEMBER 14, 3:00 P.M.: Cho is triaged in person at the Cook Counseling Center for the third time in 15 days.[1]

When Cho had sought out the center and requested help, his requests had not resulted in any meaningful assessment or diagnosis. It is not clear what happened during the December 14 appointment.

In the chapter on Seung-Hui Cho's mental history in the Panel Report, there is a description of the efforts Cho made to seek counseling: "A note attached to the electronic appointment indicates that Cho *specifically requested* [my italics] an appointment with Cathy Betzel, a licensed clinical psychologist, and indicated that his professor had spoken with Dr. Betzel."[2] The fact that he had asked, by name, for one of the counselors I recommended is telling. The difficulty he would probably have had requesting a specific counselor, given his condition of selective mutism, must have been extreme. In the "Summary of Key Findings," there is a list of reasons given for the unresponsiveness of the CCC:

The system failed to provide needed support and services to Cho during a period in late 2005 and early 2006. The system failed for lack of resources, incorrect interpretations of privacy laws, and passivity. Records of Cho's minimal treatment at Virginia Tech's Cook Counseling Center are missing.[3]

---

*A "preliminary screening" meant that no diagnosis could be made.

I understand that it can be incredibly challenging to work in an understaffed facility, but the information that had been provided to the CCC should have alerted counselors to the seriousness of the situation. The Panel Report revealed that Cho had been repeatedly flagged—by female students he harassed, by his roommate who was worried about his state of mind, and by faculty in English who had taught him. But he still fell through the cracks.

Several of the warnings received by various units pointed to Cho's instability and threatening behavior. It was in November and December of 2005, for example, that Cho harassed female students. According to the Panel Report, "Cho had made 'annoying' contact with [a female student] on the Internet, by phone, and in person"— behavior that mirrored the problems Professor Nikki Giovanni had reported about his cell phone use.[4] He had also gone in disguise to a female student's room.

Reports surfaced in the media and it was confirmed in the Panel Report that Cho had been advised by his family and his high school counselor not to attend Virginia Tech. They all felt it was too large and impersonal a school for someone like him—that he would do better at a small liberal arts college. They were afraid he would get lost. Cho had not taken their advice.

On December 13, 2005, Cho's roommate (called a "suitemate" in the Panel Report because students in Harper Residence Hall shared a common sitting area) had reported that he had received an instant message from Cho threatening, "I might as well kill myself now." The roommate called the VTPD and Cho was taken to the police department and evaluated by someone from New River Valley Community Services (NRVCS). The prescreener concluded that Cho was "an imminent danger to self or others," an evaluation that was critical because it meant that a magistrate could issue a temporary detention order. Cho spent the night at Carilion St. Albans Psychiatric Hospital, known locally as "St. Albans." At last, in spite of the fact that the first two calls had resulted only in triage—a temporary, stop-gap response—he would receive the treatment he needed.

But the next day at 7:00 A.M., psychologist Roy Crouse conducted another evaluation of Cho and concluded that he did not present an imminent danger to himself after all. This conclusion was seconded a few hours later by a staff psychiatrist at Carilion St. Albans, who recommended that Cho receive outpatient counseling. A little later that day, Special Justice Paul M. Barnett conducted a commitment hearing that lasted about thirty minutes. His ruling was in accordance with the one by Roy Crouse, that Cho did not present an imminent danger to himself. However, Special Justice Barnett ordered Cho to receive follow-up treatment as an outpatient. The staff psychiatrist concluded in his evaluation summary at noon, "[T]here is no indication of psychosis, delusions, suicidal or homicidal ideation." Cho was released on the understanding that he would receive follow-up care from the CCC.[5] Unfortunately, what the staff psychiatrist at Carilion St. Albans failed to take into account was an obstacle that I had encountered when I tried to get Seung-Hui Cho into counseling: The CCC did not see students unless they sought counseling *voluntarily*. The huge irony here, of course, is that this is precisely what Cho had tried to do. This policy could perhaps explain why, on each occasion, Cho was "triaged."

Seung-Hui Cho returned to his classes the next semester without medication, without counseling, without any support system whatsoever. He returned to a 2,600-acre campus, filled with twenty-six thousand students. A campus where he could easily get lost.

By the spring of 2007, Cho seemed to be listening only to the crazed voices in his head. But in the fall of 2005, that transformation does not appear to have been complete. He was in deep trouble, but he sought help. It was a window of opportunity. Often that is all you get with people suffering from severe mental illness. When you read about his troubled history, his twenty-year struggle with a severe social disorder, his chronic depression, and his fascination with Columbine, it's obvious that this opening was small.

Ultimately, it was Cho who killed and injured people at Virginia Tech, and it's quite possible that nothing could have prevented his rampage, especially if despair and rage had been churning inside him for years. It's also quite possible that he only sought help because he was afraid of the police, who were questioning him repeatedly about his behavior during that period. In other words, his desire to seek counseling could have been a reaction based upon fear rather than yearning. We will probably never know which it was. Ultimately, it doesn't matter. The point is that he sought help repeatedly. I wish that he had received it.

The Panel Report concluded that, in spite of the fact that there had been numerous "red flags," no one unit was in possession of all of the necessary information. In the "Summary of Key Findings," the lack of communication was described this way:

> During Cho's junior year at Virginia Tech, numerous incidents occurred that were clear warnings of mental instability. Although various individuals and departments within the university knew about each of these incidents, the university did not intervene effectively. No one knew all the information and no one connected all the dots.[6]

In the aftermath of the tragedy, I mistakenly believed that I hadn't heard anything more about Seung-Hui Cho between January 2006 and April 2007. But I later realized that two faculty members had mentioned him to me, though I hadn't been shown any samples of Cho's work. Professor Robert "Bob" Hicok had contacted me about Cho during the spring semester of 2006 and asked me if I had any suggestions about how to deal with his shyness (class participation was a part of the grade). I told him about my own experience of working with Cho. I had volunteered to meet with Cho again—something I had forgotten in the aftermath of the tragedy, when I had been wishing I had done so—but Bob had felt that this was not necessary. Cho had not, at the time when Bob spoke with me about him, produced work for the class. Then in the fall of 2006, while I was on research leave, I received a call from Professor Ed Falco. He, too, had been concerned about Seung-Hui Cho's excessive shyness, but Cho had not written much for Ed's class at that time, either. Like Bob Hicok, Ed asked for advice. He said that Cho was cooperative and polite, and I was relieved to hear it. I recommended that he speak to Carolyn Rude, the chair. Ed also conferred with Lisa Norris, who was then working as an instructor in the English department. I learned that Lisa had voiced her concern about Cho to the College of Liberal Arts and Human Sciences just as I had done, but nothing had come of it, perhaps because the college was hampered by Virginia Tech's strict enforcement of student privacy.

I had stepped down from serving as chair by the time Ed called and so would not have been privy to any work Cho may have produced. But somehow that didn't make me feel any better. I did not learn about the angry outburst Seung-Hui Cho had had in April 2006 with Carl Bean—an instructor in our department—until after the tragedy. It wasn't surprising, given the size of the department, that some of Cho's behavior and work had been unknown to me. Did the fact that it was almost impossible to get a student into counseling unless he made an explicit threat hinder the faculty from voicing their concerns? Some faculty members knew that I had reported very disturbing material written by another student in the spring of 2005, and that the whole process had been unbelievably frustrating.

The Panel Report emphasized that it was Seung-Hui Cho who committed the atrocity, and that, in the public's rush to assign blame, this should not be forgotten. But in light of Cho's suicide, public outrage had to be redirected and someone else had to be blamed for what had happened. I was fortunate in that I had reported my concerns and then spoken openly about doing so. Perhaps because of this I was not subjected to the barrage of public criticism that the Virginia Tech administration faced. Though I had received the occasional racist threat—something I have, sadly, come to expect as a person of color—and although the department took some harsh criticism from right-wing bloggers who assumed that Seung-Hui Cho's state of mind was the result of what he had studied in his English courses, almost all the mail I opened was positive.

For President Steger and his core administrative team, on the other hand, things were very different. The two-hour delay in notifying the campus that a killer was on the loose infuriated many members of the public and many of the victims' families. Understandably, they wanted to know what on earth the Policy Group (made up of the president, vice presidents, key advisers, and support staff) had been thinking when it had decided not to cancel classes after the first two homicides. Why hadn't the campus been notified that a killer could be on the loose, and why had the e-mail notifications that had eventually gone out understated the seriousness of the first attack, or come too late to do any good?

By the end of that first week following the tragedy, President Steger and his key advisers had "battened down the hatches," a phrase I have often heard utilized by one of his team to describe the administration's approach to the media. This wasn't just an attempt to keep outsiders away; the hatches were battened down internally also. From Tuesday, April 17, when the identity of the shooter was confirmed up until the time of writing this book, there has been no meaningful internal investigation with regards to specific incidents related to Seung-Hui Cho. As far as I can tell, apart from the development of some guidelines about how to evaluate and refer troubled students, Cho's history at Virginia Tech has been erased from the upper administration's collective memory.

After tragedies like this, people clam up. They are warned that it is too dangerous to talk about the specifics of a case when lawyers are chomping at the bit, when the media is lying in wait like a lynch mob. But people also remain silent when they are worried that what they have to say could injure them somehow.

In the days and weeks that followed the tragedy at Virginia Tech I was reminded of how much silence has to say to us if we listen with care.

SADLY, THE tragedy at Virginia Tech did not usher in an era of openness on the part of the administration. Questions that related to the specifics of the shootings, to Cho, or to troubled students in general were viewed in the wake of the tragedy as verbal grenades. In *Rampage,* a thoughtful study of two school shootings written by the sociologist Katherine Newman and a group of her graduate students, the authors point out that the influence of the media on a smaller rural community can be particularly damaging.[7] There is no doubt that reporters were rabid at times in pursuit of their stories. Interestingly, however, the community itself wasn't divided. The college deans made a point of coming over to the department to meet with us, as did the provost, Mark McNamee—gestures that were greatly appreciated. It is regrettable that, so far, the president has not visited the English department. I think it would have been meaningful to the faculty and staff had he done so.

While there was a sense of unity there was also a sense of foreboding. Being at Virginia Tech after the shootings sometimes felt like being inside a *Harry Potter* book where characters are forbidden to utter the name "Voldemort." "The Dark Lord" (aka "You-Know-Who") cannot be spoken about because it would be calamitous to do so. Voldemort is the unutterable, maleficent presence who lurks on the outer edges of the community intent upon committing harm. He is so odious that people refuse to acknowledge him at all until he attacks them.

Part of the reason for keeping silent is obvious: We worry that evil will beget itself. Better to remain silent lest we inadvertently wake the monster again. We do not want to be accused of sensationalizing or exploiting a tragedy; we do not want to be accused of glorifying a killer by focusing on his larger-than-life persona. All of these reactions are understandable. But silence is an impediment to understanding. What could we fail to learn about the tragedy if we refused to respond to the most basic questions? Wouldn't it look as if we were trying to hide something if we didn't speak?

Once I learned the identity of the shooter, I assumed that what would be emphasized over the summer would be student safety and campus security. I assumed that there would be transparency, and I also assumed that there would be an earnest attempt by the administration to find out what had gone wrong. There is no doubt that law enforcement in particular was fully invested in campus security after the tragedy. Law enforcement officials worked around the clock to keep the campus as safe as possible. We would not have been able to return had they not committed themselves to the investigation, even though many of the local officers in the VTPD and the Blacksburg and Christiansburg police departments were themselves trying to come to terms with the attack on their community. Alongside campus safety, however, the Virginia Tech administration seemed to be establishing a new priority, one that I found hard to comprehend in light of what had happened. In the next few months, until Governor Kaine issued Executive Order 53 on June 18, 2007, which allowed the review panel to look at Cho's academic and mental health records, the Tech administration would be obsessed with the right to privacy of a single individual. And that single individual whose rights the Tech administration would be so concerned about protecting was none other than Seung-Hui Cho.

On June 7, 2007, Marc Fisher of the *Washington Post* wrote the following in his column, "Raw Fisher":

Virginia Tech officials have refused even to tell the state investigative panel whether Cho ever went to the school's counseling center after a court ordered him to do so in December 2005. University president Charles Steger said that he is "concerned about our inability to know these things. . . . Just saying we don't know is not good enough. We have to do better, but we must follow the laws."

I was soon to experience firsthand how determined the administration was to protect Cho's privacy.

Although everyone agreed that it was most unlikely that anyone would ever sue the university for sharing Cho's records in the interests of security, and although Cho's family had made it clear that they wanted to cooperate in whatever way they could, the university's upper-level administrators still dragged their feet. Even when documents were eventually obtained, it was discovered that some of them, particularly those relating to the treatment Cho received at the CCC, had disappeared. Yet it was urgent that we obtain answers, and we didn't have time to waste. In spite of the tragedy, the largest entering class in Virginia Tech's history would be coming to campus in August. It was obvious that we needed to do whatever we could to ensure student safety, and that included finding out as much as we could about Seung-Hui Cho's troubled history.

At the end of his *Washington Post* column on June 7, Fisher, reflecting the sentiment of some victims' families who were outraged by what appeared to be the administration's aversion to transparency, wrote: "The records of how public institutions dealt with dead people should be an open book."

So why on earth would the president and some of his closest advisers risk incurring the wrath of impartial observers, especially when everyone from the governor to the review panel to victims' loved ones felt that transparency was essential?

It seems to me that the administration had boxed itself into a corner. Silence, which had often been used by the administration during times of crisis, needed to be maintained. In the past (apart from this one tragedy) silence seemed to have worked pretty well for the administration. Chronic problems at Virginia Tech tended to be shelved rather than solved. If you didn't talk about it, perhaps it would go away.

It therefore became necessary for the president and some members of his administration to construct an ethical framework on which a culture of silence could be rebuilt. The most convenient strategy was one that had been used before—i.e., a rigorous enforcement of state and federal laws related to student privacy. The irony of doing this may not have been immediately apparent to the administration because it was, by this time, thoroughly closeted. The same laws that had previously prevented people from sharing information before the tragedy could now be utilized to prevent people from sharing information after the tragedy. It was such a brazen solution to the thorny problem of full disclosure that had Governor Kaine and his review panel not been doggedly persistent about obtaining Cho's academic and health records, there's a good chance it would have worked.

I felt at times as though I were living in an absurdist drama. The president's approach, which seemed to make a mockery of justice, was initially questioned in Blacksburg, both by reporters from the *Roanoke Times* and by those on campus. In other parts of the country—particularly in the Northern Virginia region where there is a lot of sympathy for victims' families, some of whom live in the area—there was even more skepticism that Seung-Hui Cho's privacy was paramount.

I should point out that President Steger and his advisers had a legitimate concern. It was a violation of state and federal laws to make public a student's health and academic records. But there is no doubt that, had the administration taken it upon itself to lobby aggressively for a suspension of those laws, given the scale of the tragedy, they would have received unanimous support. The Cho family seems to have been more than willing to share information. In fact, one of the remarkable things about the Panel Report is the extraordinary access panelists had to Cho's family, access that makes the section on Cho's childhood and mental health the most compelling in the entire report. Notably, the president's voice throughout the report is muted.

When Executive Order 53 was issued, granting the panel access to Cho's academic and health records on a day when faculty from the English department were being interviewed by two of the panelists, it was heralded with relief by many observers. It looked as if there would be more transparency at last. It looked as if people would finally be provided with some answers.

IT TOOK me a while to realize that the dot that bore my name was not supposed to be connected to the dots that bore the president's name or the names of anyone who reported to him. This was because it hadn't occurred to me that communication between the central administration and me was forbidden.

At first I was told that the reason for the ban on communication was that I had engaged a lawyer. That didn't make sense, particularly as the ban seems to have been in effect prior to my doing so. Besides, dozens of Virginia Tech employees have their own lawyers, and my attorney had made it absolutely clear from the beginning that she wanted to work collaboratively with Virginia Tech. In fact, she sent a letter to university counsel stating that fact.

I had felt the need to engage a lawyer partly because I had received a troubling note that I felt I should report to the FBI. I had no one else with whom to consult because the two Virginia Tech attorneys were overwhelmed by the crisis. However hardworking they were, they simply could not serve the hundreds of people affected by a tragedy of this magnitude. It had never occurred to me that my having an attorney would be an issue because it was my right as an individual, as far as I knew, to have one. So when a trusted friend of mine, a lawyer herself, had suggested to me that her firm may be able to represent me pro bono, I gratefully accepted the offer. I assumed that I would be assigned an attorney with somewhat limited credentials, given the fact that I wouldn't be paying him or her. My friend had never given any indication that the firm she worked for was located in multiple cities and employed a fleet of attorneys, so I was surprised when I discovered that it did. I was assigned an extremely savvy and accomplished lawyer, Kathryn Ruemmler, who had been one of the lead prosecutors in the Enron case.

In the beginning, I assumed people were just too busy to return my calls and e-mails. I had known some members of President Steger's administration for more than twenty years. I thought very highly of some of them, and some were friends of mine. Gradually, however, I began to realize that the situation was not one that could be easily remedied.

The first indication I had that told me I had offended the president and some of his advisers occurred within a few days of the attack. Someone in the president's administration demanded to know why I was speaking to the press, and what had been included in the file I had handed to the police. Up until that moment I had thought that I would be one of many to step forward and talk about Seung-Hui Cho. I had assumed that everyone who knew about what had happened—and there were many people to whom we had reported our concerns—would come forward as well.

I reviewed what I had said to the press. The fact that Cho's behavior had been noticed by faculty testified to our vigilance, even though, in the end, the tragedy had not been averted. On the other hand, I could understand why President Steger in particular could have been hurt by what had transpired. While he had been giving interviews saying that Virginia Tech had no idea Cho was troubled, I had been giving interviews saying the opposite, though I had never intimated that the president knew about Seung-Hui Cho himself. Although I had declined more than 90 percent of the requests for interviews and only spoken with the media for part of that first week, from the administration's point of view the damage had been done. In England some headlines inferred that it was my innate British wisdom which had enabled me to see that Cho could be a threat. Local and national papers also contrasted the English department's story with the official account from Virginia Tech, and the contrast often seemed to be to the detriment of the administration. It was likely that the president and his advisers, struggling to deal with the backlash from the two-hour delay after the double homicide was reported, had not seen an interview I did with Soledad O'Brien in which I insisted that assigning blame prior to an investigation was ludicrous.

I was increasingly discouraged by the wall of silence that had been erected, and I hoped it was temporary. As long as the administration was communicating regularly with the families and friends of victims, and as long as it intended to review and improve campus safety and communication, other things were secondary. I had to admit, however, that the question about the file I had handed to police had thrown me a little. First of all, it struck me as odd that the administration would be concerned about this because it was precisely what it had asked everyone to do. Secondly, it seemed like a strange comment because much of what I had handed over—copies of e-mails sent to various units about Cho, copies of his work, etc.— duplicated materials they already had in their possession, most of which should already have been provided to the police. It was beginning to look as though I and others in the English department who handed in the documents to police as soon as they were requested weren't supposed to have interpreted the request so literally.

The first people who told me that communication between me and anyone who reported to the president had been banned were staff in Burruss. What they did was brave, and it put them in a very awkward position. Following this disclosure, I stumbled out of Burruss Hall in a state of disbelief.

A few days later, another member of the central administration told me he was risking his job by speaking with me. It was then that I became genuinely concerned. What was it they thought I had done? I told the person that the policy was ridiculous. It wasn't the first time that I had done something to offend the current administration, whose style was the opposite of my own. There is no doubt that I can be annoying—I have even been known to annoy myself at times. Virginia Tech was under a microscope. For a man like Charles Steger who abhorred scrutiny, it must have been a mortifying process.

I was still confident that things would be cleared up soon when yet another member of the central administration stopped by to see me at my home. It was clear now that this was becoming a pattern. My visitor verified that things were seriously amiss in the administration, where lines of communication were being shut down, even between the president and the victims' families. It was this comment that troubled me the most. These were members of our extended community who had lost loved ones. If we didn't show them compassion, what did it mean to be a community?

The next week I received a phone call a little after 5:00 A.M. and I lost all patience. The caller (another member of the president's administration) repeated what I'd heard before—that he could be fired for speaking with me. But, he said cavalierly, he didn't care. He thought it was wrong that I was being treated this way and couldn't cut me off any longer.

Instead of being grateful, however, I was furious. I asked him why he didn't stand up to this kind of idiotic behavior. I reminded him that there had been a horrific tragedy at Virginia Tech, and that the strategy being adopted by the president could be catastrophic. We needed to be honest about what had happened and then try to rebuild. It was a painful and brutally frank phone call. I considered the caller to be a close friend, and the fact that he had gone along with the policy and felt the need to contact me in secret hurt me deeply.

After that conversation, a counselor arrived at my office to talk with me about how I felt about the tragedy. I had never seen her before, and she seemed like a nice woman. One of the questions she asked me, however, was whether or not I was angry with the Virginia Tech administration. I paused before I answered because the question was a bit odd, coming as it did out of the blue. I said that any sane person would be angry if she had been punished for speaking up about reporting troubled students. It was quite possible that the poor woman had simply been making an innocent inquiry.

I decided then that it might be worth a shot to communicate with President Steger himself, in hopes that he would lift the ban that he himself had imposed. I therefore wrote to the president and several other members of the administration to try to reassure them that we could still work together, and that I had never said or done anything to deliberately harm anyone else at Virginia Tech. I wanted to reassure them that my attorney, as we had tried to make clear, would be working collaboratively with them. I was still laboring under the impression that it had been my admission to the media that had caused such consternation, so I tried to explain that I had done my best to represent the university as well as I could. The silence that greeted my note did not surprise me. I did receive a response from Kimberly O'Rourke, special assistant to the president, however. She informed me in her note that Charles was too busy meeting with victims' families to speak with me. I had to admit that it was a good excuse. I hoped it was true.

Because I didn't want to get anyone fired, I tried my best to keep a low profile when it came to my old friends and acquaintances in the Virginia Tech administration. I also tried not to be seen speaking too much with people in the English department. The last thing I wanted to do was to get colleagues in trouble by associating with them. The department had been traumatized enough already.

A campus was in mourning, and, to my dismay, it looked as though I wouldn't be able to do as much as I'd hoped to help the bereaved.

AFTER THE shootings, classes were canceled for a week. You saw your friends and colleagues wandering around the supermarket like zombies, unable to process what had happened. A memorial service was held and attended by President Bush, who spoke:

> Yesterday began like any other day. Students woke up, and they grabbed their backpacks and they headed for class. And soon the day took a dark turn, with students and faculty barricading themselves in classrooms and dormitories—confused, terrified, and deeply worried. By the end of the morning, it was the worst day of violence on a college campus in American history—and for many of you here today, it was the worst day of your lives.
>
> It's impossible to make sense of such violence and suffering. Those whose lives were taken did nothing to deserve their fate. They were simply in the wrong place at the wrong time. Now they're gone—and they leave behind grieving families, and grieving classmates, and a grieving nation.[8]

It struck me that the students hadn't, in fact, been in the wrong place at the wrong time, they had been in exactly the *right* place, trying to learn. It had been Seung-Hui Cho who had been in the wrong place at the wrong time when he'd burst into their classrooms and opened fire in Norris Hall.

A petition in support of President Charles Steger and Chief Wendell Flinchum was circulated soon after the tragedy and delivered to Governor Kaine's office. It was signed by 37,371 people, many of whom were alumni and friends of the school. The online version of the petition features photos of President Steger and Chief Flinchum side by side. Eighteen thousand people expressed their support in short messages they posted.

There was gnawing anxiety on campus. Had Seung-Hui Cho acted alone? Would classes resume peacefully? Everyone was reeling from the horror, but there was also a feeling of determination unlike any I have experienced before. Students were resolute about returning to class; faculty members were equally stoic; and classified staff people, in their critical but often underappreciated roles, were determined that Virginia Tech would move forward.

ON MONDAY, April 23, classes were set to resume for the first time since the shooting. I had spent the weekend fretting. I had stumbled upon information that was supposed to be confidential. Towards the end of that first week, I was told by someone who assumed I already knew about it that Seung-Hui Cho had written a letter to the English department and mailed it on the day of the shootings.

At first, I didn't believe it. There had been no announcement about any letter to the department in the news. Instead, reports were filled with information about the package Cho had mailed to NBC.

I went to see Carolyn Rude, the department chair. I learned that the letter contained a diatribe against one of our instructors, Carl Bean, and that it had been delivered to the Office of University Legal Counsel. As Carolyn understood it, the letter was now part of an ongoing investigation so it was not the kind of information that should be shared. I promised her I would keep quiet about it. I didn't wish to do anything that could place Carl in jeopardy. Now that it had been handed over to the administration, the letter would be shared with the appropriate people.

A little while later, I asked colleagues, who steadfastly remained in contact with me throughout the next few months, whether or not the president and the provost were aware of the letter. They told me in confidence that they didn't think either of them knew anything about it. I was surprised by this, but I also understood that things must be crazy over in Burruss as they scrambled to get ready for the resumption of classes. In all likelihood, the president's and the provost's offices would hear about it soon enough. After all, the campus police, state police, FBI, and ATF—to name just some of those stationed in and passing through Burruss—would be sure to bring it to their attention.

Early Monday morning, however, I realized why something still bothered me. Classes were due to begin that day, but no one was yet 100 percent sure that Seung-Hui Cho had acted alone. The first two homicides had not been definitively connected with the later killings. If Cho hadn't acted alone after all, and if the letter he had written about Carl Bean was as full of venom as it was reported to be, was it possible that Carl's students could be at risk?

Even though Carl had canceled his four classes and was meeting his students online—a precaution that seemed prudent under the circumstances—some students may not have received the message that class had been canceled, which meant they could show up for class. Was it possible that, if Cho hadn't acted alone, this last letter he had mailed to the English department was not simply a reference to things past but a threat of an attack to come?

Another thing troubled me. I had called the FBI the previous week because I had received an e-mail which stated that those of us in the English department needed to read things carefully if we wanted to avoid tragedy in the future. It ended with a quote from *The Three Musketeers:* "One for all and all for one."

The FBI had been helpful and reassuring. They had investigated the e-mail and did not feel it was something I needed to worry about. I tried to quiet my concern. But what prevented me from doing so was the realization that Cho may have assumed that I would read the letter he had sent. Although from what I could gather it had been addressed to "The English Department" rather than to anyone in particular—something that should have reassured me—I wasn't certain that he would know I wasn't chair anymore. A terrible feeling gripped me. For a while it felt as though Cho would never stop living inside my head, leaving a trail of blood for me to follow. I tried to shake the idea that I should notify someone that Carl's classrooms should be monitored, even though he was only meeting the students online.

I have never seen the letter Cho wrote but I gather, from the Panel Report and other reports in the media, that it was much like a posting Cho seems to have made to a site called RateVTTeachers.com. The site is notorious among some Virginia Tech faculty because any student with a Virginia Tech e-mail address can post comments to it. Students check it before they select their classes. If indeed the letter was similar, it was full of invective—a very immature tirade.

I was frustrated with myself for not being able to let things go. If I rushed up to campus to try to warn people, I would look like an idiot. The last time I was in Burruss it was a mortifying experience. Once again, I would have to endure people's embarrassment as they pretended not to see me because many of those who worked in Burruss reported, directly or indirectly, to the president.

There was a critical piece of information to which I did not have access because I have never seen the letter. As was revealed in the Panel Report, the letter to the English department was sent close to the one-year anniversary of Cho's argument with Carl in his office. In other words, Cho could have been trying to punish Carl by selecting that particular Monday as the date for his brutal attack. Not realizing, however, that Cho had indeed devised a cruel way to try to punish his teacher, I was afraid that Cho would not be satisfied with merely sending a letter. In addition, I was concerned that students in nearby classrooms could be at risk should Carl's classes be empty.

Which was why, not long after 8:00 A.M., I found myself driving down Main Street in Blacksburg, exceeding the speed limit by some eight miles for the first time in living memory. I knew it was possible no one would listen to me, but I thought it more likely they would if I showed up rather than called on the phone. I doubted that I would be put through to anyone in authority, especially as lines of communication between the administration and me had been severed by this time.

I pulled up in front of Burruss Hall and parked in a disabled parking spot. First speeding and now this. But time was ticking, and Carl's first class would start within the hour.

I hurried up to the sheriff's deputy who was patrolling in front of Burruss and tried to explain to him what was going on. To put it mildly, the deputy was not impressed. He couldn't have moved more slowly had he been made of molasses. I refused to give up, however, and eventually he agreed to call the FBI agents to whom I had spoken previously about the e-mail I'd received. From his squad car, which was parked on the grass next to Burruss Hall, placing it just in front of Norris, he made some calls. I waited anxiously by the car, trying not to look at Norris because, each time I did, my eyes began to water—which wouldn't do at all, not if I were going to persuade anyone to take me seriously.

After about twenty anxious minutes waiting outside of Burruss Hall, I was told that I would be permitted to speak with someone. By this time, I was genuinely concerned. Even though it was likely that there was nothing to worry about, even though it was possible that my information was wrong and the president and the provost both knew about the letter (why wouldn't they know about it if it had been hand-delivered to the Office of University Legal Counsel?), I still felt I needed to warn someone.

It struck me as I stood in front of Burruss Hall that I had spent much of the past two years trying to warn Virginia Tech about potential danger, all to no avail. It had turned out to be a horror story after all. The slaughterhouse of Norris Hall was a few yards away. I could almost smell it. The student-killer, "Seung" or "Cho"—Lost Soul or Monster, Cowering Boy or Sadistic Brute—was still forcing me to look for signs. I resented his savage silence; I didn't want him attached to me anymore. And it was only a week that had gone by. How would I find a quiet place to sit and rest when Seung-Hui Cho's silence took up so much room?

I wouldn't let myself think about it. Not now. All that mattered was getting someone in law enforcement to connect the dots and see if they led anywhere.

At last a couple of agents showed up and I was ushered into Burruss. I was shown up to the floor where the various law enforcement agencies were headquartered. No one seemed to know what to do with me, and I was, at first, left in the corridor. I spotted a man with a kind face and appealed to him. I believe he was an FBI agent. Soon he was joined by another agent, I believe from ATF. The second agent clearly felt that I was wasting their time and was therefore aggressively dismissive. But the first agent was helpful, a fact that seemed to annoy the second agent, who pushed past us both roughly and stormed off. His reaction surprised me because of its intensity, but, in those days, everyone in Burruss was on edge. He'd probably had as much sleep as I'd had—which wasn't much.

After a few minutes I was ushered into an office where I sat and waited. I kept looking at my watch: Carl's classes were due to start soon, and I hadn't managed to get anyone to check on them. If worst came to worst, I would have to run over to the building where his classes were to meet and keep an eye on them myself. I didn't believe I would be particularly effective at preventing an attack, but I was armed with a cell phone and determination. That would have to do.

At last, four men entered the outer office where I sat, then went on through to an inner office. To my great relief, one of the four was Wendell Flinchum. For some reason, as soon as I saw him I knew that my concerns would be taken seriously—that he would know why I was worried about Carl's classes, and that someone would be sent to check on them.

When they called me in I was asked to sit on a chair on one side of the fairly small room—someone's office, one that was unfamiliar to me. On the other side of the room from me sat the four men, one of whom was the ATF agent who had pushed past me in disgust in the hallway earlier.

I discussed the letter to the English department and the e-mail

I'd received. I then made the connection to Carl's classes and security. One of the men who seemed to be the highest ranking of the
four spent much of the time trying to persuade me that they had
things under control and that I shouldn't worry.

At last I appealed directly to Chief Flinchum because I felt I
could trust him. I said something like "I know you understand why
this is so important. It can't happen again here—not at Virginia Tech.
It can never happen here again."

I provided the four men with Carl's schedule, and, much to my
relief, they assured me they would take care of it. And that was it.

I don't believe I made much of an impression on the agents, but
I was confident that Chief Flinchum had heard me, and that was
all that mattered. He had shown courage by his willingness to be
present at the interview. Wendell Flinchum, in his role as chief of
the VTPD, reported—though indirectly, via the Office of the Executive Vice President—to President Steger. I assumed, therefore, that it
would be awkward for him to speak with me. It was an unexpected
gift during a time of trial, and so it was especially welcome.

Later I learned from someone in the administration that President Steger had "hit the roof" when he had been told about the letter
from Cho to the English department. According to the person who
shared this with me, neither the president nor the provost had been
aware of its existence. If this was indeed the case, it must have been
irksome to discover that someone who was supposed to be out of
the loop had provided the information. I hoped that part had not
been emphasized.

People didn't realize that Carolyn Rude had handed the letter
over to Virginia Tech's legal counsel as soon as she had received it.
Given the fact that a number of people in the English department
were aware of the letter, it is a testament to all of them that no one
said anything. They demonstrated their concern for the instructor's
safety and the safety of his students. Carolyn had relied upon law
enforcement and the administration to let her know how to proceed

as far as the letter went. Unfortunately, as far as I know, no one ever contacted the department about the letter again until the administration decided to share it with the governor's review panel, at which time some of the media outlets assumed that the English department had failed to report it. For the record, it was indeed reported.

I have thought about the department's discretion since that time and compared it to the way the video package was handled by NBC. The contrast is striking.

As I headed down the steps of Burruss Hall, I felt relief that I had reported my concerns, however foolish I may have seemed for doing so. I ran back to my illegal parking space on the edge of the Drillfield in front of Burruss Hall, thinking about Wendell Flinchum's expression. I was confident that there would be at least one officer checking the classrooms where Carl had been scheduled to teach.

Classes had begun. I looked around. Students were hurrying across the Drillfield. I kept my eyes fixed on them and didn't turn to look back at Norris Hall, situated on a slight incline behind and to the right of Burruss Hall.

The resumption of classes was proceeding smoothly, even though some students had opted to go home after the tragedy. The campus looked almost serene.

4.

Prey

ABC, NBC, CBS, Fox, CNN; local news crews; international teams like the BBC and Sky News from the United Kingdom and from Canada, Japan, and Korea; print journalists—all were in Blacksburg, drawn by a story that generated worldwide sympathy.

The setting was the campus—pastoral, photogenic. The students and faculty members who had been killed and injured were recognizable as people everyone could love. From a United Nations of countries, the victims were not the privileged "brats" Cho had railed against in the video clips he sent to NBC News:

> You had everything you wanted. Your Mercedes wasn't enough, you brats. Your golden necklaces weren't enough, you snobs. Your trust fund wasn't enough. Your vodka and cognac weren't enough. All your debaucheries weren't enough. Those weren't enough to fulfill your hedonistic needs. You had everything.[1]

In fact, many of the undergraduates and graduates he killed had overcome economic hardship and had worked diligently for their success.

Many were about as likely to have trust funds as he was. They were eager to make positive contributions in the world and had already been engaged in activities with those who were underprivileged— something Cho himself never was. They were local; they were from other regions of Virginia; they were from other states; and they were from other countries. But Seung-Hui Cho's hatred was all-encompassing by that time—he didn't discriminate when it came to his victims. He didn't care whether they were students or faculty, white or black or brown, men or women. Even though, in the video package he sent to NBC, Cho claimed he was targeting privilege and immorality, this was a ruse. By then, it wasn't about politics at all; it was about vengeance. Unfiltered, as raw as Cho's own sense of victimhood, the video diatribes testified to Cho's delusional state.

As I have mentioned before, the media's role in the tragedy is much more complicated than it seems at first glance. In their "rush to assign blame" and their attempts to "find a scapegoat"—phrases commonly uttered on the Virginia Tech campus by those critical of the media's role—the media failed to do either. In fact, within a few weeks of the shootings, the media, at least on the Virginia Tech campus, were seen as the "evildoer." Instead of finding scapegoats, the media themselves were scapegoated. Instead of rushing to assign blame, reporters were blamed (and sometimes this blame was completely justified) for their reckless, insensitive pursuit of the story, and for the ways in which the tragedy was being sensationalized. All were equally guilty: the print journalists who invaded the campus like a foreign army, the NBC executives who released Cho's video diatribes, National Public Radio, PBS, CNN, and the BBC. If you were a member of the media, you were despised. And if you spoke to the media, you were complicit in wounding the community.

One of the reasons for the antipathy people felt at Virginia Tech towards the media was the action taken by NBC News.

The package Seung-Hui Cho had mailed to NBC on the morning of April 16 contained photos, writings, and videos. Referred to in the media as a "multimedia manifesto," it contained a twenty-three-page written statement, twenty-eight video clips, and forty-three photographs, only some of which were released to the public. It outlined the fact that, in the world according to Cho, Cho himself was the victim:

> You had a hundred billion chances and ways to have avoided today, but you decided to spill my blood. You forced me into a corner and gave me only one option. The decision was yours. Now you have blood on your hands that will never wash off.[2]

The release of these videos and photographs was so disturbing to victims' families that some of them canceled interviews with NBC after the videos and photos were aired. NBC News president Steve Capus defended the actions of the network, saying, "This is as close as we'll ever come to being in the mind of a killer," a statement that did nothing to persuade those traumatized by the event that the release of the video so soon after the tragedy was justifiable, especially as some of the images selected were designed to force the viewer to assume the role of victim. Three days after the shootings, Cho was on the screen enumerating a litany of injustices he felt he had experienced, letting everyone know what he was about to do, and why he would be compared to Jesus Christ. It is impossible to convey to those who have not experienced this kind of travesty how painful it was to see these videos and the photos Cho had taken of himself. They accosted us. This visual/verbal attack aired again and again.

It was his face that was on the screen each morning when people sat down to breakfast, his image that loomed over us on the evening news. Many in Blacksburg felt it was an image conveyed to us by a media machine intent upon profiting from what they called "the massacre at Virginia Tech," a phrase that CNN used to preface every report it did on the tragedy. The words appeared on the screen in a savagely disintegrating font. "Virginia Tech" and "Massacre" were fused together in a visual depiction of horror, accompanied by menacing music. People who cared about Virginia Tech and who saw it as much more than a setting for Cho's revenge drama were deeply offended by this depiction. The guns were being pointed at our faces because Cho was enacting his role in a real-life, first-person-shooter killing spree. He was poised to kill all over again. No wonder the outcry against the media echoed across campus.

Seung-Hui Cho's disturbed persona morphed into the archetypal anarchist courtesy of his NBC videos and his own horrific attacks. Like Eric Harris and Dylan Klebold, he was well aware of the power he wielded; he knew that his videos would appeal to other disaffected young people. He knew there was a market for this kind of brutality, and he played it to the hilt. Cho the Antagonist had two lives—one in the mainstream media, and one in the shadowy subculture of youthful disaffection. He could be found online with ease, his verbal torrents a startling contrast to the selective mutism that he must have felt emasculated him in other arenas. He could speak to the camera and the camera would listen. He wouldn't stutter or stumble. He could say anything he wanted and no one would mock him, no one would tell him no. It was a free country and an open university. He could take his prey by surprise.

What was largely forgotten in the rush to condemn the media was that, for all its faults, media coverage is one of the main tools we have for uncovering the truth. Investigative reporting, when it is undertaken with sensitivity and integrity, is an essential component of a democratic society. Having lived in Sierra Leone at a time when a free press was not countenanced and everything was subject to censorship by then president Siaka Stevens, I am grateful that the U.S. media are, in most cases, free to publish and present what they want. Print and broadcast media are rightly accused of being vindictive and rapacious. School shootings, which are particularly enticing because they can so easily be transformed into compelling human-interest stories, tend to bring out the worst when it comes to news coverage.

The Virginia Tech community had witnessed what had happened at Columbine—the media invasion, the commercialization of the carnage, and the sensationalizing of a tragedy. It wasn't simply that a president and his administration wanted privacy, most of the campus yearned for it.

The backlash against the media at Virginia Tech manifested itself with surprising speed and efficiency. This itself became a story. By April 19, the day after NBC had released its video, ABC News's Daniel Marotta and journalists from other media outlets began reporting that the backlash was well under way. Notices were put up around campus to let reporters know they were not welcome. In the online posting of Marotta's report, entitled "Media Backlash at Virginia Tech: Community Chafes at Media's Constant Coverage," there is a description of the campus's furious reaction to the media invasion:

> The media frenzy at the Virginia Tech campus in Blacksburg, Va., has spurred resentment among family and friends who continue to mourn for the victims of Monday's shooting. . . .
>
> Students have also been handing out a flier that reads: "We are Hokie Nation and we need to mourn and heal. We need each other. The media has taken advantage of our situation and are exploiting us for their own sensationalism. We will not tolerate the abuse; we love our community far too much to stand for this anymore.
>
> "We, the students of Virginia Tech, are asserting ourselves. We are taking back our campus. All media, if they have any respect for Hokie Nation, will no longer attack our administration. They will no longer hound our students. Leave us to heal. Leave us to ourselves. Hokie Nation needs to be UNITED. Return our campus to us."[3]

Those who spoke with the media could be accused of conspiring with the enemy; those who remained silent were loyal to Virginia Tech. I was surprised by the line in the flier about the administration because, at that point, President Steger hadn't yet responded to the legitimate questions many people had about what occurred on April 16. As early as April 19, however, students appear to have been persuaded that Steger's administration and Virginia Tech were one. To be part of Hokie Nation, you needed to stop asking questions and let people heal. It was a powerful and popular argument on campus. Few wanted to openly oppose it. Some of those who had accused the media of rushing to judgment rushed headlong into judgment themselves.

On Saturday, April 21, five days after the shootings, media talking points were sent in an e-mail to university employees by University Relations. Among the things we were asked to emphasize were the following: that we would not be defined by this event, that we were still confident we could invent the future, and that we were a "unique, special family—more enduring and closer to one another than a typical university community." When I read the e-mail, I realized that, if Virginia Tech was indeed a family, I had become one of its black sheep.

It could be argued that an aggressive media campaign was completely justified. It was essential that the university not be seen as dysfunctional. The administration, the faculty, and the staff had to make sure people knew that we were not cowed by this tragedy because the survival of Virginia Tech was at stake. We needed students to return in the fall, and the entering class had to be as robust as ever. Unfortunately, the need for positive PR became embroiled with the need to avoid responding to a series of difficult questions, and this fact sometimes resulted in a refusal to address key issues.

What was almost forgotten during this time was how much we had all benefited from the more thoughtful and informative aspects of the coverage. As a number of the faculty members pointed out, the reports provided by TV and newspaper reporters were the community's main way of discovering what was going on. It was on television, along with the rest of the country, that we had watched the tragedy unfold, and we continued to do so. We read the *Roanoke Times* because it was clear that the newspaper was invested in our community. We saw interviews with courageous students who prevented Cho from reentering his German class. We learned about the courage of faculty members. But a tragedy like this isn't only a story of heroism, much as we may wish it to be. It is also a story of messier human interactions, of missed signals and lost opportunities. And it was that part of the story that some members of Tech's upper administration seemed intent upon concealing.

The media were not the only casualties during this backlash. The very people whose voices should have been heard—those whose loved ones were dead or injured—had been drowned out. People who anxiously awaited scraps of news about what had actually happened that Monday morning were left wondering why a president who said that a lockdown would have been impossible for a campus this size had managed, nevertheless, to impose a lockdown that same morning immediately after all the shots had been fired. They wondered if anyone else noticed that this didn't make sense.

By Wednesday, May 23, just two days after a meeting with the gubernatorial panel in Blacksburg where he had chosen not to speak in detail about what had happened in the President's Boardroom on Monday, April 16, President Steger was throwing out the first pitch at Yankee Stadium. The Yankees had donated $1 million to the Hokie Spirit Memorial Fund, and it looked as if things were getting back on track. The huge crowd cheered for the besieged president and for Virginia Tech. By now, it was hard to see them as being separate entities. The outcry about accountability was beginning to die down.

Many of us limped towards the end of the semester, holding in our grief so that we could function. Graduation had been particularly challenging because posthumous degrees had been awarded to all of those killed. The media had been in attendance, but their posture had been respectful and they had kept their distance. By then, everyone had been schooled about how to deal with the media. We had been reminded that we could just say no, that we didn't have to speak to anyone.

Shortly after the Panel Report was issued by Governor Kaine, an article by Tom Breen of the Associated Press appeared in *USA Today*. Under the headline "Few on campus blame Va. Tech president," the online posting depicts a community determined to support its embattled leader:

> BLACKSBURG, VA.—With an independent panel saying Virginia Tech's actions might have cost lives and some victims' parents wanting him held accountable for the rampage, university president Charles Steger must look no further than his campus for support.
>
> "I don't think he should resign," said Samantha Cavanaugh, a junior from Manassas. "Considering what he knew at the time, he couldn't have really done anything differently."[4]

Even though the governor's panel had concluded that lives could have been saved if there had been some notification given to the campus, the sense that no one could have predicted this tragedy because it had been so cunningly planned and executed had become an accepted fact. In the same *USA Today* article, however, there is a lone detractor, Celeste Peterson, the mother of one of the victims:

> Support for the university doesn't have to mean backing its leaders, said Celeste Peterson, whose freshman daughter Erin was killed. She called on Kaine to fire Steger and the police chief.
>
> "I love Virginia Tech, too. My daughter loved Virginia Tech," Peterson said, but "we have to separate Virginia Tech brick and mortar from the administration, which is inept."

Governor Kaine, however, disagreed. In his statements that followed the release of the Panel Report, he said he did not feel President Steger should be held accountable for what had happened. In an article by Hank Kurz Jr. and Vicki Smith, also in *USA Today,* Governor Kaine made his position clear:

> The panel, appointed by Gov. Timothy M. Kaine, released its report late Wednesday, and Kaine said he was standing by Steger and other top administrators and not pressing for their firing because they have suffered enough.
>
> "This is not something where the university officials, faculty, administrators have just been very blithe," Kaine said. "There has been deep grieving about this, and it's torn the campus up."[5]

This particular argument was premised upon the notion that those who had suffered were exempt from accountability—precisely what the administration had been arguing for some time.

I am not suggesting that the entire Virginia Tech administration was attempting to manipulate the story. Most were still trying to find ways to cope with their grief. The vast majority who serve in the current administration do whatever they can to assist the institution. This is true even when you look at those administrators who were in the President's Boardroom that Monday when the fateful decisions were made. I think people understood from the outset that a president in that terrible situation does the best he can. Most simply wanted an account from the president of what transpired. It was reasonable to expect that this would be forthcoming.

We all know that there are times when, in spite of our best intentions, we are unable to prevent catastrophe. The administration could have acknowledged from the outset that there were chronic problems we were facing—some of which were unique to Virginia Tech, and some of which plague all large, state-subsidized universities. It could have admitted early on that we had no staff psychiatrist in the Cook Counseling Center, for example, that the center is understaffed and underfunded, and its employees—many of whom are exceptionally dedicated—are overworked. The problem was that the administration's silence suggested—rightly or wrongly—that people had something to hide. It was a reaction prompted by panic rather than common sense. A president who had lived in a small college town for almost his entire life had suddenly been thrust onto a global public/political stage. The town had been invaded by strangers looking for blood. As is typical in almost all cases of school shootings, people were terrified of giving the media more on which to feast. So the administration decided to say nothing in hopes that the questions circling the campus like a swarm of locusts would eventually move on.

Students had no way of knowing that there were so many things left unsaid. What they saw when school opened in the fall of 2007 was a campus revived—one that they could rightfully claim as their own. Once again, Virginia Polytechnic Institute and State University was a place of beauty and peace. How could they possibly know that there could be other angles to this story?

5.

The Panel
Review

SEUNG-HUI CHO's sinister persona cast a shadow over a pretty campus on May 21. A distinguished group of panelists hand-picked by Governor Kaine would hear from the university's upper administration. It would not be trial by media this time; it would be a methodical examination of the events of April 16. Some of the victims' families and friends were in attendance, together with members of the campus community, all of them eager to discover the truth.

The meeting was reported by Michael Sluss and Greg Esposito in the May 22 issue of the *Roanoke Times* with a simple headline, "Panel convenes":

> By the end of the panel's public meeting on the Tech campus, the group had been given a detailed timeline of the shooting deaths of two students in West Ambler Johnston Hall and the shootings 2½ hours later in Norris Hall.
>
> They also heard Tech President Charles Steger and other university officials defend their decision to keep the campus open after the first shootings, saying that nothing about the

two deaths in a dormitory suggested that a much larger crisis would unfold later that morning.

"It's a judgment call, but we believe we did the right thing," Steger told the panel.

What wasn't reported in the *Roanoke Times* was that something very strange had occurred during that meeting. In fact, a very sketchy account had been provided by the president and the Policy Group to the panel review.[1]

In his introductory remarks, President Steger reminded the panel that the Virginia Tech attorney also serves as "Special Assistant Attorney General." This implied that the Office of the Attorney General in Richmond was overseeing the entire procedure on behalf of the Commonwealth of Virginia, and reinforced the notion that whatever was said by university legal counsel had been approved by the state. In this tricky situation—i.e., a state-controlled system of education was being investigated by the state that controlled it—potential conflicts of interest should have been apparent. Not only was one arm investigating another arm, the two legal offices—the state's and the university's—were, all the while, shaking hands. Although a full list of Policy Group participants has not yet been made public, university legal counsel was present on April 16. This means that the office responsible for representing all the administrators, faculty members, and staff at Virginia Tech was placed in the unenviable position of having to defend itself and its clients at the same time. I can't imagine how any attorneys, however dedicated they may be, could manage this task.

At the May 21 meeting, President Steger also announced that all communication between the university and the panel would be routed through Lenwood McCoy, a retired university controller and thirty-five-year veteran of Virginia Tech "who has agreed to serve as the liaison between the university and the Review Panel to ensure that the Panel receives a thorough response to all requests for information."

Lenwood McCoy's role became very important. As the only conduit to the panel members, he was the person who was charged with contacting faculty and staff to let us know if the panel wanted to speak with us. Although, in theory, it was possible to submit an e-mail directly to the panel, if it were done on a university computer through the university's server, the e-mail could easily be traced. In addition, because those involved in the case had been instructed by the administration to work exclusively through Lenwood McCoy, bypassing the administration in this way could be seen as disobeying the advice of university legal counsel and could therefore result in a loss of representation. The president ended his introductory remarks by saying that the university wanted to "learn from these events."

President Steger relied upon university counsel Kay Heidbreder to explain why it would be so difficult for the university to comply with the request to share Seung-Hui Cho's medical and academic records. This became the lynchpin of the administration's argument, and it was to plague the panelists for some time.

Kay Heidbreder, like Charles Steger, also read from a prepared statement. By the time she had finished speaking, it was clear that the obstacles confronting the panel in their quest to uncover the truth would be significant. Her argument was one I had heard before at Virginia Tech—one that was respectful of the law, but it also meant that critical information could not be shared under any circumstances:

> At any institution of higher education in Virginia, there are a number of laws protecting the privacy of students and student records. These laws include The Family Educational Rights and Privacy Act, 20 U.S.C.A. 31232g, HIPAA 42 U.S.C. Section 1320, the Virginia Freedom of Information Act, Section 2.2-3700, Code of Virginia, as amended, and the Government Data Collection and Dissemination Practices Act, Section 32.2-3800, Code of Virginia, as amended. The Family Educational Rights and Privacy Act (aka FERPA or Buckley Amendment)

sets forth criteria for the dissemination of information to protect a student's rights of privacy.

The University is restricted in its ability to share a student's
educational records with third parties, external to the University, absent a properly executed release or a court order. While
it is debatable whether the FERPA protections end at the student's death, the other laws contain no such limitation.[2]

As I look back on what occurred during that pivotal May 21
meeting, I am struck by the fact that it was a meeting at which the
Virginia Tech administration explained, in some detail, why it couldn't
speak. This point is critical because, at the time, it was hard to be
100 percent certain that Cho had acted alone, nor were we any clearer
about his motivations. For all we knew, he'd said something to counselors that could be helpful to the investigation. It was urgent that
information be shared because otherwise the campus could still be in
jeopardy. But five weeks after the shootings, there was no urgency
on the part of the Virginia Tech administration. We still didn't know
whether Cho had even visited counseling services, and we weren't
about to find out anytime soon.

When it was time to describe what had happened on April 16,
the presentation was not made by President Steger, who served as
the head of the Policy Group. Instead, it was delegated to David
Ford, vice provost for Academic Affairs, who was, quite possibly,
the lowest-ranking faculty member of the Policy Group.*

While the president sat and listened, Ford recounted the sequence of events:

Shortly after 8:00 A.M. on Monday, April 16, I was informed
that there had been a shooting in West Ambler Johnston Hall
and that President Steger was assembling the Policy Group

---

*It is hard to know for sure if Ford was the lowest-ranking faculty member be-
cause, as of this writing, it is not entirely clear who was present at the Policy Group
meeting on April 16.

immediately. By approximately 8:30 A.M., I and the other members of the group had arrived at the Burruss Hall Boardroom and Dr. Steger convened the meeting.

. . . In the preliminary stages of the investigation, it [the double homicide] appeared to be an isolated incident, possibly domestic in nature. The Policy Group learned that Blacksburg police and Virginia state police had been notified and were also on the scene.[3]

If this had been dialogue from a play I had assigned to my class, students might wonder why the main character isn't speaking. What happened before this? What happened afterwards? Who was making calls to whom? Was the attorney general's office in Richmond contacted, for example? What did the president want to do? If the president and the Policy Group are not one and the same thing, what was it that President Steger himself assumed? We don't know for certain when he was first notified of the double homicide, nor do we know what his plan of action was, as one report after another came into Burruss Hall. We never find out who actually made the decision *not* to notify the campus, though we can assume it was the president because he had the responsibility to do so. Was a vote taken? Did the group reach a consensus? Were there any naysayers? What we get instead is a valiant attempt by the vice provost for Academic Affairs (wrongly identified in this instance in the Panel Report as "Vice Provost for *Student* Affairs" [my italics]) to summarize his impressions of what happened that morning.

I wish to add at this juncture that, having worked with David Ford, I think it is very likely that he was simply one of the only people (if not the only one) willing to take on the onerous duty of representing the group. In all the dealings I have had with Dr. Ford, I have found him to be an ethical person who is deeply committed to Virginia Tech—a kind and generous man. It was regrettable that the president asked him to speak on behalf of the group, especially as it seems Dr. Ford was on the margins of what occurred. There would be certain things he could not address, many issues he could not elaborate upon in any detail.

Dr. Ford's role as spokesperson for the Policy Group—arguably the most powerful group on campus—is particularly puzzling when you look at the group's makeup. According to the Emergency Plan 2005 (hereinafter referred to as ERP-2005), most of the other members of the Policy Group are vice presidents, with the exception of university legal counsel Kay Heidbreder, Associate Vice President for University Relations Larry Hincker, and some support staff.[4] David Ford had been at Virginia Tech since 1998, and although his title as of this writing is vice president and dean of Undergraduate Education, Ford was not a vice president at the time of the tragedy. As I understand it, the Policy Group was set up to function like a presidential advisory group, which would mean that key advisers would likely hold the rank of vice president. In fact the "Vice President in Charge"—a position clearly spelled out in ERP-2005—is the person who is authorized to take a lead role in the Policy Group. (To date, his identity has not been publicly released.) The vice president in charge reports directly to President Steger, so his account of what happened would have been particularly helpful, if we were not permitted to hear the account of the president himself. In fact, when the Panel Report was published four months later in August 2007, it was surprising to see that the president's name rarely appears.

Had the panelists been more firmly acquainted with university culture they might have asked why David Ford spoke for the Policy Group. One panelist, Gordon Davies, held a supervisory role in higher education as the head of the State Council of Higher Education of Virginia (SCHEV) prior to his retirement. The other panelists who worked in higher education—panel vice chair Dr. Marcus L. Martin, assistant dean of the School of Medicine and associate vice president for Diversity and Equity at the University of Virginia, and Dr. Aradhana A. "Bela" Sood, professor of psychiatry and pediatrics at Virginia Commonwealth University Medical Center—are likely to have been more familiar with the culture that exists at medical schools. Panelists such as the Honorable Tom Ridge, former secretary of homeland security, would have been unfamiliar with Virginia Tech protocol, and so, like others on the panel, probably relied upon the Virginia Tech administration for their information.

Using the timeline included in the Panel Report and details from numerous articles, it is possible to piece together some of what happened on the morning of April 16.

The members of the group began to gather at 8:00 A.M. in the President's Boardroom (referred to in Ford's account as the "Burruss Hall Boardroom," but more commonly known by the name I am using here). According to Ford's first-person account, President Steger had been in constant contact with the VTPD:

> I learned subsequently that as he awaited the arrival of other group members, President Steger had been in regular communication with the police, had given direction to have the governor's office notified of the shooting, and had called the head of University Relations to his office to begin planning to activate the emergency communication systems.[5]

The President's Boardroom is situated on the second floor of Burruss Hall. You get to it by walking through the president's and the provost's suite of offices, or you can approach it from a corridor that runs between the presidential suite and Burruss auditorium. It is an imposing room filled with oil portraits of past presidents, and you are struck by the weight of Virginia Tech's history. You would think from this opening statement that the emergency communication systems would be activated any minute now. But that's not what happened.

The Policy Group convened shortly after 8:00 A.M. The double homicide had been discovered at 7:24 A.M. after a student who was nearby heard a noise coming from room 4040 in West Ambler Johnston Residence Hall and suspected that someone had fallen out of bed. The investigating officer had requested additional resources and those had been provided by the Blacksburg Police Department.

According to the Panel Report, the Office of the Executive Vice President—a title held at that time by James A. Hyatt, who has since left Virginia Tech—had been notified of the shootings at 7:57 A.M.[6] While the investigation was under way, classes commenced as scheduled at 8:00 A.M.

President Steger would have been under tremendous pressure. It's likely that the president behaved as he usually did in meetings, listening carefully first, mulling things over, and then responding, usually erring on the side of caution. Sometimes it could be difficult to know what conclusion he had come to because he is a guarded person. There is nothing excitable about Virginia Tech's fifteenth president. Introverted, perspicacious, and discreet, he manages to convey an air of authority. He tends to be ill at ease in a crisis situation and most at home when surrounded by the familiar. He relies heavily on his advisers, especially those in his inner circle.

Across the Drillfield in West Ambler Johnston, the double homicide was being investigated by Chief Flinchum and the Virginia Tech police. The Blacksburg Police Department was also on the scene. The police chief did not have the capability to send out an alert to the community because the order had to go through the prescribed chain of command first. According to ERP-2005, the police chief's reporting line was through the emergency response coordinator, who would then report to the vice president in charge, who would then report to President Steger. In an article by David Ress that appeared in the *Richmond Times-Dispatch* on September 13, 2008, a parent of one of the victims claimed that Chief Flinchum had said he wanted to close the campus but that it wasn't his call—a claim that was immediately refuted by university spokesperson Larry Hincker. In a September 25, 2008, article by Rex Bowman and Carlos Santos, Hincker's assertion is corroborated by some newly released documents, including notes from Ralph Byers, director of government relations for Virginia Tech. Byers wrote in a note he took while in the meeting that morning: "Police don't believe lock down is necessary or advisable." What is most surprising in Ress's article, however, is the revelation that Chief Flinchum does not appear to have been questioned about this himself by the panel. Therefore, it is still unclear what exactly was conveyed to the group:

> Former State Police Superintendent Gerald Massengill, who led the state's April 16 review panel, said he didn't remember Flinchum saying he had recommended closing the school. But Massengill added that he didn't recall anyone on the panel asking, either.[7]

I found it regrettable that President Steger (to my knowledge at least) did not convey to people that it was he who was empowered to make the decision about the lockdown, empowered to make the decision about notification, empowered to run the university, and that Chief Flinchum's role was marginalized by the cumbersome hierarchy that existed at Virginia Tech. There are still people out there who believe that Chief Flinchum had the capability to close the campus and notify the community. He did not. The VTPD chief was not empowered in this situation, though in the news conferences that followed, given the prominence afforded to Chief Flinchum, it was easy to forget this fact.[8]

As Ford revealed in his prepared statement, the president and the Policy Group were advised by the police that a suspect was being tracked—slain student Emily Hilscher's boyfriend.

> Information continued to be received through frequent telephone conversations with Virginia Tech police on the scene. The Policy Group was informed that the residence hall was being secured by Virginia Tech police, and students within the hall were notified and asked to remain in their rooms for their safety. We were further informed that the room containing the gunshot victims was immediately secured for evidence collec-

tion, and Virginia Tech police began questioning hall residents and identifying potential witnesses. In the preliminary stages of the investigation, it appeared to be an isolated incident, possibly domestic in nature.[9]

It's difficult to know why this last assumption was made, though there is little doubt that the term *domestic violence* has connotations which can lead people to assume that the violence has somehow been contained within the domestic sphere and is therefore less likely to be visited upon those outside it.

When the passive voice is used in sentence construction it is hard to pin down who the subject is. In the first sentence of the above quote, for example, we would normally say "So-and-so continued to receive information," but instead we have "Information continued to be received," which makes it hard to know who was actually receiving it. Although this description begins as what appears to be a first-person, eyewitness narrative, it seems to dissolve into an account of an event viewed at a considerable distance. The phrase "The Policy Group was informed," for example, begs the question of who did the informing. It seems by the end of the paragraph as though everyone is receiving all the information at the same time, but given how chaotic the situation must have been, this seems somewhat unlikely. Usually teachers of writing try to dissuade students from using the passive voice construction because it tends to result in accounts that lack specificity and removes a subject from his or her own actions, as it does in this case.

One of the things the Policy Group discussed was how to break the news to the campus that two students had been killed. The president wanted to make sure that he didn't compound an already difficult situation by making matters worse.

Although the administrators in the room would have had limited experience dealing with a shooting, they would have been able to draw upon the experience of the Morva incident. When William

Morva—the gunman who killed security guard Derrick McFarland and Deputy Sheriff Eric Sutphin—had been on the loose in August 2006, a SWAT team responded to an erroneous report of a possible hostage situation in Squires Student Center. According to Ford's account, this episode had influenced the Policy Group's decision. The members therefore decided not to alarm anyone by issuing an alert.

> The Policy Group was further informed by the police that they were following up on leads concerning a person of interest in relation to the shooting. During this 30-minute period of time between 8:30 and 9:00 A.M., the Policy Group processed the factual information it had in the context of many questions we asked ourselves. For instance, what information do we release without causing a panic? We learned from the Morva incident last August that speculation and misinformation spread by individuals who do not have the facts cause panic.[10]

It is true that the campus was somewhat on edge on April 16. Bomb threats had been left in Torgersen, Durham, and Whittemore Halls on April 13, all of which had turned out to be hoaxes. But the notion that the Policy Group would cause panic if it issued a warning is unwarranted. In fact, when warnings had been issued during the Morva incident, no one panicked. Although there had been some confusion in Squires, no one was hurt. Similarly, when notified of the bomb threats three days earlier, the campus responded calmly— which is not to say that there had not been some disruption. As Virginia Tech visiting professor Patricia Mooney Nickel pointed out in her insightful essay "There Is an Unknown on Campus," classes had been canceled on three prior Mondays in the 2006–7 academic year "due to the threat of violence on campus."[11]

It is quite possible that the administration was aware, as it tried to think about how to proceed, that classes had frequently been disrupted. Had there been a nonadministrative member of the teaching faculty present, or indeed a member of the VTPD, the Policy Group could have been reassured that, though it would indeed be yet another disruption in what was already a difficult year, panic would not ensue.

A barrage of information would have been received by the Policy Group by now. The members needed to decide what to do with it, but they had numerous questions. They began to draft an e-mail:

> Beyond the two gunshot victims found by police, was there a possibility that another person might be involved (i.e., a shooter), and if so, where is that person, what does that person look like, and is that person armed? At that time of the morning, when thousands are in transit, what is the most effective and efficient way to convey the information to all faculty, staff, and students? If we decided to close the campus at that point, what would be the most effective process given the openness of a campus the size of Virginia Tech? How much time do we have until the next class change?[12]

The question about whether or not there was another person involved—"(i.e., a shooter)"—is, quite frankly, absurd. Of course there is "a possibility" that someone else could be involved. What is most distressing about what comes next is the list of questions: "and if so, where is that person, what does that person look like, and is that person armed?" These questions appear to have been asked between 8:30 and 9:00 A.M., well before any kind of notification was issued to the community. So well before the first e-mail alert was sent the Policy Group and/or the president had determined that it was quite possible that an armed gunman could be on the campus, someone who had already killed two students.

At 9:01 A.M., while the Policy Group was trying to decide whether or not to notify the campus, Seung-Hui Cho was mailing his crazed, misanthropic video missive to NBC. He was also mailing a rambling, rage-filled letter to the English department at Virginia Tech.

The second class period of the day began on time at 9:05 A.M. Thus far, no warnings had been issued.

At 9:24 A.M., Emily Hilscher's boyfriend was apprehended off campus by police who proceeded to question him. The poor young man must have been devastated when he realized that he not only had lost his girlfriend but also was suspected of having been involved in her murder. A seasoned officer would have suspected as soon as he questioned the young man that something wasn't right—that perhaps they had been tracking the wrong person all along. But not until 9:48, following a gunpowder residue test, was it confirmed that Emily Hilscher's boyfriend was not the perpetrator.

At 9:25 A.M., a VTPD captain joins the Policy Group "as a liaison," and within a minute an e-mail is sent at last to campus staff, faculty, and students to notify them of the shooting in the dorm room. But it is too late to prevent people from coming to campus for the second class period of the day.[13] The captain's arrival is absent from the Ford statement and is found instead in the meticulous timeline provided in the Panel Report.

What comes next in Ford's account is, perhaps, the most distressing passage of all:

> And so with the information the Policy Group had at approximately 9 A.M., we drafted and edited a communication to be released to the university community via e-mail and to be placed on the university web site. We made the best decision we could based upon the information we had at the time. Shortly before 9:30 A.M., the Virginia Tech community—faculty, staff, and students—were notified by e-mail as follows:
>
> > "A shooting incident occurred at West Ambler Johnston earlier this morning. Police are on the scene and are investigating. The university community is urged to be cautious and are asked to contact Virginia Tech Police if you observe anything suspicious or with information on the case. Contact Virginia Tech Police at 231-6411. Stay tuned to the www.vt.edu. We will post as soon as we have more information."[14]

The message was carefully worded, but it was not nearly as direct as it could have been. The "shooting incident" was really a double homicide. Even though the Policy Group now suspected that the shooter could be on the loose, the e-mail did not make it clear to the community that this was the case.

Between 9:15 and 9:30 A.M., Seung-Hui Cho chained the doors of three of the main entrances to Norris Hall from the inside. He left notes on the chained doors that bombs would be detonated if anyone tried to remove the chains. A faculty member saw one of the notes and took it to the Office of the Dean of Engineering on the third floor of Norris Hall.

Around 9:40 A.M., Seung-Hui Cho entered the second-floor classrooms of Norris Hall.

Just as someone in the dean's office was about to call in the bomb threat, the shootings began.

Shots were heard in the President's Boardroom in Burruss, a stone's throw from Norris Hall.

The police responded to a 911 call from students in Norris. They reached Norris Hall in a mere three minutes. By 9:50 A.M., they had shot open a lock on an unchained door and entered the building to search for the shooter.

At roughly 9:51 A.M., Seung-Hui Cho committed suicide.

IT IS quite possible that, had a warning been issued, it would have resulted in a similarly tragic outcome. Seung-Hui Cho was determined to kill as many people as he could that morning. But when President Steger told the media that it could have turned out much worse than it did I can't help thinking about those who lost loved ones on April 16.[15] For them, the horror is superlative not comparative. There is no "worse" scenario than the one they are living inside because the worst has already happened to them. Their beloved children or husbands, brothers or sisters, mothers or fathers, students or teachers, wives or friends are dead. In light of this, whatever explanation was provided for what happened needed to be as forthright and as honest as possible.

Families are still struggling to get access to critical papers. Some have been provided but there are others that have been omitted. There is no explanation as to how or why Cho's counseling records were "inadvertently destroyed." University spokesperson Larry Hincker defends the university's right not to share all the documents pertaining to the case in this way:

> Hincker, who wrote the notes from the Policy Group meeting, said last week that he couldn't remember enough about that time to put them into context.
>
> He said some documents the family lawyers obtained were removed by Virginia Tech lawyers before allowing *The Times-Dispatch* review.
>
> Hincker said documents not released were not public records because they were Steger's working papers, covered by attorney-client privilege, or Cho's student records.[16]

Although more material has been recently released in accordance with the settlement between the victims' families and the public, and it's possible that other documents will be released in the future, it would seem that those lobbying for full disclosure still have a long battle ahead of them.

Some years ago, a friend gave me a quote by the late Audre Lorde, an African American poet who fought a courageous battle with cancer. On the top and bottom of the thin strip of blue paper are pinholes where I stuck it up on a notice board in my studio. When times get tough, I recite Audre Lorde's words: "When I dare to be powerful—to use my strength in the service of my vision, then it becomes less and less important whether I am afraid." I like the idea that fear diminishes when we focus on serving our visions; I like to think that there is a type of empowerment we can cultivate within ourselves that is nurturing rather than acquisitive or destructive.

We all make errors in judgment. Sometimes these errors result in tragedy. It must have been an agonizing morning for the Policy Group, unaccustomed as it was to dealing with security issues of this magnitude. In all likelihood members relied upon those with longer tenure for guidance.

Many of us under the same circumstances could have made some of the same mistakes the Virginia Tech administration may have made on the morning of April 16. I, like others, was willing to accept that the president had done the best he could. I thought that, within a few weeks, after the university had time to digest the horror of what had happened, the president and his advisers would understand that there was an urgent need for open communication. So far, this has not happened. One result is that the most insistent narrative has become Seung-Hui Cho's. Because it was the most dramatic, it was the one to which the media responded. But there should have been a counterpoint to that narrative provided by the Virginia Tech leadership.

Sadly, the president ended up silencing himself at a time when everyone desperately needed to hear him speak.

Part Two

BACKSTORY

6.
The
Setting

WHEN SEUNG-HUI CHO mailed his multimedia package and letter from the Blacksburg Post Office on April 16, he would not have been seen as remarkable—just another Tech student mailing a package to someone. People are friendly in Blacksburg; they are often willing to assist you, even on April 16, a particularly busy day at the downtown post office because it marked that year's tax-filing deadline. One of the postal clerks went out of her way to help Cho. He was confused about the address on the package he wanted to mail to NBC. By then, it was after 9:00 A.M. He had killed two students already. That morning, no one suspected Seung-Hui Cho of anything at all.

In *Rampage: The Social Roots of School Shootings,* Professor Katherine Newman and her coauthors devote part of a chapter to defining the difference between what they call "rampage shootings" and inner-city violence. They make important distinctions between rural/suburban versus urban settings. Among them is the following:

In rural communities, school is one of the few "public stages" where an attention-seeking shooter can create a spectacle. In the city, there are many other (potentially more meaningful) stages available. . . . The school itself is a highly symbolic target of the attack.[1]

Virginia Tech offered the kind of "public stage" that would appeal to a desperately insecure, obsessively self-centered and aggrieved young man like Seung-Hui Cho. Cho knew that he would be able to create "a spectacle." He knew that his attack on a campus in small-town America would guarantee national and, quite possibly, international coverage.

The setting could well have been as important as the act itself. It would represent the overthrow of authority and be seen as the ultimate violation of a space previously thought to be sacrosanct. From Cho's perspective, it had to be an attack that outstripped all others, one that would prove his significance.

It was not an accident that Cho had chosen writing as his career path. That way he could project his voice without having to speak. Like many young writers, he yearned for fame, but his yearning went unfulfilled when his book proposal was rejected by a publisher. One way or another, Cho was determined to make a name for himself.

When I spoke with Cho about a poem he had written about his high school teacher and fellow students, a poem full of anger and resentment, he indicated that high school had been traumatic for him. His experience there made him feel persecuted. He attended Westfield High School in Chantilly, in Fairfax County, Virginia, from 2000 to 2003. Various accounts from classmates suggest that he was ridiculed for the way he spoke:

Chris Davids, a Virginia Tech student who graduated with Cho from Westfield High School in Chantilly, Va., in 2003, re-

called that Cho almost never opened his mouth and would ignore attempts to strike up a conversation.

Once, in an English class, the teacher had the students
read aloud and, when it was Cho's turn, he just looked down
in silence, Davids recalled in an interview with The Associated
Press.

Finally, after the teacher threatened to give him a failing
grade for participation, Cho started to read in a strange, deep
voice that sounded "like he had something in his mouth,"
Davids said.

"As soon as he started reading, the whole class started
laughing and pointing and saying, 'Go back to China,'" Davids said.[2]

Two of his victims were Westfield High graduates, but investigators
do not believe they were deliberately targeted. (Westfield High has
an excellent academic reputation, and many of its graduates come to
Virginia Tech.)

I understand what it can be like to be singled out because of the
way you look or sound. It happened to me as a biracial child growing up in London before it was acceptable to be mixed race. Cho's
experience seemed, in many ways, typical of the kinds of things that
happen, unfortunately, at school. Students sometimes carry grudges,
and it is not unusual to find manifestations of them in their writing,
so I had seen angry work like this before, from young men in particular. One of the things that troubled me about Cho's writing, however, was that it indicated both intense resentment and an extreme
level of immaturity. Most of us have been rejected or ridiculed at one
time or another; most of us find ways to cope with it. But for Cho
there was a recurrence of the original hurt, a restaging of it in his
mind, as if time for him were not linear but cyclical. Cho's exaggerated sense of his own victimhood was worrying because it was what
you would expect to find in a much younger person.

I have since wondered whether Cho transferred some of the fury he felt growing up in Centreville (a community near Chantilly) to Virginia Tech, especially if, in his unbalanced state, he found it difficult to differentiate between his earlier experiences and his experience as an undergraduate. If the timeline that existed in Cho's head consisted of repeating and replaying past injustices, then what happened years ago at school could be as vivid to him at the age of twenty-three as it was when it first took place. Even in 2005, when he was still capable of socializing with others to a limited degree, Cho's behavior and vision were out of step with his surroundings. Although the work I saw of his was by no means the angriest or most disturbing I have read, there was a hollowness to it, as if the author inhabited a cavernous space crowded with tormentors, as if he were looking for a way out. In the fall of 2005, he seemed to be searching for the one exit that did not lead to self-annihilation, but he was not able to get to it alone. He was still allowing himself to feel things back then, and his anger hadn't completely overwhelmed him.

One of the most difficult aspects of living in Blacksburg after the tragedy and continuing to teach at Virginia Tech is that I am obliged to live and work side by side with Cho's indifferent ghost. Indifference is often worse than rage because it can be divorced from causality. Someone kills simply to kill; his victims are randomly selected. His skewed perspective results in a self-imposed countdown to catastrophe that cannot be avoided.

I have learned since the shootings that there were students at Virginia Tech who tried to reach out to Cho. Almost invariably, their kindness was rebuffed, perhaps because it was important to Cho that he be seen as different. You have to work hard at Virginia Tech to remain isolated. There are more than six hundred registered student organizations, and many students claim it's impossible not to find a group of like-minded students who share an interest in something you enjoy. There are organizations at Tech built around a common faith or ethnicity, the love of a sport or a career, and organizations focused on activities as varied as belly dancing, cigars, croquet, philosophy, and spying. But if Cho allowed himself to have fun with other students, to actually enjoy himself when he went out with them, to truly be their peer, how would they recognize his power? In the fall of 2005, when he grabbed a knife and stabbed it into the carpet as his roommates watched in surprise, he was emphasizing the fact that he would never be one of them. As the scene was described in the Panel Report:

> At the beginning of the school year, the roommate and the other suitemates took Cho to several parties. He would always end up sitting in the corner by himself. One time they all went back to a female student's room. Cho took out a knife ("lock blade, not real large") and started stabbing the carpet. They stopped taking him out with them after that incident.[3]

After a while, having been rejected by a publisher and by various young women he had pursued unsuccessfully at Virginia Tech, Cho turned the tables on the community and rejected everything it had to offer. He wanted to straddle the stage alone, guns in hand, wreaking havoc and instilling terror. It is generally believed that he committed suicide because he heard the police coming. I also believe that this is what happened, but I suspect that a contributing factor to his decision to take his own life at that moment, when he still had more than two hundred rounds of ammo left, was that he wanted to make sure there were witnesses to the carnage—people who would be able to testify to his callousness. He knew he had left people alive, and like a performer, he needed an audience.

Seung-Hui Cho was one of twenty-six thousand students at Tech. Blacksburg residents are accustomed to seeing international students. Even though Cho's demeanor and mannerisms may have struck some people as strange they would have been unlikely to alarm many people. He was able to cultivate his isolation in this community, in part because he was free to become whoever he wanted to be. For the most part, he wasn't monitored or questioned.

His privacy was respected and he was treated as an adult. The assumption was that he would try to fit in and be eager to learn. It is the assumption schools always make about students, one on which the entire learning enterprise is premised.

I don't think that Cho found nearly as much opposition as he had anticipated at Virginia Tech, which could be why he had to manufacture some of it by stalking young women and making sure that they would find his attempts to get to know them frightening. (Cho harassed female students at Virginia Tech and was twice warned against stalking by the VTPD.) In the encounters he had with these women he did things to ensure they would be afraid of him. He wanted to be remembered, and instilling fear was one of the most efficient ways of accomplishing that. It seems contradictory to say, on the one hand, that Cho yearned for an end to his isolation and, on the other, he prized it. But it seemed to me at times that this was the case, perhaps because he had lived in a state of isolation for so long. After a while, behavior becomes habit, and habit can become compulsion. It may have been difficult for him to stop being the campus loner without, in his mind at least, losing face.

When Cho arrived in Blacksburg, it was likely that he found a town which was, for the most part, tolerant of difference, and a school where, with a few exceptions, he could be as silent as he wanted to be. In Virginia Tech and in Blacksburg, Cho found a community willing to accept his differences and afford him his privacy. On 4/16, he took full advantage of that.

IN 2003, Seung-Hui Cho joined hundreds of other foreign-born students and faculty who found their way to Southwest Virginia. International students and faculty are attracted by Virginia Tech's strong research programs in engineering and the sciences. Apart from the international community, however, the town and the university have relatively little to boast about in terms of racial diversity. In a state where 17 percent of the population is African American, Virginia

Tech can point to less than 4.6 percent of its student population and less than 2 percent of its teaching faculty who are classified as "Black." It can be challenging for those who decide to reside here. If your heritage is African American or Caribbean, for example, it can be tricky to find a beauty salon. (My own quest has taken me to various salons in Blacksburg, nearby Christiansburg, and Radford. At one salon, years ago, an impromptu meeting was held to find out who was willing to tackle my hair. I felt like Mount Everest.) Hispanic and Native American students are also in short supply at the university. Diversity is therefore provided by international students and faculty, who have come to Tech in increasing numbers. We hail from countries like China, the United Kingdom, South Korea, France, Vietnam, Iran, Indonesia, India, Pakistan, the Côte d'Ivoire, Tanzania, Mexico, and Australia. This international presence has helped energize the town and bring fresh perspectives into the community.

It is easy to turn Blacksburg into a caricature, especially if you drive through the downtown—a drive that lasts for all of three minutes, assuming you have to stop for a traffic light. Like Holcomb, Kansas, the town depicted in Truman Capote's blistering "nonfiction novel" *In Cold Blood,* Blacksburg is an easy target. Like Holcomb, it, too, seems helplessly ordinary to the untrained eye; its residents, particularly its indigenous ones—those who possess accents it's fashionable to ridicule—are tempting prey. Like Holcomb, Blacksburg received international attention because of murders so savage that they spoke all languages at once. But Blacksburg defies easy categorization. The community values an old-fashioned concept of community, but it is also eager to embrace modernity. It welcomes difference and values artistic expression. Touted as the first "electronic village" in the country, Blacksburg got online faster than any other town in America but seemed to lose interest when everyone else in the country got on board.

As the largest employer in the region, Virginia Tech is the behemoth you don't mess with if you're sensible. To some extent, this makes Blacksburg a "company" town—a place where it's almost impossible to escape the institution's influence. Students tend to view Blacksburg as a mere extension of the campus. Some of them barely seem to see the town as an entity in its own right, which is why there has been a concerted effort at Virginia Tech to ensure that students, faculty, and staff engage more fully with the local community. Generally speaking, however, Locals and Imports live in relative harmony with each other—more so than is often the case when Town and Gown rub up against each other.

Students are guests of the town for the four years they are here. There are no walls separating the campus from Blacksburg; in fact, in certain areas, it can be hard to tell where Blacksburg ends and the campus begins. So it makes sense that Tech residents are the town's residents also. This is one of the reasons why Blacksburg grieved alongside Virginia Tech—Tech's tragedy was the town's. Even now you see the black-ribbon VT logo—in the windows of downtown stores, at the beauty salon on the lapels of beauticians, displayed in doctors' and dentists' offices, in local banks, in used-car lots.

Cho could just as easily have attacked a local restaurant or bar in Blacksburg. But he seems to have selected the campus because it was a way of usurping authority, wrenching it from the hands of teachers and parents. But because the town and the university are so tightly knit, the violation in one locale was a violation against the other. The blood spilled out from the campus and stained the region red.

I first set eyes on Blacksburg in February 1985. It had been snowing and the streets were a pristine white, as though people had taken off their boots before they walked on it. I had been invited to interview for the position of instructor, a non-tenure-track position given to those who were assumed to be unworthy of permanent employment, people like composition specialists and creative writers. Even if I got the position I would be forced to relinquish it after five years. Well before my contract was up, however, and well before I had published a collection of poetry and been moved into a tenure-track position, I had come to the conclusion that Blacksburg wasn't half bad. By then I had lived and taught in England, in Sierra Leone, and in Arkansas, and each time the move had resulted in culture shock. I had expected to endure the same degree of culture shock in Blacksburg. It never came.

Some of the features of Blacksburg replicate those found in other college towns. There is the local theater, for example, and the local vegetarian restaurant. The theater is located on College Avenue—the road that runs along one edge of the campus and marks the beginning of Blacksburg's downtown area. Called the Lyric, it was meticulously restored by townspeople several years ago. Near the Lyric is Gillies, the compulsory college restaurant. Gillies is a hangout for Blacksburg's bohemians—a hippie-flavored gathering place where artsy types can take up residence at one of the wooden tables and complain about the world's excesses.

When my son was young, I would take him to Gillies for ice cream. Slow fans churned the sultry air in the summertime when no one was ever in a hurry. Once in a while, writers from the English department would hold poetry and fiction readings amid the clatter of ceramic dishes and the pungent smell of herbs and brown rice. We were earnest about our craft because we were under the gun: We had only five years to become famous before Tech would compel us to move on. We read standing up without a podium. Poised in front of the old wooden ice cream counter, we sent our words up with a gusto born of sincerity and panic. We were making art; we could say whatever we wanted. Even if Tech fired us we would still have our words.

Nothing symbolizes the fusion between Town and Gown more than a flock of recent additions to the town's artistic ambience. To honor the close relationship between Virginia Tech and Blacksburg, and as a way to encourage tourism, the town decided a couple of years ago to honor its most famous resident, the Hokie bird, Virginia Tech's beloved turkey mascot. Seventy-five fiberglass Hokie bird statues were manufactured by a group of concerned citizens who launched a project whimsically entitled Gobble de Art in 2006. Several Hokie bird statues now stand guard along Main Street; others were snapped up by patrons; and some, alas, have been kidnapped.

It's not surprising in an area where farming is still a viable occupation and agricultural extension agents employed by Virginia Tech fan out into the region to serve the community that Tech's mascot is a loving tribute to the pulchritude of poultry. The Hokie bird statues are as imposing as the Virginia Tech mascot itself (though the mascot head has to be supersized because it is stuffed with a student's). Each 120-pound fiberglass bird embodies the Town-Gown fusion: Each has been painted to depict a variety of the town's virtues. In a clever reversal of the power dynamic, the university mascot became the canvas upon which the town painted its own highlights.

At A Cleaner World, the dry cleaners on South Main, you can find *Freedom Hokie* swathed in stars and stripes. Then there is the Hokie bird that looks like a financier: He stands proudly outside one of the local banks and is called *A Bird You Can Bank On.* He sports a copy of the *Wall Street Journal,* a class ring, and a smug expression. Not to be outdone, another local bank commissioned *Something for Everyone,* a Hokie bird statue on whose head is balanced a minuscule replica of Burruss Hall.

The popularity of the Hokie bird mascot rivals that of Burruss Hall, the most instantly recognizable symbol of Virginia Tech. It was a crime worthy of prosecution, therefore, when in 2006 a gaggle of undergraduates from the University of Virginia unceremoniously grabbed hold of *Farmer Hokie*—a magnificent specimen in his flannel shirt and denim overalls—yanked him off his foundations near the town library, and flew off with him to Charlottesville. All that was left were two gargantuan feet and a ruff of torn fiberglass where his ankles should have been.

Although many residents saw the funny side of the kidnapping, some were outraged. What was to become of young people who demonstrated so little respect for the town and the university that they would trash the Hokie bird? This kind of incident wasn't a college prank, it was a deliberate violation, the kind of thing that didn't happen in a sleepy little town like Blacksburg. There were articles about it in the local paper. Older people shook their heads and younger people giggled. There was mock horror in the community as people saw what was left of *Farmer Hokie*. It seemed like a cruel prank to play. The birds didn't belong to Virginia Tech, after all. They belonged to the town. It was hard to understand why the students were compelled to do such a thing.

Things shifted after 4/16, of course. Violations were not measured in terms of vandalized fiberglass statues nor were they carried out by a group of pranksters from a rival university. The innocence that characterized the kidnapping of *Farmer Hokie* seemed vague and unfamiliar. Something much larger had shoved it out of the way.

Blacksburg is a place where people still leave their doors unlocked. The town prides itself on a tradition of making strangers feel welcome. "Nothing happens in Blacksburg" is a saying I have heard hundreds of times, a sentiment that is as distressing to Generation Y-ers as it is comforting to aging baby boomers. Before April 2007, there were the usual crimes and misdemeanors in Blacksburg, many involving students who were drunk and disorderly. There were robberies, rapes, and frequent binge drinking and drug taking—the crimes and misdemeanors you encounter regularly in college towns. On rare occasions, there were murders. Before April 16, our crime stories tended to feature fairly predictable plots and fairly recognizable characters. Each year the college students would arrive, then most of them (thankfully) would leave. We would wave good-bye, feigning to be disheartened, and relish the few summer months when the town was liberated from the hormonal frenzy of youth.

For the most part, Virginia Tech and the town of Blacksburg live in relative harmony with each other. Although there is some resentment about Virginia Tech's power and influence, the town is dependent upon revenue generated by the university. Town and

Gown work in harmony, welcoming the students, assisting them as they mail their letters from the local post office, letting them know that, for four years, Blacksburg will be their home.

THERE IS nothing that serves as a better example of how closely the town and the university work together than a football game. Football games are the major events of the year in Blacksburg, drawing more than sixty thousand fans from across the country to each game and generating millions of dollars for the Athletics division of the university and for the town. Many fans see the football field as the nucleus of the campus, the place where the heart and soul of the institution resides.

The football field at Lane Stadium became the venue for public tributes after the tragedy. It was a place where Hokies could mourn and celebrate. Victory became much more than overcoming a rival team. It was about vanquishing horror. Players announced that they were playing in memory of the victims. Sports commentators got choked up as they talked about what the game meant and why this 2007 season, more than any other, had to be a triumphant one for the team. This was a battle for Virginia Tech's identity. Winning was a way to prove that Hokies were invincible, as evidenced by the Hokie cheer that erupted spontaneously at the end of the memorial service in Cassell Coliseum on April 17.

The football season that followed the shootings wasn't only revealing in terms of what it said about the need to find victory on the playing field. It also partly shaped the way the Tech community and the town of Blacksburg responded to the tragedy.

After 4/16, Hokie fans wanted to show their support for Virginia Tech and present a positive image of the school. They flocked to the campus wearing orange and maroon, determined not to be defeated. Football—the most splendid, the most sentimental, the most unequivocal, the most patriotic, and the most romanticized of American sports—became the perfect metaphor as commentators claimed that a triumphant season could go a long way in healing a ravaged community.

I cannot pretend I am immune to the Hokie spirit. Each year I spend hundreds of dollars on season tickets. I have written Hokie poems and song lyrics, and I have T-shirts of burnt orange and Chicago maroon. I have a pair of turkey earrings, tastefully crafted, and I have been known on occasion to wear them in public. Though I like to think that I approach the whole football thing tongue in cheek, I enjoy the camaraderie of the fans and the fact that, for a day at least, we can put aside serious matters and focus on an achievable goal that has a beginning (the kickoff), a middle (halftime), and an end (hopefully, victory). There is something merciful about competitive sports because they demand closure, and their unpredictability is constrained by the rules of the game. In football things can be redeemed. If the team doesn't win this time around there is always next season.

After April, however, the games played in Lane Stadium claimed a much larger territory for themselves. It wasn't about winning a game anymore, it was about what it meant to be a Hokie, and how important it was to show your support for the university. The word *Hokie* became synonymous with the word *patriot,* and was imbued with quasi-religious fervor. And if there was some irony in the fact that a game as brutal as football was being used to exorcise violence from the community, most fans didn't seem to feel conflicted about it.

The tragedy made Virginia Tech even more marketable in the world of TV sports where sentiment and athletics go hand in hand. Sports commentators, using the kind of imagery reserved for sermons, exhorted us to believe that this wasn't about winning a game, it was about ousting something sinister from our midst. Some fans seemed to make the transition easily, investing themselves in the ready-made symbolism, confident that something amorphous and unutterable would be toppled with a win. Others were more circumspect, knowing that there is a big difference between the game on the field and the game off it. They pointed out that this game would be played by the rules and would not end in tragedy—defeat, perhaps, but not tragedy. But in the frenzy of Lane Stadium, fans could buy into the notion that all would be well as long as we declared that it would be. It was an intoxicating vision: We could look forward to a future that would be as clear and uncomplicated as the sky overhead.

Because of Virginia Tech's strong military ties, a Stealth bomber flies over the stadium during some games. The Stealth is an awesome and terrifying creation. A shadowy presence, the Stealth personifies its own name. There is nothing extraneous about it as a plane or a weapon. Its muted roar boasts of its own potency—a machine that doesn't brook any disagreement. It is dark and brooding, but when Stealth is on our side it is welcomed. Fans cheer as it hurtles along on a trajectory we cannot anticipate. We applaud on cue as Stealth disappears into the horizon. A few of us remember another manifestation of that quality and shudder. But irony only works through juxtaposition and comparison, and American football—like other fan-based, high-octane sports—does not allow anything else to intrude upon its own point of view.

Athletics plays a key role not only in the characterization of the university but also in its bottom line. If a college football team (or basketball team if it has enough star power) has a successful season, this fact alone can save a university from low enrollments and attract students with higher grade point averages. It can also help generate sizable donations to the university. For this reason, the role of savior is a typical one that athletics plays. But it can also play another role. Athletics has the potential to become the campus bully, the power that cannot be challenged. Football games remind us that it's important to cheer for the team, but they also encourage us to ignore any reservations we may have about how the game is being played. Football players I have taught in the past have told me that they sometimes feel like slaves. Given their typical workweek this is hardly surprising. Sadly, the underside of big-money college sports is a story in which exploitation and hypocrisy are common. The college football player who hails from a poor black or poor white background, who will never be selected for the pros, and who stands a pretty good chance of not earning a degree isn't the player you hear about, but he is far more common than the star who makes it professionally.

The culture at Virginia Tech was not responsible for Cho's actions, but the culture shaped the response of the community after the tragedy. The emphasis on cheering the administration to victory encouraged blind affirmation rather than thoughtful questioning. When the students erupted into a Hokie cheer at the end of memorial services, it was a way for them to proclaim their unity and their loyalty to the institution, and to banish any fears they might have had about the unpredictability of tragedy. We could simply move on as long as we cheered loudly enough. As people waited for answers to the important questions, the administration's silence went largely undetected in the roar of the crowd.

HIGHER EDUCATION in the United States has changed over the past decade, and these changes have been felt most acutely at public institutions that rely on a steady infusion of state funds and at smaller private institutions that cannot draw upon hefty endowments to shore up their budgets. Nowadays, some of those in leadership positions at universities have little experience working with students and almost no experience in the classroom. It has become more important to hire administrators who know how to raise money than it is to hire those who know much about students.

If you examine a typical state-funded university, you will find that many of its resources are dedicated to generating funds. As the public began to opt out of subsidizing public education in the past two decades, something had to fill the gap. A university that is focused on staying afloat cannot pay as much attention to students as it did in the past. The problem is compounded if the university leadership does not have a clear understanding of the importance of student support services. In the case of Virginia Tech, as I have mentioned previously, there was no staff psychiatrist for several years at the Cook Counseling Center (CCC). The fact that this does not appear to have been a major concern until after the shootings suggests that it was not seen as a top priority.

The Office of the Dean of Students (ODS) was abolished in 2003 when Dr. Barbara Pendergrass retired. Some of the responsibilities of the office were reassigned to a newly created unit called the Office for Student Life and Advocacy (OSLA). But the OSLA had neither the authority nor the funding of the defunct ODS. No attempt was made to find out what the impact would be on the students, faculty, and staff at Virginia Tech. In fact, many people at Virginia Tech had no idea the transition even took place.

The ODS had a central role at Virginia Tech as it does on other campuses as the main advocacy and intervention office for the student population. When the ODS was abolished, James Thomas "Tom" Brown, who had served as Barbara Pendergrass's exemplary second in command, was appointed as interim director of the OSLA. The other duties previously performed by the dean of students were divvied up between people in leadership positions in Student Affairs.

It was extremely hard to persuade the upper administration that the ODS needed to be reinstated. When Bevlee Watford, the associate dean for academic affairs in engineering, and I lobbied aggressively for the restitution of the dean of students position, we were told at first that the university was fine without it. When we were joined by other faculty and staff who had been similarly dismayed when they had learned that the ODS had been abolished, Provost Mark McNamee eventually agreed to reinstate it. In May 2007, more than a month after the shootings, Tom Brown was at last appointed as the new dean.

At times in the Panel Report, there seems to be an assumption that the ODS was in place in 2005 when the English department alerted various units across campus about Cho, as well as in 2007 when the shootings took place. Yet, from 2003 to 2007 that particular office didn't exist. Even though Tom Brown and his staff did a heroic job throughout the period when the ODS was abolished and were always responsive when it came to troubled students, it should have been recognized by the upper administration that the ODS had a pivotal role to play on the campus, and that summarily abolishing it was unwise. The office is a key component of the Care Team, for example, the body charged with coordinating the university's initial response to troubled students.

Since the shootings, a Virginia Tech working group, led by Jerome A. Niles, a former dean of the College of Liberal Arts and Human Sciences, has developed a series of solid recommendations designed to address deficits in the makeup of the Care Team (prior to this it contained no law enforcement official, for example). The group also recommended that a threat assessment team be put in place. But it took years for the university to reexamine its approach to handling troubled students.

In the aftermath of Seung-Hui Cho's attacks, it was important that life on campus resume swiftly so that recruitment would not be jeopardized. But it would be impossible to make the physical campus completely secure before the fall semester began. There simply wasn't money for dozens of surveillance cameras and the communication devices recommended by the internal reports and by the Panel Report. What would be more important, therefore, than physical security would be a *sense* of security—a belief that the community was safer because the university administration said it was. Even though guns were readily available, even though there still weren't enough counselors, and even though the new locks on the doors were unlikely to prevent a determined perpetrator from causing severe harm, the campus community and the general public had to be persuaded that the campus was safer. They had to make a leap of faith.

Virginia Tech was not the only university or college to proclaim that its campus was now secure; colleges and universities all over the country were reassuring parents that their campuses were safe. Some cited their student support centers, some spoke about their cutting-edge technology and emergency notification systems, some reminded everyone how unlikely it was that an attack like the one on Virginia Tech would ever happen again. It is not surprising that some students didn't buy the hype and lobbied to carry weapons themselves.

Ironically, one of the things that could have made an immediate, substantive difference in terms of security at Virginia Tech would have been open communication about the specifics of the tragedy. But this would have meant acknowledging the fact that Cho wasn't completely invisible after all.

IN "CRISIS of Leadership: A Response to the VT Panel Report" crime prevention specialist Vincent J. Bove cites numerous examples showing where the administration was not prepared to handle an emergency.[4] From the perspective of the Steger administration, however, it must have seemed very unlikely that anyone would ever attack the campus. The president has spent almost all of his adult life at Virginia Tech, and he knew it as well as anybody. Far removed from the problems of troubled students, it could have been difficult for the administration to imagine there were students whose anger against the community was palpable or whose writing was deeply disturbing.

When Charles Steger came to office in 2000, his primary goal was to make Virginia Tech a top 30 research institution by 2010. In order to achieve this goal, the university would need to rise steadily in the annual National Science Foundation (NSF) rankings, something that would be difficult to do without a significant infusion of new funds. It was an ambitious goal, but many people thought it was a worthy one, as long as it didn't jeopardize undergraduate education. "Top 30" became a mantra that dominated conversation in administrative circles in much the same way as the chant "Let's go, Hokies!" does at football games. Strategic planning was geared towards the achievement of that single goal. Like prom party planners, the administration had a theme and it was insistent. Gradually, however, as budget crises cycled in and out, and Tech found itself moving steadily south in the rankings, the chant became more muted. (Since the quest to enter the top 30 began, we have slipped out of the top 50 for several years, returning to it again in 2008 when we were ranked 42nd. It is unclear whether or not impending budget cuts will result in a significant drop in 2009 rankings.)[5]

The corporate model of the jet-setting, entrepreneurial CEO is a model university presidents have been forced to adopt. Their boards expect them to raise funds, their governors expect them to do so as well, their faculty complain when they don't, and voters are increasingly reluctant to fund education. Some state institutions have opted to raise tuition to levels comparable to those of private institutions. Tuition and fees at Penn State, for example, will be over $13,500 in 2008. Contrast these with Virginia Tech's in-state tuition rate of roughly $4,100 and it becomes clear why the university faces some tough fiscal challenges.

Whenever budget cuts are announced at a college or a university, one of the easiest cost-cutting devices is to increase class size. Unfortunately, it's impossible for faculty members to get to know each student in a class unless that class is a manageable size. A question students and parents should ask when they visit a campus is this one: "What percentage of classes offered at this university have a class size of twenty-five students or under?" The answer may be surprising. Even at some of the most prestigious institutions, students may have relatively little access to faculty. Although large classes can be wonderful when they are used to complement smaller classes (I know of teachers at Virginia Tech who are adept at handling the demands of a large class and who do a wonderful job relating to students in these environments), a diet made up exclusively of large classes is far from desirable, especially for the student who is in need of special assistance or intervention. Class size and healthy communication between faculty and students are directly related.

Like other state institutions that have seen rapid growth from the 1960s onward (Tech has seen a nearly fivefold increase in enrollment during the past five decades), Virginia Tech has been obliged to deal with its own popularity and the demands created by an expanding student body. As the university metamorphosed from a technical school into a comprehensive university with 60 bachelor degree programs and 140 master's and doctoral programs, it was hard to keep pace with growth. Between 2001 and 2002, the university endured a series of budget cuts that resulted in the loss of tens of millions of dollars, and a base reduction of 28 percent. Virginia Tech has never fully recovered from these cuts. Another round of budget cuts was slated for 2008, and yet another will be enacted in 2009. Meanwhile, some state legislators like to boast that enrollment has skyrocketed at state institutions. They portray this as a sign of success because it pleases voters if their children get into the university of their choice. But it is not always healthy for a university to grow, and it can be positively unhealthy if funds lag behind a university's growth rate. There is no president I know, however, who thinks we're likely to return to the "good old days" when allocations by the state covered the cost of a student's education.

At Virginia Tech, one of the most pressing problems is class registration. Although it would appear from our course catalogs that students have a vast array of classes from which to choose, incoming students at Virginia Tech are sometimes unable to get into a single course of their choice because not enough sections of these courses are being offered. This means that they have to begin all over again, selecting their second, third, and fourth choices, just to ensure that their ticket is full. This isn't the only bottleneck when it comes to serving students. Increasingly, students are being admitted to Virginia Tech under the umbrella of University Studies, which means that they haven't yet declared a major. Some of them are happy not to do so because they want to sample courses and find out which major is for them. But others are desperate to get into majors in the colleges of engineering and business, or majors such as Communication, a particularly popular selection for students eager to work in broadcasting. In response to growing demand and dwindling resources, some departments have placed caps on majors, and some have raised GPAs to 3.5 or above in an effort to stem the tide of students hoping to be admitted after their first year.

At several points during my time as chair of the English department we were asked not to notify students when we had no one to staff the courses they wished to take. On almost every occasion, we were given funds to hire instructors at the last minute, but there were several occasions when we were asked to fire these instructors first and then rehire them a few days before classes started — a money-saving strategy that seemed to me to be unethical.

Although Virginia Tech has lost some excellent faculty and staff, particularly in the last few years, this is still a strong university with a wide range of outstanding academic programs. The current economic crisis, however — a crisis likely to be more serious than we have seen in years — will prove challenging to those state universities that have, like ours, been chronically underfunded for nearly a decade. Not just in higher education, but throughout public education, our ability to respond to troubled students is likely to be undermined.

In many ways, Virginia Tech is a typical state university. But it also has its own unique signature and its own way of doing things. Sometimes known as the "Tech Way," it is an approach to governance and protocol that is the result of more than 135 years of evolution. But the hierarchical system that holds sway at Virginia Tech can seem positively medieval. Reporting lines can place key individuals working on the ground below bureaucrats who haven't seen the ground for years (as was reflected in ERP-2005, when the campus police chief was supposed to route information through several layers and was not empowered to send an alert out to the campus). Virginia Tech prides itself on its military heritage, but there can be a dogged adherence to old-style protocol—the kind of bureaucracy that modern military thinkers no longer embrace, especially not in emergency situations.

Earlier in Tech's history, all of the students were required to participate in the Corps of Cadets, but this is no longer the case. This military legacy is one that has helped to define Virginia Tech since its founding in 1872. The university has an ROTC program as well as the corps. At major events, the young men and women who are pledged to serve their country (if they are ROTC students) or who participate in the military lifestyle (if they are members of the Corps of Cadets) are featured prominently. In April 2007, these young men and women were ubiquitous—some of them learning about death and dying as a prelude to what they would soon face in Iraq and Afghanistan. To faculty and staff who come here from other places it can seem strange to have a military presence on a civilian campus, but there is remarkably little tension, in large part because ROTC students are almost invariably the most conscientious and disciplined members of the student body.

Having taught at Virginia Tech for more than twenty years, I have experienced four different administrations and several very different leadership styles. I had limited experience under the first president, William E. Lavery, who served from 1975 to 1987. Lavery stepped down after questions arose about both the management of Tech's athletics program and his handling of a land-swap deal that resulted in Virginia Tech receiving farmland in exchange for prime real estate along Route 460, the main business corridor of the region, an exchange that was highly controversial. The scandals swirling around athletics at Virginia Tech in the early eighties were significant, as reported in the *New York Times:*

No basketball players admitted to Virginia Tech from 1981 to 1986 have been graduated from the school, administrators said yesterday in releasing a report on an investigation into National Collegiate Athletic Association violations. "In reviewing the academic records of basketball athletes, it is evident that most are not serious students," the report said. "Individuals have been advised to take courses in order to remain eligible, not to make progress towards a degree."

The report said 30 reported N.C.A.A. violations were reviewed, and 12 violations were found to have occurred. But the university president, William E. Lavery; the interim athletic director, Raymond Smoot, and the vice rector, W. S. White Jr., declined to say whether they planned to dismiss Coach Charlie Moir.[6]

After Paul E. Torgersen served a year as interim president, James "Jim" McComas was selected to serve as Virginia Tech's next president (1988–1994). Jim was beloved by the students, and he could often be seen walking around campus chatting with them to find out how they were doing. A teacher at heart, he was determined to keep the focus of the campus squarely on education. He surrounded himself with students, and his primary concern was how he could enable them to succeed. The atmosphere on the campus when Jim McComas was president was warm and inviting. People knew him as Jim, and he hired a new provost, Fred Carlisle, who was exceptionally skilled and dedicated. Fred was able to recruit dozens of minority faculty because he invested himself in the process of recruitment. When President McComas died of cancer in 1994, the entire campus mourned.

Paul E. Torgersen was selected by the Board of Visitors to succeed Jim McComas as Virginia Tech's fourteenth president. Paul didn't give a hoot about what others said about him. He was admired as a scholar and a teacher, and as the university's most successful dean of engineering. Like Jim McComas, Paul Torgersen was a dedicated teacher who continued to teach throughout his presidency. Although there were a number of decisions Paul made with which some of us disagreed—the most notorious being the restructuring of the College of Education—no one could fault him for his courage.

If he wanted something done he made it happen, and he didn't give a damn if he offended someone in the process. You could disagree with him without fear of consequences for doing so. He called people "jackasses" if he thought they were ignorant or weak, and he demanded in every meeting that people get to the bottom line within fifteen minutes. If they didn't they were asked to leave. It was a time when Burruss Hall was, for the most part, bereft of empty rhetoric. Like all Tech presidents, Paul Torgersen reported to the Board of Visitors, but board members did not exert undue influence over the university. In fact, many people were intimidated by Paul. He was fond of going on unannounced walkabouts around campus, popping in to see people, asking them what wasn't working and what was, then deciding on the spur of the moment what to do about it. By the time Paul Torgersen retired from the presidency in 2000, it seemed as though Virginia Tech was on the verge of reaching its potential.

Charles Steger's administration began that same year, and it stands in stark contrast to the two previous administrations. Charles is neither gregarious nor impetuous. Intelligent and prudent, he has a quiet exterior that belies a dogged determination. Although he would never stand out at a party, he would quickly find a way to become an influential guest. He often says he likes to work "behind the scenes," and he is shy of speaking in public, even though he can be an effective public speaker. Charles does not enjoy the limelight and is often happy to see others in the foreground, such as Provost Mark McNamee and university spokesperson Larry Hincker. For the most part, Mark and Larry are the voices of the institution. Mark McNamee fields tricky questions from faculty and speaks on a wide variety of topics, many of which would commonly come under the president's purview.

There have been a number of notable achievements since 2000—numerous new buildings on campus, the launch of many strong graduate programs, a promising focus on twenty-first-century research areas like bioinformatics, and an emphasis on student engagement with the community, to name just a few. Gradually, however, internal communication, particularly across units and divisions, has become more difficult. The administration lacks internal checks and balances. It has become a place where voices that are not in lockstep with the official view are often ignored. Towering over the tiny town of Blacksburg, Virginia Tech has developed a strong sense of its own invincibility and an alarming lack of familiarity with some of its most pressing problems.

When Charles Steger took office it marked not simply the rise of one man but the rise of an entire class of men. Not many people realize that when Charles came to power the triumph was not his alone. It marked the culmination of a remarkable trajectory enjoyed by five members of Tech's class of 1969.

In the beginning, the five alums referred to themselves openly as "the class of '69." Soon afterwards, however, they were advised by people close to them that having five members of the same class in positions of tremendous power and influence throughout the university could unsettle some faculty members. Charles W. Steger, the Virginia Tech president; Thomas C. Tillar Jr., the vice president for Alumni Relations; Raymond D. Smoot Jr., the university treasurer and the chief operating officer of the Virginia Tech Foundation; and Joe W. Meredith Jr., the president of Virginia Tech's Corporate Research Center are all members of the class of '69. In addition, the most famous member of that class is the man coaching the football team to victory. The return of Frank Beamer to Virginia Tech was celebrated by alumni and fans alike, making the university, as the alumni newsletter proudly proclaimed, "the only university in the country to have as many as five classmates serving their university in major leadership roles."[7]

Joe Meredith and Frank Beamer in particular have done outstanding jobs building a corporate research center and a football team, respectively, both of which are the envy of many other schools. But there are also disadvantages to having a core governing group consist of people who share the same education and background;

namely, they run the risk of being too similar in their outlook. I do not feel that a graduate of an institution is unsuitable for employment at that institution, though I know a number of colleagues who would argue that this is the case. I think it can result in dedicated faculty and administrators determined to devote their lives to the betterment of their alma mater. But when a group moves up the ranks together it is essential that their ascendance be balanced by the hiring of other people with a wide diversity of backgrounds to complement those already in positions of influence. In Virginia Tech's case, this has happened at the college level, where we have hired a number of progressive, visionary deans, several of whom are women. But, with some notable exceptions (the late Zenobia L. Hikes, who served as the vice president for Student Affairs, and Elizabeth A. Flanagan, the vice president for Development and University Relations, for example), the inclusion of new perspectives has been harder to achieve at the university level.

Today's students present us with challenges we have not faced in the past. As large state-funded universities become more impersonal, it is increasingly important to persuade "customers" (students and parents) that campuses are genuine communities. The pressure to define a campus as a secure learning community has resulted in claims being made about the university experience that can be inaccurate and misleading. It convinces parents that they can safely leave their troubled son at a university, or that their anguished daughter will receive assistance if she needs it. In some cases this is true, of course. Academic departments, Student Affairs, and student support services work hard to create a sense of community among students. But the community works best for those who are already comfortable living and working inside community structures. For those who have difficulty navigating them, and for those who suffer from certain types of disabilities, the very notion of community can cause feelings of panic or isolation. Students arrive on campus with differing needs, and many universities are not ready to meet them.

7.

The First
Amendment

*Congress shall make no law respecting an establishment of
religion, or prohibiting the free exercise thereof; or abridging
the freedom of speech, or of the press; or the right of the people
peaceably to assemble, and to petition the Government for a
redress of grievances.*

—First Amendment to the U.S. Constitution

B Y THE summer of 2007, it wasn't clear who was permitted to
say what to whom about Seung-Hui Cho. The media talking
points provided by the Office of University Relations were in part
responsible for this. But for me at least, it was the high priority
placed on Cho's privacy by the administration that caused the greatest confusion.

Those who knew anything about Cho were balanced precariously on the rim of free speech. A variety of critics perched next to
us, waiting to dissect every word. The media had taken up residence
on the rim, secreting the tabloids underneath their jackets. Next to
the media sat the twins FERPA and HIPAA, coy and tight-lipped,

unwilling to reveal much about what you could and couldn't say about the academic or medical records of the perpetrator, and next to them the National Rifle Association (NRA) stood poised to ambush those who mentioned guns in the same breath as Seung-Hui Cho because, as the NRA has proclaimed for years with its perverse logic, "Guns don't kill people, people kill people." Next in line were the accusers eager to blame someone for something—anything at all, it didn't really matter. And alongside them was the supreme deity—the Internet. Patient and brooding, it was capable of consigning you to the everlasting purgatory of recycled bad news. Once snared by the Web, you could never really escape. Say the wrong thing and the Net could multiply it a million times over before you could stutter, "I d-d-didn't mean it." Was it any wonder that people, including those in the administration, were reluctant to say anything?

Throughout the rest of 2007, communication across the campus was severely curtailed if it pertained to the specifics of the tragedy. Nevertheless, a cluster of administrators tried to reach out to the departments and programs most severely affected. Provost McNamee and Dean Jerry Niles, for example, visited the English department, and deans in other colleges did the same with their own departments. When he met with us the provost encouraged us to write about what we had experienced.

The Panel Report criticized the university for its narrow interpretation of laws relating to student privacy. The approach led to widespread misunderstanding and is the primary reason why essential information was not shared. As cited in the report:

> University officials in the office of Judicial Affairs, Cook Counseling Center, campus police, the Dean of Students, and others explained their failures to communicate with one another or with Cho's parents by noting their belief that such communications are prohibited by the federal laws governing the privacy of health and education records. In reality, federal laws

and their state counterparts afford ample leeway to share information in potentially dangerous situations.[1]

But it proved difficult for some to determine what was "potentially dangerous," especially if the main evidence to support that claim was a student's own poetry, fiction, or creative nonfiction. In such cases, concern over betraying a student's right to privacy was complicated by a desire to protect his right to free speech.

On April 20, 2007, Christopher Flynn, Virginia Tech's director of counseling services, explained the following in the *New York Times*:

> The university had played no role in monitoring Cho's psychiatric treatment.
>
> "The university is not part of the mental health system nor the judiciary system, and we would not be the providers of mandatory counseling in this instance," Flynn said at a news conference. "This is not a law enforcement issue. He had broken no law that we know of. The mental health professionals were there to assess his safety, not particularly the safety of others."[2]

Neither Dr. Flynn nor the previous director of the Cook Counseling Center, Dr. Robert Miller, was unconcerned about student safety. But if mental health professionals were not there "to assess . . . the safety of others," who was? At Virginia Tech, no one was designated to do so. If a student was ordered to seek treatment, he could not get it from campus counseling services because he was not seeking treatment voluntarily. Because the records of Cho's interactions with the CCC have been lost, it remains unclear what happened when he reported to the center on December 14, 2005, for mandatory treatment, as Special Justice Paul M. Barnett ordered earlier that day. The situation described by Dr. Flynn may explain why Cho was only triaged "for the third time in 15 days" when he showed up at the

CCC.[3] Students had to take it upon themselves to seek treatment elsewhere. The policy created serious problems for students if their insurance coverage did not extend to mental health care providers outside campus counseling. Those who most needed treatment could be turned away by the only facility on campus set up to assist them; they could be routed back to departments and programs that would not even be informed of the fact that this had happened, nor would those departments be provided with any guidance at all about how to deal with them. This meant it could be easier to get a prompt response if you reported a case of plagiarism than if you reported a deeply troubled student.

The role of the counseling center was not the only problematic one. The Panel Report cited the Virginia Tech Judicial System as one of the units that failed to react to the threat posed by Seung-Hui Cho. Unfortunately, many campus judicial systems are designed to cope with transgressions that tend to be relatively minor—plagiarism, for example, or excessive drinking or drug taking. The system is premised on the notion that students, once they are made accountable, will be eager (or at least willing) to rectify the situation. At Virginia Tech, as at other campuses, students often play a major role in the judicial process. The Judicial System at Tech is overseen by the Division of Student Affairs. It was not intended to function as a mechanism to respond to deeply disturbing writing or behavior.

Another recommendation of the Panel Report was that a threat assessment team be put in place at Virginia Tech, something that a number of other universities implemented after the shootings at Columbine. This recommendation was echoed in the August 2007 report from the internal working group chaired by outgoing CLAHS dean Jerry Niles and charged with examining the interface among counseling services, academic affairs, judicial affairs, and the legal system.[4] However dedicated and well-trained threat assessment teams may be, thorny issues remain. If, for example, a threat assessment team concludes that a student may pose a danger, but that he or she has not broken any law or violated any of the school's rules and regulations, what are the legal options? An issue that may prove to be even more difficult to handle is this one: How do you evaluate a potential threat if the primary catalyst for the complaint is the student's creative writing or artistic expression? Even so, these teams, when constituted correctly, can play a vital role in evaluating and monitoring troubled students—a responsibility that should never have to be assumed by academic departments and programs.

IN THE summer of 2007, I wanted to speak openly with panelists about my experiences with troubled students, and I hoped that an upcoming interview would provide an opportunity to do so. As I mentioned previously, the only official conduit to the panelists was through Lenwood McCoy, the former university controller—an unfortunate title, under the circumstances—who had been appointed by President Steger to serve as the liaison between Virginia Tech and the panel. The panelists probably felt that this would be a good way to manage the flow of information from Virginia Tech. After all, there are more than seven thousand employees at the university: Trying to process all that information could be a nightmare. It also meant, however, that unless they specifically requested it, most of the critical information the panelists received was selected and/or monitored by the administration.

Second, if Virginia Tech employees wish to be represented by the university attorneys, they must abide by their advice. The Tech administration can deny them representation, if it sees fit. The result of this arrangement at Virginia Tech was that free speech was severely curtailed, and advice for those outside the upper administration could be hard to come by.

During the summer of 2007, I saw with increasing apprehension that the English department did not appear to be receiving guidance about how to handle the crisis, even though it had been made clear from the beginning that Cho was an English major, which had resulted in the media turning its sights on the department. In the first few weeks following the tragedy, I asked repeatedly if faculty in English who had taught Seung-Hui Cho could meet with the upper administration and/or legal counsel and get some advice about what we were permitted to say, especially as I had been told by people close to the president that he was very displeased with the job I had done when I had spoken with the media myself. It seemed reasonable to expect that faculty who had taught Cho should be advised about what documents could and could not be shared, and what they were and were not permitted to say to the panelists and the media about their experience with him.

Our first request elicited no response. Eventually it occurred to me that the reason it was impossible to arrange such a meeting was because I planned to be present. As soon as I offered not to attend, a meeting with faculty in English who had taught Seung-Hui Cho was set up. While it was upsetting to realize that I had to absent myself from this meeting in order for it to occur, I was relieved that faculty in the English department would be receiving some guidance at last.

Following the meeting, an e-mail was sent in early June 2007. It came from Valerie Hardcastle, an associate dean in the College of Liberal Arts and Human Sciences, who had been selected to represent the college administration. As far as I know, it marked the only time that an administrator issued a written statement in support of our efforts to report troubled students. In her note, Valerie (who has since left Virginia Tech) praised English department faculty for going "above and beyond the call of duty." She thanked us for our service to Virginia Tech and dedication to students. She also said that the college and university stood behind us—something that I trusted would prove to be the case. It was a courageous act on Valerie's part.

On June 18, the same day that Governor Kaine issued Executive Order 53, I was scheduled to be interviewed by two of the panelists, Gordon Davies and Judge Diane Strickland. I had let Virginia Tech know that my lawyer's associate, Jeffrey Shrader, would be accompanying me to the interview because, by then, I had no idea what I could and couldn't divulge. The other members of the English department would have a university attorney present during their interviews with the panelists, so this would protect them from being castigated later by the administration for revealing something that could violate state or federal privacy laws.

The meeting did not begin auspiciously. We were about to commence when we were joined by the associate university counsel, Mary Beth Nash. I was surprised by this because I had not been told that she planned to do so. When asked why she had joined us she informed the group that Charles Steger wished her to attend. Although I could understand why the president would want to monitor what was said to the panelists, it would have been common courtesy to be notified ahead of time that university counsel would join us for the interview. It was another indication that I was not considered part of the group being defended by the university but had instead been identified as a potential liability.

Governor Kaine's executive order giving the panelists access to Seung-Hui Cho's academic and medical files had been issued that morning. Unfortunately, Mary Beth Nash had not yet seen it, and at first denied its existence. Much of the thirty or so minutes I had been allotted with the panelists was taken up with disputes about whether or not the executive order had been issued. Eventually, a fax of the order was sent to the English department. Even then, however, there were numerous objections from university counsel.

The questions from the panelists were insightful, and I was grateful to learn that Seung-Hui Cho had sought help from counseling, as he had told me he would. It wasn't clear from the interview whether there would be a follow-up interview at a later date. But as it happened, there was not. I recount this episode because I think it illustrates how difficult it was for the panelists to obtain information even from those who were more than willing to share it.

When the Panel Report was published, the university administration received lavish praise for its cooperation—praise that I found surprising given my own experience. The Panel Report indicated that there were some problems obtaining documents, and that some interviews were "monitored" by the university attorneys, but concluded nevertheless that the university was "extremely cooperative." The paragraph entitled "Virginia Tech Cooperation" appears at the beginning of the report and contains sentiments echoed by Governor Kaine when he spoke later to reporters:

> VIRGINIA TECH COOPERATION—An essential aspect of the review was the cooperation of the Virginia Tech administration and faculty. Despite their having to deal with extraordinary problems, pressures, and demands, the university provided the panel with the records and information requested, except for a few that were missing. Some information was delayed until various privacy issues were resolved, but ultimately all records that were requested and still existed were provided. University President Charles Steger appointed a liaison to the panel, Lenwood McCoy, a retired senior university official. Requests for meetings and information went to him. He helped identify the right people to provide the requested information or obtained the information himself. The panel sometimes requested to speak to specific individuals, and all were made available. Many of the exchanges were monitored by the university's attorney, who is a special assistant state attorney general. Overall, the university was extremely cooperative with the panel, despite knowing that the panel's duty was to turn a critical eye on everything it did.[5]

There are some worrying phrases in this evaluation. That some records no longer existed is a reference to the fact that key documents related to Cho's interactions with the counseling center were missing. In addition, there is no reference to the fact that only minimal documentation was provided to the panel about the Policy Group's meeting on the morning of April 16.

Gathering pertinent material proved to be a very tricky thing for the panelists because the panel was not empowered to issue subpoenas. Therefore, in theory at least, people could simply decline the invitation to speak to the panelists—an option that was conveyed to some of us by the administration. I was concerned by this suggestion. As I understood it, we ultimately reported to the state and should therefore cooperate fully with the panel's requests. The example provided by the administration—of students who had decided not to meet with the panelists, and were perfectly within their rights to do so—didn't persuade me that this would be an acceptable response from faculty and staff, whose responsibilities are very different from those of the student population. It seemed unwise for the administration to indicate to some employees that appearance before the panel was optional because it could result in a report that would be full of holes, and could even suggest that people had something to hide. I therefore concluded that accepting the invitation to appear before two of the panelists was the only option for people who wanted to assist the investigation.

Another complicating factor regarding the gathering of documents was that the English department had followed the guidelines laid down by the university itself. As I have described earlier, I had handed over to the police any documents I could find related to Cho because that is what we had been instructed to do. I advised department members to do the same, as had the chair of the English department, Carolyn Rude. No definitive guidelines were ever issued about where documents should be submitted, even though it soon became obvious that such guidelines were needed. It was never made clear whether or not these documents were passed on to members of the Virginia Tech administration, which was one of the reasons I offered repeatedly to share whatever documents I had in my possession. In fact, when I inquired why it was that the president and the provost had not been made aware of the letter from Seung-Hui Cho to the English department, a member of law enforcement stated that it was not their job to share that kind of information.

The administration must have been keenly aware of the potential conflict. On the one hand, it needed to see any documents related to Cho so that it wouldn't be blindsided by them later. On the other hand, if the administration saw these documents, it would have to share them with the panelists. As a result, some of us were caught in the middle. When it looked as if there would be litigation, however, it became critical that the university administration obtain all the documents relating to Seung-Hui Cho. This process to preserve documents and information relating to the tragedy was absolutely justified. I knew that all such documents had to be preserved, not just in the event of litigation but also to ensure the thoroughness of the investigation.

In the summer of 2007, faculty in the English department who had taught Cho were ordered to hand over every single file we had on our computers. The administration said that it wished to employ a process called "computer imaging," which would mean, essentially, that the hard drives of those who had taught Seung-Hui Cho were to be reproduced, then stored indefinitely, and accessed when needed by the Virginia Tech administration. The administration claimed it needed to do so in case litigation was filed. The copying process would mean that our scholarship and writing would be held by the university administration indefinitely. As some of us pointed out, the administration would, in effect, be in possession of the virtual keys to our offices.

The university's demands seemed excessive to some of us. The only teaching faculty members targeted for the imaging process were in the English department, even though Cho's first major was Business Information Systems, not English, which meant that he would have taken many courses with other faculty members outside of our department. It wasn't clear at all why only teaching faculty in Cho's second major had been asked to submit to the imaging process. If those of us who objected to having our hard drives imaged refused to submit to this process we could be accused of trying to withhold information from victims' families.

I did not feel personally at risk should my hard drive be imaged because I have always been careful about what I put on university computers, and because I have a habit of speaking my mind. The administration was therefore fully aware of any problems I had related to their policies or actions. But other faculty and staff, many of whom were without tenure or job security, had confided in me their reservations about the current administration. Sharing these private documents without raising objections to doing so would be a violation of the trust they had placed in me. Because I had served as chair of the department, I also had personal information relating to health issues of faculty and staff on my computer, information completely unrelated to Seung-Hui Cho. I was concerned about this information being "imaged" unless very careful attention had been paid to security issues, because it could place others at risk.

Although there were a few faculty members in our department who had no qualms about the imaging process, particularly if they rarely used the computers provided by Virginia Tech and so had nothing of value on them, others were very upset. Some of us proposed a compromise. We asked if it would be possible for us to remove the most sensitive documents that had absolutely no bearing on the tragedy prior to having the hard drives imaged. We offered to do so in the presence of university lawyers who would be able to oversee the process and make sure we were not trying to hide anything.

At first, this compromise was dismissed out of hand. But, eventually, the administration agreed to meet with members of the English department to discuss it. On this occasion, I was allowed to attend. Much of the meeting was spent trying to get assurances that the material, once provided, would be secure. It was reassuring to hear Dean

Jerry Niles advocate on behalf of the faculty, but distressing to realize that Provost Mark McNamee did not feel compelled to do the same.

Unfortunately, the administration's arguments were not very convincing, in part because the Virginia Tech security system had been compromised not long before. Moreover, in the process of trying to collect data from faculty in the English department who had taught Cho, the administration inadvertently attached one individual's private response to a survey seeking the location of university computers. When the administration was informed of this gaffe, it expressed surprise, not having known it had done so. The violation of privacy did little to reassure some of us that our hard drives would be secure. At a time when Seung-Hui Cho's privacy was being zealously guarded by the administration, the privacy of faculty and staff seemed to have no value.

It is likely that one of the main reasons the administration felt the need to image the hard drives of faculty and staff in the English department were my notes to various units as I tried to seek assistance in handling troubled students. This was a painful hypothesis because, if it were true, it meant that, as a direct result of my reporting this problem, my colleagues would be subjected to a very invasive process.

But by July 2007, it seemed as though things had calmed down somewhat in that we were close to a compromise. I was taken aback, therefore, when we received another memo, this time from the Office of the Attorney General of the Commonwealth of Virginia. The memo, dated July 10, 2007, bore the state's official seal and was signed by a person I had never heard of: Ron Forehand, chief, Education Section. (Ronald C. Forehand serves as the senior assistant attorney general in the Health, Education and Social Services Division in the state attorney general's office.) It was addressed to university counsel but its subject related to faculty in English who had lingering questions about the imaging of their hard drives. For those of us who had hoped that the administration would be responsive to our security concerns, the contents and tone of the memo were shocking. Ron Forehand made it clear that the punishment for non-compliance would be extreme:

> Employees who refuse access to Virginia Tech–owned electronic equipment for this data preservation project may be subject to a range of sanctions, to include discipline (including discharge) and denial of a defense by the Attorney General's office in the event litigation is filed as a result of April 16th.
>
> In the even [*sic*] an employee is not cooperative, I suggest that the university simply confiscate the equipment, take appropriate action in respect to copying, and then take appropriate personnel action against the resistant employee.
>
> I'd be happy to speak personally to any employee should that be necessary. Please know that you, the legal department, and the university have the full support of the Office of the Attorney General in your endeavors.

I didn't know exactly what was meant by the adjectives *cooperative* and *resistant,* but the fact that the memo contained an explicit threat to terminate the employment of all those who didn't "cooperate" had some serious implications. Faculty in the English department who did not comply could lose everything—jobs, health care coverage (which is tied to employment), and legal representation, even though the university had not yet determined how it would safeguard the information it was seizing.

It was impossible to tell from the memo whether or not these threats were being delivered by the state or by the university administration or by both, though the fact that the memo bore the official state seal meant that it originated in Richmond. Did this mean that all the strategies adopted by the university administration, including the one not to disclose information because it could violate Cho's privacy, were preapproved by Attorney General Robert F. McDonnell, whose name appeared at the top left-hand corner of the memo in small font, and, by extension, Governor Tim Kaine? If so, what implications did it have for the panel investigation? Eventually, we were obliged to submit to the imaging process.

Since that time, I have been given to understand that the matter is out of the university's hands because the threatening memo was initiated by the commonwealth. One member of Tech's central administration told me that the Office of the Attorney General was responsible for the tenor and content of the letter, and that the university administration had felt obliged to go along with it. But having heard exactly the same tone from members of the Virginia Tech administration prior to receipt of this memo, I am not entirely persuaded by this argument.

In my role as a distinguished professor at Virginia Tech, I had been asked on numerous occasions to speak on behalf of the university, and I had done so gladly. After the shootings, my status was unclear. (The college officer who handled media requests, for example, was unable to determine whether or not she could communicate with me for more than a year.) I realized that it was not only the case of Seung-Hui Cho that had created concern on the part of the administration. There was an earlier experience we had had in the English department with another student. It was the first time I learned how difficult it could be to obtain a comprehensive evaluation of disturbing writing by a student at Virginia Tech.

IN THE section entitled "University Setting and Campus Security," the Panel Report concluded:

> Although the 2004 General Assembly directed the Virginia State Crime Commission to study campus safety at Virginia's institutions of higher education (HJR 122), the report issued December 31, 2005, did not reflect the need for urgent corrective actions. So far as the panel is aware, there was no outcry from parents, students, or faculty for improving VT campus

security prior to April 16. Most people liked the relaxed and open atmosphere at Virginia Tech.[6]

Yet in 2005 several faculty members, including myself, had alerted various units to issues of campus security, vandalism, and troubled students. We had spoken with a number of people about our concerns, including representatives from the College of Liberal Arts and Human Sciences, Student Affairs, the VTPD, Judicial Affairs, the Women's Center, and the Cook Counseling Center. Everyone had agreed that the problem needed to be addressed, particularly in light of what had happened in two departments that year, one of which was in English.

In the spring semester of that year, faculty members contacted me about the writing of an older student who was enrolled in their classes. For the purposes of this book, I will call him "Student A." Since his graduation, Student A has posted a number of critiques to various websites describing how unjustly he was treated by some in the English department. Due to the fact that he has posted his work to a public forum and thus entered into a public debate about his time at Virginia Tech, I feel it is legitimate for me to refer to his work in general terms. I am not citing this example as a way to point fingers at those who tried to assist me. In fact, I am grateful to them for doing what they could, given how challenging it could be to intervene in cases like this at Virginia Tech. Nor am I suggesting that Student A was a threat to the campus. I don't know whether he was or not. I cite this case because it demonstrates how difficult it can be to respond to writing that is deeply disturbing and so has relevance to what happened later with Seung-Hui Cho. The case highlights issues that go far beyond Virginia Tech and have serious implications for students' *and* teachers' civil rights. As a writer I am leery of censorship, and I usually object when limits are imposed on free expression. But in 2005, I learned how difficult it can be to address this issue effectively.

Student A was brought to my attention in March 2005 when a faculty member came to my office with a short essay he had written. The class was an undergraduate creative writing course, and students had been asked to describe the main influences on their work. Under those circumstances, most students cite accomplished writers like John Cheever, Seamus Heaney, Toni Morrison, and Derek Walcott. Instead, Student A claimed that his main influences were serial killers Jeffrey Dahmer and Ted Bundy. The essay contained graphic descriptions of the murders Dahmer and Bundy had committed.

The work was deeply troubling, and I consulted with my colleagues in the English department's administration. When they, too, found the essay profoundly disturbing, we sought guidance from those charged with dealing with student issues. I learned that this same student had submitted an article in support of rape to the *Collegiate Times,* the campus newspaper, some time before. The paper had declined to publish it.

Everyone with whom I consulted agreed that the work Student A had produced for his creative writing class was cause for concern, particularly given the nature of the assignment. Because there were no explicit threats in the writing, however, and because we could not require him to seek counseling or get a psychological assessment unless he submitted to it voluntarily, we were left with very few options. In the end, I felt I had no choice but to offer to serve as Student A's adviser. I could not ignore the teacher's request for assistance, and I didn't have anyone else I could ask to do this.

Our first meeting seemed to go fairly well. He was intelligent and well read. He understood that postmodernism had lifted many of the limits placed upon artistic expression, and he seemed to enjoy shocking his readers. He was well aware of university regulations and protocol, and was confident that, as long as his work didn't contain explicit threats or break specific university regulations, he could feel free to express himself. He made some good arguments in defense of artistic license, and it seemed as though he understood why his work could be interpreted as threatening.

At first it seemed as though Student A understood that his "satires" had gone too far, and that he was willing to moderate his work for his creative writing classes so that it did not focus on reenactments of mutilation, rape, and serial killing. I became increasingly concerned, however, as I began to hear from other professors, instructors, and graduate students, especially when it was not simply the student's writing but also his behavior that was causing concern. Graduate students were alarmed, for example, when Student A showed up in an obvious disguise in Shanks Hall. I learned that, on another occasion, he had come to the campus in a gas mask and that he claimed this disguise was part of a "performance art" piece. A sickeningly graphic poem celebrating the rape of a disabled woman was posted anonymously on a faculty member's door. It contained the same kind of imagery found in Student A's first essay about his literary influences. Student A later attached his name to the poem and submitted it to one of the creative writing courses he was taking. He also submitted other work to me that featured even more disturbing material. He had now submitted enough creative writing to constitute a sizable manuscript of work. In each case, the same themes were evident. The personas he adopted were invariably obsessed with one or more of the following: rape, necrophilia, pedophilia, fecal matter, racism, mutilation, and serial killing. The descriptions were very detailed, and the rape and mutilation of little girls was one of the dominant themes. Much of the work seemed to be nonfiction and contained philosophical assertions about the inferiority of women, disabled people, and African Americans, who were usually referred to pejoratively when they appeared.

I learned that several creative writing teachers had tried hard to persuade Student A to rethink his work, but he seemed unable or unwilling to do so. If Student A's work was for his literature classes—as opposed to creative writing—it was often well reasoned and astute, and did not contain the same kind of highly disturbing material. He was therefore quite capable of producing strong work that demonstrated his keen intelligence. The creative writing classes Student A took in 2005, however, became an outlet for him to write about rape, mutilation, and murder—perhaps because he wanted to see how far he could go at Virginia Tech without being confronted, or perhaps because he wanted to test the limits of the discipline of creative writing, a discipline premised upon free speech. I felt that the department— and particularly Student A's creative writing teachers—were being goaded into a response.

By this time, not surprisingly, two of Student A's teachers were no longer comfortable having him as a student in their classes. They had not been able to persuade him to submit less inflammatory material and they were, quite justifiably, concerned about what would happen if he insisted on submitting this kind of material for peer review. (In creative writing courses, the students' own work is the primary text, and students review each other's work in class.)

Throughout this process, I consulted with my contacts in various units and made it clear that the situation was placing severe stress on the department. I considered simply removing Student A from creative writing classes, but Virginia Tech protocol required that, if I do so, I had to offer him an equivalent academic experience. This would mean transferring him into another creative writing class or teaching him myself. Given the fact that it was creative writing that triggered his most disturbing work, transferring him to other creative writing teachers was something I would not do. After multiple attempts to do so, we had been unable to persuade him not to submit incendiary work for peer critique—a proposal that he felt impinged upon his civil rights. We were so uncomfortable with the situation in one class we had to request that security be in attendance. Removing Student A from classes and teaching him myself, or simply awarding him a grade as he was so close to graduation, seemed to be the only options the department had left.

Student A's determination to "perform" in the guise of a serial killer and rapist in his writing was alarming. Carrying that performance into a class full of undergraduates would have violated the learning space, especially as his teachers had told him not to do so. Although it was possible that Student A's obsession with killing and rape was, as he claimed, a form of literary expression designed to challenge what he saw as the provincialism of the university, having someone else evaluate it and let us know how best to proceed seemed to me to be essential.

Once again, I shared the student's work with my contacts in the college, counseling services, Student Affairs, and the police, and asked for guidance about how to handle this situation. Some of those with whom I consulted said they were unable to finish reading the material I had sent them because they found it so offensive.

In 2005, there was no threat assessment team at Virginia Tech and no staff psychiatrist. Although there was a Care Team charged with assisting departments, and although its members did their best to respond, the team did not include people trained to evaluate writing or threats, and usually did not include anyone from law enforcement. Tom Brown, in his role as director of student life and advocacy, was especially helpful, even meeting with the student on one occasion. But he, too, was thwarted by the system.

In a last-ditch attempt to obtain assistance, I contacted the campus police again to see if they had any suggestions. To my amazement, the officer to whom I spoke offered me another option. He said that all I needed to do was invite security to come to my office when I met with Student A. At that point, the officer would ask Student A if he would be willing to come for a psychological evaluation. If he agreed to this, he could be evaluated by a psychiatrist who would have access to the work he had produced for his creative writing classes.

I could hardly believe that a solution as simple as this one had existed all along and that no one whom I had contacted before had thought to tell me about it.

The officer explained to me that he would need to make it clear to Student A that he was being invited to accompany him voluntarily. I understood that it was a somewhat risky approach in that the student could easily refuse, or be infuriated by the fact that the police had been notified about his writing and his refusal to comply with his teachers' requests. Since the meeting was scheduled to take place in my office, Student A would immediately realize that I had shared his work with the police. But at least it was better than my trying to handle this alone. After weeks of trying to get help, it was the only option I had that could result in a comprehensive evaluation by a mental health professional. I consulted with several people to make sure that the officer's idea was the best option. I told the teacher who first reported concerns to me about Student A that he would not be in class.

Unfortunately, I forgot to ask the officer a critical question: What was likely to happen *after* the student had been interviewed by a mental health professional? I had assumed that any mental health professional who read Student A's work would be so concerned that he or she would want to have a more comprehensive assessment done. Under normal circumstances, I would have asked more questions about possible repercussions, but I was, by that time, exhausted. I had tried every option I could think of, contacted every office, met with the student myself, forwarded his work, and made numerous calls to see what options there were. It had consumed dozens of hours of time I did not have as I struggled to keep the department functioning on a budget that was woefully inadequate. Hearing that there was an option I hadn't known about before was like a gift from heaven.

I asked Student A to come to my office. As soon as he arrived, two officers entered and asked him if he would be willing to submit to a voluntary evaluation. Student A seemed to find it all pretty amusing and agreed immediately. I was surprised that he did so because I

had assumed he would ask me questions about it. But I was also relieved that he didn't appear to be angered at all that the police had
been contacted.

For about two hours, I felt an enormous sense of relief. At last a
mental health professional would meet with the student. I knew it
was unlikely I would learn anything about what had happened, but
Student A's work would be carefully evaluated. Moreover, he had
gone voluntarily, which suggested that he understood why we needed
to act. He had been posting and submitting shocking material for
years—sometimes to newspapers, on the doors of faculty members,
and to classes. (Later, Student A himself would reveal that, years earlier, he had been fired from one job he held because of e-mails he'd
sent that he claimed had been misinterpreted by people of inferior
intelligence.)

My sense of relief was abruptly shattered that afternoon when
I received a frantic call from the person teaching the creative writing
class. He told me that Student A had shown up for class after all. I
was so surprised by this that I thought at first that the teacher must
be mistaken. Surely someone would have notified us that he would
be going to class, especially as we had made it clear that the teacher
wanted security if Student A were present. I assured the teacher that
there must have been some mix-up and that security would be provided at once. I then called the police to request that security be sent
immediately to the teacher's classroom. To my dismay, I was told
that there were no officers available at that time. I wanted to scream
in frustration, but I didn't have the time. I had promised the teacher
that he would have security, and it wasn't a promise I intended to
break. I called my husband, Larry. His office was closer to the classroom in question than mine was so he could get there quickly. I asked
him if he could hurry over to the classroom and discreetly monitor
what went on from the doorway while the class was in session. Larry
didn't hesitate. I then took off for the classroom myself, running
across the campus as fast as I could.

As I ran I realized that my efforts to assist the teachers who had reported their concerns to me had made a bad situation even worse. I was angry with myself for not anticipating this scenario, given the fact that mental health services provided to students often seemed cursory at best. Yet I found it difficult to imagine that a mental health professional who had read Student A's writing would not have been alarmed.

I was not permitted to know the details of what had transpired during his meeting with mental health services because of privacy laws. Much later, however, I learned from Student A's own Internet postings that one of the people who had interviewed him—a woman referred to pejoratively as "The Gimp" in one of his lengthy postings—had indeed been very concerned about his work. Social services was contacted, and, according to Student A's postings, his home had been investigated to see if his child was safe. (Student A had a toddler.) Student A assumed that I was responsible for alerting social services and was incensed. Sadly, the option the officer offered me turned out to be stressful for all those involved. But I believe that he was genuinely alarmed by the student's work and behavior, and suggested this option because he could see that the department should not be obliged to handle this alone.

Student A did not insist on sharing his work with the class that afternoon after all. Larry and I monitored the class from the doorway until it was over. Student A claimed later in his postings that he had not realized he had the option of declining to accompany the officers, though this was certainly made clear to him at the time. His anger was directed primarily at me and his creative writing teachers. He demanded to be excused from attending the two classes where he had produced his most disturbing work. I consulted with the college and then granted his request. At least this meant that the undergraduates would not be exposed to his writing and the teachers he had would not be obliged to read it anymore.

A Care Team meeting followed. I felt it was essential that we try to discover how the university could have responded more effectively. I was worried that the underlying message which had been sent was that if you reported students you did so at your own risk. The university needed to be aware of the fact that departments and programs were in urgent need of assistance. Even though this was an extreme case, we had seen a marked increase in angry students, and it seemed that, increasingly, students could be struggling to manage their medication and also struggling with alcohol and drug abuse.

Later that same year, a small group of concerned faculty from two creative arts programs met with representatives from various units on campus to discuss this issue. Creative arts departments and programs are a haven for those with different and daring perspectives. It makes teaching creative arts subjects especially rewarding. But if a student decided that performance art could consist of removing all the screws from the doors in a building, is that really performance art or is it vandalism, especially if people could get hurt? If a student consistently submits work for his creative writing instructors that is designed to provoke a reaction through its excessive use of sadism, misogyny, and racism, how should a department respond? We agreed that the issues related to troubled students, disturbing writing, and the limitations of artistic expression needed to be addressed by the university. But none of those present at that meeting were in key policy-making positions, which was why I alerted others in the administration about this incident, in hopes that it would result in change.

In October 2005, about six months after the encounter with Student A, Professor Nikki Giovanni contacted me about a student who had written a poem her class had found frightening. The poem was a tirade that seemed to be directed at his teacher and classmates. His name was Seung-Hui Cho.

AFTER THE shootings, Student A posted a series of denunciations of the English department. The tenor of some of them suggested I needed to be even more attentive to my own security and that of my students. I anticipated that Student A would identify strongly with Seung-Hui Cho. Included in the denunciations he posted to the Web were links to work he had produced as a student at Virginia Tech and work he has written since then, including his series of poems about raping the disabled woman, and a story excerpt that featured a character named "Lucinda," who was deriving pleasure from the lynching of a black man. This story excerpt was linked to the page where he castigated selected English faculty members at Virginia Tech. He describes his poems as bombs, and claims that to interpret his black humor as pathological rather than comic is a testament to the reader's stupidity. It is hard to laugh at his description, however, when a little girl is being fed body parts while she is being raped; it is impossible to laugh at his gruesome reenactments of serial killings and mutilations, particularly of disabled people and little girls with Africanized features. He has posted a long letter devoted to praising the man accused of killing JonBenet Ramsey. In it, he reenacts her rape and murder. He argues at great length that his work should be read as satirical—much like Swift's "A Modest Proposal," or work by William S. Burroughs.

At the end of a letter he posted online after the shootings in which he sympathized with school shooters, Student A used his own last name, but substituted another first name for himself. The name he chose was "Cho."

THE PAST few years have taught me that, in many ways, I am a traditional, somewhat conservative teacher, even though my political leanings are liberal or independent. There are many books I do not include on my syllabus because I still believe—unfashionable though it has become to do so—that great literature is more than an obsession with a stark realism and raw verisimilitude, that the greatest work teaches us how to live with dignity, courage, and compassion. Experience has taught me that words are more powerful than we give them credit for, and that we have no way of knowing how sophisticated students may or may not be when they enter our classrooms. I therefore do not assume that all students are ready to devour all texts at the same time.

It would be easy to assert that Student A had no right to submit such disturbing material to his teachers, but, if we adhere to the spirit of the Constitution, he had every right, and still does, to say whatever he wants. What I would assert, however, is this: His teachers had every right to be appalled by what Student A had written and to react accordingly. People can be easily intimidated by violent writing, especially when it is by men and directed primarily against women.

Student A's teachers were absolutely right to confront him about his work and to demand that he not submit such disturbing material to class. As chair of the department at the time, I had every right to demand that he comply with those requests. At some point, people have to say no. That is what the English department did. That is what the officer who offered to help me also did. That is what Tom Brown—then serving as director of student life and advocacy—did when he met with the student himself. But the university lacked the mechanisms needed to react more appropriately to what became an urgent and distressing situation.

Any guidelines about the handling of troubled students should include an acknowledgment that those who confront these students—whether they be faculty, staff, counselors, parents, or administrators—take on a *significant personal risk,* one that can negatively impact their lives for years. I have not seen this acknowledgment in the guidelines offered by Virginia Tech, which are premised on the notion that the mental health and judiciary systems will be appropriately empowered and funded well enough to respond to a crisis. This is one of the reasons that, as yet, I have not been able to subscribe to any of the guidelines produced by the university. We need to acknowledge that, in most cases, unless a student voluntarily seeks help and that help is provided, it is enormously difficult to respond effectively at all, however detailed the guidelines may be.

The vast majority of students are receptive and empathic. We should acknowledge that rage manifests itself most commonly in creative and artistic expression, but that this alone does not indicate that a student is troubled. In the vast majority of cases, if a student claims his or her work is satirical that's exactly what it is. But rage is not satire—and schools and universities have to do a better job of recognizing it and responding appropriately.

To deny the right of free speech to others while reserving it for myself would be hypocritical. At a time when the unpredictable response to terror by the Bush-Cheney administration has resulted in egregious violations of the U.S. Constitution, the Bill of Rights, and the Geneva Convention, I am loathe to suggest that we should explore ways to curtail students' right to free speech. And yet, the tragedy at Virginia Tech obliges us to take another look at some of our assumptions about education and about creativity.

8.
Teachers and Students

THE TRAGEDY at Virginia Tech called into question a number of prevailing assumptions about students and teachers. The Ideal Teacher, who knows instinctively how to teach, can reach any and all students. Although she has always been a myth, this person is nevertheless called upon to transform even the most recalcitrant pupil. Because the Ideal Teacher is a comforting figure, with an abundance of maternal qualities, she is often resurrected after attacks on schools. The Perfect Student is another idealized projection that has been even more instrumental in shaping education. The Perfect Student is always receptive to new ideas, ever eager to learn. The Ideal Teacher and the Perfect Student work in harmony—so much so that the authority of the teacher can be jettisoned because it is unnecessary. Education isn't a matter of coercion for these two. It is a matter of inspired teaching on the part of the teacher, and receptive learning on the part of the student. Dedicated teachers can enlighten all of their students if they only try hard enough.

Paolo Freire, the Brazilian educator and one of the most influential educational theorists of the past century, proposed a new kind of relationship between teacher and student in books such as *The Pedagogy of the Oppressed,* published in the late 1960s. Although some have argued that Freire was deeply indebted to others such as John Dewey, Freire has had a significant influence on education throughout the world. Through a process of democratization, teacher and student learn to work together in partnership. In this student-centered, problem-solving, reflective approach to learning, the teacher isn't a fount of knowledge from which the student drinks. Instead, for both student and teacher, the learning process is transformative and reciprocal.

Freire's work had a profound effect on the way teachers thought of their roles. Often imbued with religious imagery, the gospel of engagement Freire proclaimed was (and is, for many educators) a powerful one. Teachers were validated, and education was thoroughly integrated with political action. Many believed that Freire's vision of education, premised as it was on the concept that hope must be nurtured, was radical and revolutionary. As he called for social engagement, he emphasized the need for critical awareness as a tool of self-liberation. Paolo Freire didn't want to transform only the student; he wanted to transform the world.

Nowadays, it is possible to trace Freire's influence in schools and campuses throughout the United States. His vision was particularly appealing to those who saw teaching as a vocation. His ideas, and the spirit of engagement he personified for many educators, have influenced campus rhetoric. We now refer to learning as "student-centered," and to students as "reflective learners." We talk about "learning communities," as if they magically appear when students set foot on campus, and many teachers strive to create a nonthreatening, nonauthoritative communion between students and themselves. Words like *discipline, authority,* and *teaching*—unless, of course, the teacher acknowledges him- or herself as a learner—don't have as much currency anymore in progressive circles. Ironically, scholars like Freire are often called upon to validate a pedagogy they would have serious reservations about because of its overreliance upon a mass-market delivery system.

The kind of education offered at many large public institutions co-opts the two perennial figures as protagonists—the Ideal Teacher (charismatic and selfless) and the Perfect Student (industrious and focused). In reality, however, each new wave of students brings a new series of challenges.

Seung-Hui Cho and the series of school shooters who preceded him shatter any neat assumptions we may have about homogeneity in the student population. But there are risks involved if we assume that thousands of students are potentially lethal. Administrators who are justifiably concerned about school safety could intercede aggressively, setting up punitive systems designed to detect any and all potential threats, however unlikely they may be, not realizing that some of the things we cherish most—young people's energy and imagination, for example—could be jeopardized in the process.

Seung-Hui Cho felt that he was different from other students. It was a difference he seemed to both resent because it isolated and embarrassed him, and cherish because it made him intimidating and memorable. He was someone who was incapable of responding to the usual methods teachers utilize when communicating with students. In fact, Cho's condition of selective mutism meant that he was unable to communicate at all in certain social situations.

From the account in the Panel Report, provided mostly through interviews with Cho's family, it seems that he suffered from chronic shyness and a dislike of being touched by anyone from the age of three onward. The family speculated that he could have been emotionally traumatized by a medical procedure he underwent at the time, possibly cardiac catheterization.[1] Cho was diagnosed with selective mutism in 1997 when he was in the sixth grade. He was also diagnosed with depression. He was prescribed the antidepressant paroxetine from June 1999 to July 2000, but was taken off medication after about a year because he seemed to be doing so much better. By the time Cho attacked students and faculty at Virginia Tech, therefore, twenty years had passed since his condition had first manifested itself. For his entire childhood, adolescence, and early adult life, he had been unable to communicate normally.

The demands that a student like Seung-Hui Cho places on an overtaxed education system, which does not begin to resemble the idealized campus where every student receives customized attention, are substantial. However, it is important to guard against the notion that this attack tarnishes all youth and signals a rebirth of an era of "superpredators," described by Princeton criminologist John J. Dilulio Jr. in 1995. According to forensic clinical psychologist Dewey G. Cornell, Dilulio's theories about superpredatory youth persuaded a frightened public that we were about to experience a crime wave of unprecedented proportions (270,000 additional superpredators by 2010, according to Dilulio's estimates) and resulted in a frantic rush to incarcerate juveniles and impose stricter penalties on juvenile offenders.[2]

But if Seung-Hui Cho, himself inspired by Columbine shooters Eric Harris and Dylan Klebold, could well inspire others to follow in his footsteps, what is the best way for schools to address this serious issue without impinging upon the rights of innocent students in the process?

The Panel Report concluded that there should have been more information sharing when it came to Seung-Hui Cho's medical history, and that Virginia Tech should have been informed by Cho's high school, or by his parents, or by Cho himself, that he suffered from selective mutism and depression.

Schools can be confused about what information can and cannot be disclosed when it comes to laws relating to student privacy. At times, federal law seems to offer conflicting imperatives, depending upon whether you consider, say, the Americans with Disabilities Act or the Family Educational Rights and Privacy Act (FERPA). Schools caught in the middle of this confusion are likely to err on the side of caution and decide not to share information because it could make them vulnerable to litigation. The Panel Report compares mental health and special education records to immunization records, and asserts that there are times when collective security outweighs an individual student's privacy. In light of this, the panel made the following suggestions:

> Perhaps students should be required to submit records of emotional or mental disturbance and any communicable diseases *after they have been admitted but before they enroll at a college or university,* with assurance that the records will not be accessed unless the institution's threat assessment team (by whatever name it is known) judges a student to pose a potential threat to self or others. . . .
>
> This much is clear: information critical to public safety should not stay behind as a person moves from school to school.[3]

The report recommends that perhaps there "really should be some form of permanent record" for students. The implications of this, however, are wide ranging. It presupposes that it is always possible to identify "information critical to public safety." Unfortunately, people interpret behavior and artistic expression differently. What could be a threat to public safety in the eyes of some, therefore, could well be interpreted by others as nonthreatening. Establishing permanent records of potentially threatening behavior or writing by students could even result in the assumption that conditions as nonthreatening as selective mutism or autism indicate that a student is a threat.[4]

There are other questions that need to be asked about permanent records before a protocol like this is established. For example, should the record extend all the way back to middle school? What about elementary school? Some will argue that if records don't extend that far back warning signs could be missed, as they would have been in

Cho's case. (Cho was in eighth grade when he wrote about wanting to "repeat" Columbine, and when he was diagnosed as suffering from depression.) But other cases suggest that there could be serious repercussions if we create a "permanent record" for students, accessible by higher education authorities and, at some stage perhaps, prospective employers. One of the factors that would make it hard to know what belongs in a record like this is the policy of zero tolerance in K–12 schools in the United States—a policy which assumes that violence can be prevented by harshly penalizing students whose behavior may or may not pose a threat. Should the eight-year-old boy in Arkansas who brandished a chicken finger at a teacher and said "Pow-pow" have this incident recorded on his permanent record, especially as he was promptly suspended for it afterwards?[5] Could this chicken-finger incident become a scar on the student's permanent record, indicating that he is someone who is prone to violence, especially if poultry were in the vicinity? At some point, would the chicken finger disappear in the telling and a knife appear in its place? (Few of us have time to be as careful about details as we'd like, and fear and hyperbole are frequent bedfellows.)

The Rutherford Institute's website, "Legal Feature," lists other similar violations of the zero tolerance policies currently in place in schools throughout the country. Perhaps one of the most ridiculous examples of the policy is the following:

Robert Richardson v. Concord School District (IN)

Thirteen-year-old Robert Richardson was expelled for one semester after being accused of violating the school's zero tolerance policy forbidding possession of drugs or over-the-counter medications, "including diet aids." Richardson had expressed concern that his girlfriend was abusing a diet aid called "Fatburners" (a non-medicinal dietary supplement made of nuts, cinnamon, mustard seeds and grapefruit rind). He took the bottle of fatburners from her at school, placed them in his locker and sought special counseling for his friend's situation. An investigation revealed Richardson's possession of the diet aid and, without regard to his intent or to the non-medicinal nature of the substance, he was expelled and all administrative appeals denied. This was the seminal case that motivated The Rutherford Institute to research Zero Tolerance further and to launch a national effort to fight ZT policies. The expulsion was upheld.[6]

One of the obvious drawbacks to the zero tolerance policies is the fact that students who are suspended or expelled have to go somewhere—they don't simply disappear. Who is supposed to educate them at that point? Do zero tolerance policies result in the transference of the student from one school system to another? If other schools are not open to them, are these students meant to simply roam the streets? If so, is this policy likely to make the community safer? I speak as someone who knows how important it is to get a swift and effective response to an urgent situation posed by troubled or deeply disturbed students. But I also believe in common sense, and some of the results of the strict imposition of zero tolerance policies have been as disturbing as the behavior they are supposed to address.

Narratives related to troubled students are usually nuanced if they are to come close to capturing why there was concern in the first place. Zero tolerance policies do not allow for any nuance whatsoever. The notion that educators are going to have time to write lengthy, insightful narratives that will then be pondered over by superbly trained threat assessment teams is, unfortunately, absurd. It is likely that something akin to the infamous "Mosaic Assessment" would soon replace a longer narrative.

In the wake of Columbine, when parents and educators were desperate to find a way to predict whether or not a student was a threat to public safety, the violence prevention consulting firm Gavin de Becker and Associates, led by Gavin de Becker, the author of the *New York Times* bestseller *The Gift of Fear,* developed a computer-assisted approach called MAST (Mosaic Assessment of Student Threats). Earlier iterations of the Mosaic approach to threat assessment had been utilized by federal agencies, including the Bureau of Alcohol, Tobacco, and Firearms. Mosaic 2000, customized for schools, included an updated software program designed to predict who was likely to pose a threat to public safety. The program generated a firestorm of protest from educators, psychologists, and civil rights advocates, in part because it included a rating system for potential threats. Some saw it as an attempt at profiling—an approach that could demonize students for being different.[7] Critics feared that teachers could soon be checking a box that said one of the following: "Not a Threat," "A Possible Threat," "A Likely Threat," "A Ticking Time Bomb!!" Absurd though this sounds, no one would have imagined, pre-Columbine, that Tawana Dawson could be expelled from a school in Florida for bringing nail clippers to school—a decision that was later overturned by school board members in possession of common sense.

Before we rush to establish permanent records, we need to acknowledge that young people make mistakes, and that sometimes the policies schools enforce are ridiculous. If the system never permits erasure of incidents like these from a student's record, some young people are likely to be discriminated against for the rest of their lives. An aggressive response to attacks on the part of administrators and politicians could result in the creation of a separate and unequal system of justice for college students, who would have to surrender their right to privacy if they wanted to pursue their studies. Instead of addressing the problem we stand a good chance of compounding it. Zero tolerance policies can turn punishment into farce and penalize students who have done absolutely nothing wrong. Parents and students sensitive about permanent records would be far less likely to seek help for conditions such as depression, and it could put counselors in untenable positions as they tried to advise and protect pupils.

It's possible that I would have responded more effectively to

Seung-Hui Cho had I known that he suffered from selective mutism, though I admit the term alone would have had to be explained to me because I was unfamiliar with it. I made the assumption that he was a chronically shy student who seemed to have the capacity to be much more vocal when he wanted to be—traits that were alarming to me because they suggested that he was very volatile. Paradoxically, had I known that Cho suffered from selective mutism and that he had received treatment for it in the past, I may have been less concerned about his behavior. It's possible I could have concluded that his erratic communication was a symptom of his condition and not a symptom of anger or depression. If I had also known, however, that he had fantasized about the Columbine shootings six years before I met with him, I would have been even more concerned about the anger I saw in his work. It's therefore possible that a revelation such as this could have made a difference, but only if a mental health professional were prepared to make a comprehensive diagnosis, and only if there had been a system in place to guarantee that treatment would be forthcoming. There is evidence to suggest that medication and counseling *did* make a difference earlier in his life.

It seems only sensible that a threat assessment team should have been allowed to call his high school, and, if they were confident that this would not further exacerbate the situation, the family, to find out if they had experienced similar problems. This more moderate approach, which the panel recommended, would not curtail the privacy rights of all students and would not generate mountains of paperwork. It would allow threat assessment teams to have access to critical information that could help them determine how to proceed. Common sense tells us that a student's history is relevant to his development, and that cutting off one phase of a student's development from another (high school years from college years, for example) can result in a dangerous lack of information. There is another aspect of this recommendation, however, that probably needs to be questioned further.

The report suggests that Virginia Tech should contact parents if there are serious problems with students. The FERPA clarification letter in the report's appendix makes it clear, however, that only the parents of students who were claimed by parents as dependents for tax purposes can be contacted.[8] Not all troubled students are young, of course. Assuming, however, that the student is of traditional age (eighteen to twenty-three), and that he or she is listed as a dependent for tax purposes, it's important that threat assessment personnel weigh the risks before they contact the family.

One of the thousands of e-mails I received in the weeks following the tragedy was from a woman who wrote about what had happened to her when she was still a child, after she submitted poems to her English teacher. He had read them with growing concern and realized that they could well be an autobiographical account of abuse. It had never occurred to the student that this would be a likely conclusion, though she had, in fact, been abused by her father for years. The teacher reported his concerns to one of the counselors at the school. Later, the counselor relayed the teacher's suspicions to the family—a particularly unwise thing to do given the nature of the concerns. When the student arrived home that day, she received the worst beating of her life. She understood that her teacher was only trying to help her, and she was grateful that he had, even though it had caused her so much pain. But she warned of what could happen if people automatically assumed that a home was safe. There is another reason to be cautious: Families of deeply disturbed students can be vulnerable to attack themselves, and so it is important to consider safety issues in regard to the family as well as the school.

The other, even thornier question for threat assessment teams is what to do if indeed the student is deemed to be a potential threat. Should the student be required to seek treatment? If so, what kind of treatment? Supposing the student doesn't appear to be mentally ill, what then? Should the student be returned to the classroom while treatment is being received? Could the student be expelled on suspicion of being potentially dangerous? One of the drawbacks to zero tolerance policies is that infractions are so wide-ranging the innocent can easily be condemned along with the guilty.

The Panel Report recommended that a threat assessment team be put in place at Virginia Tech composed of "representatives from law enforcement, human resources, student and academic affairs, legal counsel, and mental health functions."

> The team should be empowered to take actions such as additional investigation, gathering background information, identification of additional dangerous warning signs, establishing a threat potential risk level (1 to 10) for a case, preparing a case for hearings (for instance, commitment hearings), and disseminating warning information.[9]

While this would help alleviate the burden in academic departments and programs, I also think teachers should be a part of the team, and preferably those with experience interpreting student writing and trained to identify threats. The assumption that it is easy to identify potential threats is faulty; almost all the students who write about homicide have absolutely no intention of killing anyone. It should be acknowledged, however, that threat assessment teams will make mistakes. In order to protect students' rights, some kind of swift appeals mechanism will have to be established if there are penalties that accompany the threat assessment process.

The chronic lack of resources in education is bound to be a major impediment to the effectiveness of these teams. My fear is that, especially if budget woes continue, threat assessment teams are likely to be drawn from existing personnel who will be asked to assume additional responsibilities. If the process is premised on the notion that people in education, mental health, security, and law enforcement will be able to do more with less, we will be creating a system that is doomed to fail.

The Panel Report remarked on how little communication there

is between high school teachers and higher education. For some time, educators have proposed that we think about education in terms of K–16 rather than K–12, and include the college years as part of the developmental process. This idea is inconsistently applied. The two cultures are very different. In high schools, the primary focus is upon teaching and learning; in higher education—especially at research-based institutions like Virginia Tech—the focus tends to shift from teaching to a combination of teaching and research and scholarship. Bringing the two cultures closer together will not be easy, especially since each has preconceptions about the other.

The truth is that there is a wide disparity in the teaching skills of faculty. Some professors are naturally gifted teachers and others are not. Some become engaged with the teaching process while some see it as a chore they have to perform in between their research and scholarship. At Virginia Tech, teaching tends to be valued by the faculty and undervalued by the administration. We have a thriving Academy of Teaching Excellence and some exceptionally gifted teachers are members of that group. Most dedicated teachers are never recognized for their contributions but this does not lessen their commitment to their students. We must acknowledge that there is still a prejudice at American research institutions against those who devote their lives to teaching. Often, they are relegated to inferior positions at lower pay. Their contribution is not seen to be as significant as that of researchers who are "the discoverers of new knowledge." It's a shame that those whose focus is teaching and who are, I would propose, "the nurturers of new intelligence," are sometimes not considered to be as valuable to the research-based institution. With the pressure to generate income more pronounced than it has ever been it is unlikely that teaching will attain the level of recognition it deserves any time soon.

The Ideal Teacher and the Perfect Student have had a profound influence on today's system of education. But the disconnect between the ideal and the real has been around for a long time. It was apparent when I first started teaching nearly thirty years ago. It allowed administrators to see the world through rose-colored glasses, and it meant that even the most glaring problems could be ignored.

IT HAS always been difficult for administrators who are not regularly in the classroom to understand the challenges teachers face. This is as true now at schools and colleges in the United States as it was in the early eighties when I was assigned to teach at Brockley County School for Boys in London.

Brockley County had already been written off by the authorities. Slated to be closed within a few years, it was deteriorating fast. In 1981, Brockley County's reputation was dubious at best. Double-decker bus conductors were forced to serve as referees at the bus stops surrounding the school because boys from Brockley County jumped the queue, pushing elderly people and small children into the gutter in the process. Although students in classes for the academically gifted could flourish, students who were not considered to be academically gifted were paired with the less gifted teachers—an arrangement that appeared to be designed to make sure that neither the teachers nor the students would succeed.

The school's wide corridors and high ceilings amplified sound so that the shouts of boys echoed as if you were in some subterranean cavern. There was a lingering smell of disinfectant and school lunches. Most teachers couldn't leave fast enough when classes were finally over.

In the smoke-filled staff room, teachers with nicotine-stained fingertips talked wistfully about the good old days when students didn't bring knives to school or tell teachers to "f——" themselves. Many of the pupils—especially those herded into less rigorous curricula—were of Caribbean heritage; almost all the teachers were white.

In those days in England, students were often "streamed" according to their academic potential, so there were entire classes made up of boys who were predicted to fail—most of them disaffected, some of them enraged by what they saw as their incarceration in a penal system masquerading as education. There were stories of knifings and muggings. The changing of class was a process that resembled a stampede on the old cowboy series *Rawhide.* Whenever the bell rang, I would grab my handbag, clutch it to my chest, and bat a frantic path through the hallways. If a male teacher happened to pass by, I would latch onto him as discreetly as possible and ride his wake to my next class—one of the few ways I had of guaranteeing I would get there without being shoved into the wall as boys tore past.

Being the youngest teacher there—and a student-teacher at that—I had the misfortune of being assigned to teach English literature to one of the most notorious classes in the school: a class of boys of about fifteen years of age. Even substitute teachers—an unusually hardy bunch—couldn't keep order. These were the discarded juveniles in the British educational system, the ones who were supposed to be marching in place until they were released into the world at sixteen. Some teachers only pretended to teach this particular class. If the door was open when I passed by, I would likely see a teacher, oblivious to the chaos around him or her, reading a book until the bell sounded. The classroom was a cage; the boys acted like animals because they could. There were times when no one at all showed up to teach, so students had large hunks of the day totally unsupervised. Although those in classes for the academically gifted were very receptive to learning, the boys in the holding-cell classes had come to expect that they would never be taught anything of value. They were understandably shocked and resentful when they were asked to learn anything.

On the first day I entered the dreaded classroom as the new English teacher I found what I thought was a gift on my chair. Being profoundly nearsighted, I mistook it for a balloon and was touched by the gesture. Unfortunately, it wasn't a balloon at all; it was a test—the kind of test a young female teacher is asked to undergo at a school made up entirely of boys. The prophylactic, which contained the full measure of a boy's manhood (or possibly several boys given how generous the offering was) smelled rancid. It was meant to send me screaming from the classroom in disgust. But by then I had already spent two years as a volunteer teacher in Sierra Leone, and, though the girls I had taught there had been very respectful, the unrelenting poverty had forced me to become accustomed to life in the raw. I'd seen lepers whose faces and limbs had been ravaged by disease; I'd lived in a town that had open sewers and rats the size of cats. I wasn't about to be traumatized by a used condom.

The boys were watching, waiting. I knew it was important not to miss a beat. In an imitation of my late English mother—a trained repertory actress with an accent not unlike the queen's—I demanded that the offending object be removed from my chair and placed in the rubbish bin *at once*. To his credit, a boy I'll call "Arnold" (not his real name), who had been laughing with particular vigor, stood up, swiped the condom from the chair, and flung it into the bin. Apart from the fact that I couldn't sit down for the rest of the class period, the experience of teaching the class that first day wasn't as bad as I thought it would be. But the fun was only just beginning. Arnold—the short, stocky student from the Caribbean islands, like my father—decided from that day onward to disrupt the class.

While I was teaching the class a few days later, it seemed at first as though I would be able to convince Arnold to learn something, or at least sit quietly while others did so. But he resented it when the other students participated. Accordingly, he punctured the classroom with "f—" this and "f—" that, railing against everything— perhaps because, as far as he could see, every single door in his future was marked "No Entry." In all likelihood, this classroom was the only stage upon which he would ever be able to strut, and he was determined to take full advantage of it. Eventually, Arnold's abuse became so extreme that I had no choice but to ask him to leave the classroom. I told him he could stand outside until class was over, at which time he could accompany me to the headmaster's office. At first I thought Arnold would call my bluff and refuse to do it. But instead he scowled at me for a few moments, shrugged his shoulders, and then loped out, giving me the finger as he went.

As soon as Arnold departed, the whole class relaxed. The students who wanted to learn could now do so without being ridiculed for it. I began to think that perhaps these months at Brockley County would not be as unbearable as I'd imagined.

Just then, who should come along but the deputy headmaster, a well-meaning individual whose creed was "There is no such thing as a bad student; there are only bad teachers." Through the pockmarked yellow glass in the upper part of the door leading to the corridor I saw his shadow bending over solicitously towards Arnold.

The deputy headmaster knocked on the door to the classroom. He opened the door and poked his head inside. His expression was kind, paternal. "Miss Roy," he said, "I need to have a word with you outside." I told the class to keep reading and stepped out to join him and Arnold in the corridor. Arnold was looking downcast and victimized, but he shot a grin at me while the deputy headmaster wasn't looking.

In front of Arnold, I was severely upbraided for having turned him out of class. "How can he learn if he's not allowed to participate, Miss Roy?" the deputy headmaster asked me. Not realizing it was a rhetorical question, I tried to explain that Arnold had no intention of learning a bloody thing, nor did he want anyone else to do so, though, understanding that profanity on my part was unacceptable, I didn't use the word *bloody*.

The deputy headmaster shook his head. "You go on inside, Arnold, there's a good lad," he told the boy, "and you make sure you behave for Miss Roy." He guided Arnold back into the classroom and reminded me that it was my job to teach these boys and that I needed to try harder. In fact, it wasn't my "job" at all because, as a teacher in training, no one was paying me a penny. Nor did I tell him that trying harder was my forte—that, in fact, it was destined to become a handicap I would have to endure for the rest of my life. I didn't point these things out because, although the deputy headmaster—who considered himself a progressive and enlightened educator—indulged the students, his indulgence did not extend to the teachers. Arnold, his back to the deputy headmaster, smirked at me before he sidled back into class, greeted by the whoops of his friends. For the rest of the period, Arnold interrupted the class and threatened me and others whenever the fancy took him.

Arnold, as it turned out, eventually decided he would try to learn. Towards the end of my time at Brockley County, he became engaged with the material and seemed to look forward to my class. He'd spent most of his life trying to hide the fact that he could barely read; when at last he was willing to admit it, it was too late. He and his classmates were cycled out of the education system at the end of the year, some of them, like Arnold, barely literate. They taught me that even the most resistant learner is often teachable, and that listening is as important a skill to bring to the classroom as speaking is. They taught me that trying harder is part and parcel of teaching, even when success is elusive.

Today in the United States, hordes of boys and girls are funneled through an unresponsive system that barely acknowledges their existence. They emerge at the other end often unable to read or write, or reading and writing at such a basic level that it can be hard for them to function. Their parents are often chronically absent from their lives, or so consumed by poverty that it can be hard to get from day to day. There has been a massive exodus of good teachers from teaching. This is a catastrophe that threatens to redefine the social landscape of the United States. In poor rural and tough urban districts there is a paucity of good teachers; those who try to remain are often treated like dirt and paid salaries that do not permit them to support their families. We acknowledge that this is happening, shake our heads, and move on, hoping that these wild young people will not encroach upon our neighborhoods. We are more likely to assume that a young person killed or injured in an environment like this one is less innocent than someone on a middle-class campus. The tragedy isn't considered to be as great when those who are lost have already been discarded.

The approach that requires teachers to indulge challenging students is, I believe, a dangerous one because it fails to prepare them for the life they will encounter when they leave school. We need to beware of giving lavish praise to students for relatively minor accomplishments. It doesn't take long for young people to become conditioned to praise and to be discouraged or angered when they do not receive it.

There are times when students yearn for boundaries. Seung-Hui Cho may have been willing to study with me because he knew what to expect, and he knew the parameters. For someone who had great difficulty controlling his emotions, and who eventually was subsumed by them, an environment of predictability and order may have been a welcome one.

Some time ago, after I had delivered a keynote address in North Carolina, a woman came up to me and began a conversation about teaching. After we had spoken for a few moments she said, "Oh, I get it. You're a teacher from the *old* school." At the time I was taken aback. What did she mean, "old school"? Wasn't I the innovative, free-thinking teacher who was always willing to adopt new methodologies? In many ways, however, she was right. I do try to create a structured, disciplined environment in my class—I always have. I think it can help if a floundering student knows there is something he can grab hold of to steady himself. I used to need that myself as a child, when it seemed sometimes as if making it to the next day and then the one after that would prove to be impossible. During that time, I took refuge in the orderliness and predictability of school. In the safe space of the classroom, at least, I was permitted to learn in peace.

The 2008 report from Alma and Colin Powell's America's Promise Alliance highlights the fact that we still haven't begun to find an effective way to reach at-risk students. Dropout rates for U.S. school-children are alarming. In Baltimore, Cleveland, Detroit, and Indianapolis, fewer than 35 percent of students graduate with diplomas.[10] If some of our schools resemble detention centers, it is not surprising that students graduate without a clue about how to conduct themselves. And if those who opt to teach in the better schools or at the college level do so in part because they are confident that they will never be confronted by deeply disturbed or violent students, it isn't surprising that these educators from sheltered backgrounds don't know what to do with at-risk, troubled, or deeply disturbed students when they encounter them.

Children who leave school prematurely don't just drop off the face of the earth, of course; they return to their communities. This is why it is important to look at school-age violence rather than simply violence that takes place *in* schools.

In schools across America, entire communities of children are being discarded on a scale that makes it impossible for teachers to tackle the crisis alone.

IMAGINE THIS scenario:

It is morning in Washington, D.C. Shareeza, a twenty-two-year-old, newly certified teacher, receives a phone call. It is her neighbor, Bill, a shy man she dated a few times over the summer. Bill has noticed that a youth named Harry, who lives in their apartment complex, has been behaving strangely. Harry has been writing graffiti on the walls of the elevator—graffiti that suggests he may be deeply disturbed. The last example scratched into the elevator wall was a four-line poem full of curse words, some of which Bill, who is from a sheltered environment, had to look up online. As if that weren't worrying enough, Bill came upon the young man in the parking lot last week when Harry was attempting to drown a litter of kittens. The six-foot, two-hundred-pound high school junior confessed that he was off his meds and had decided to "try a real life-and-death scenario on for size." He said he'd been fixating on death; he hated everyone and blamed his lousy job prospects on women, Mexicans, and black people rather than poor grades. Harry hadn't actually called them women, Mexicans, or black people—his language had been more colorful than that, but Bill tempers his account out of deference to Shareeza.

Yesterday Bill entered the elevator and was forced to ride with Harry while he was in "a terrible state," flinging expletives around and threatening his own suicide. It's possible Harry has a weapon or two, Bill informs Shareeza matter-of-factly, "maybe an arsenal," because his stepfather, "who comes and goes," is an avid hunter. It's rumored that poor Harry has been struggling with some kind of mental illness for years.

Bill tells Shareeza he'd ask Harry's mother to do something, but she appears to be consumed by the demands of her job in advertising and utterly terrified of her son. Bill isn't a teacher himself, he reminds her, he's a computer programmer with no desire whatsoever to interact with young people, which is why, on behalf of the apartment's housing association, he is contacting Shareeza. Could she monitor Harry's behavior for the next nine months or so, make sure he's not armed, and talk him down if she comes across him trying to commit suicide somewhere in the building?

Shareeza gently reminds Bill that she is a black female. Bill tells her he doesn't feel it's particularly helpful to use the race card as an excuse for inaction. "It was just blacks and females *in general* Harry said he hated, not you in particular," Bill points out. "Besides, you're a teacher. You're trained to handle this kind of thing."

When the call ends, Shareeza ponders the situation. After a moment or two, she rushes off to Harry's apartment, armed with a number two pencil and a college-ruled writing pad (so that she can take notes), a willingness to listen, her vocation as a teacher, and her winning smile. Shareeza is a mere five foot four and a hundred and twenty pounds, but, last month, she attended a workshop at the same school where she teaches entitled "Dealing with Troubled Students Who May Wish to Kill You." It lasted the entire morning. She feels prepared.

When we read an account like this one, we realize how ridiculous it would be to ask someone like Shareeza, an inexperienced young woman with limited training, to monitor and possibly disarm a young man who has given every indication that he is deeply disturbed. Yet increasingly in our schools, colleges, and universities, unlucky teachers, instructors, and professors are being asked to do just that. There is a belief that those things that have not been addressed in the home environment will be addressed by teachers who function in loco parentis. In part because of this assumption, teachers can be presented with choices that are as ludicrous as those presented to Shareeza. Because the system is flawed and demand is acute, some teachers are being obliged to take on too much responsibility for students who are in desperate need of intensive, long-term assistance. Parents are either afraid to admit that they need help or unable to get the help they say they need for children who are spinning out of control. In Virginia, the passage of recent legislation designed to address the severe shortage of in-patient treatment centers is a step in the right direction. But the problem is not just Virginia's, and it will take much bolder legislation to rectify the situation.

There has been a shift in the balance of power in higher education—a shift that has advantages and drawbacks. Nowadays, professors and instructors can be just as worried about the evaluations they are due to receive from their students as students are about the grades they receive from their teachers. A student's ability to damage a teacher's reputation has grown exponentially because of the changed environment. Complaints that were formerly restricted to campus can now be posted online. The Internet has spawned sites such as RateVTteachers.com (where Cho may have posted his rant against an instructor in English, as I mentioned earlier), which contains thousands of postings from students about professors and instructors at the university. The website's motto resonates with students: "They've graded you. Now it's your turn." In theory, the site seems like a good idea: Students post their impressions, and other students learn which classes to take and which to avoid. In practice, however, because it is difficult to monitor, some pretty outrageous remarks are posted there, none of them verifiable. It matters what students think, and they have every right to evaluate teaching. But we should be aware of the implications of this new way of speaking.

Years ago, when student evaluations were first introduced, they often came with an assurance that they would never be used to "judge" faculty members, only to help them succeed as teachers. For the most part, this idea has been gradually undermined. Awards, raises, and even tenure decisions at some institutions can be based partly on the scores you receive from your students. Twenty years ago I thought this was a good idea, but now I am glad that some of us are looking at how these evaluation scores correlate with grades students receive, and whether they limit the freedom we have to teach material that may not be accessible or entertaining but is, nevertheless, essential. The "dumbing down" of the curriculum and grade inflation are realities in education, and, although there is a reluctance to admit it, student evaluations of teachers are partly to blame. I am not speaking as someone who is bitter about her own student evaluations; in fact, they have been a source of encouragement to me over the years. It is not unusual for me to finish teaching a class and assume that I have failed in some way or other. Reading the evaluations has been enlightening. I think that all faculty should invite students to respond to their classes, but I am concerned that the weight that some institutions have attached to them obliges us to be less adventurous than we used to be as teachers, making some teachers think twice before they offend or provoke a student, and making professors and instructors less willing to report troubled students, especially if the teacher knows he or she could receive a blistering evaluation from the student in response.

EVEN IF teachers are willing to report disturbed students, the scarcity of treatment facilities makes intervention difficult. In a report from the Treatment Advocacy Center, researchers found that in 1955 there were 340 public psychiatric beds per 100,000 people; in 2005 there were 17 per 100,000.[11] This means that 95 percent of the beds have been lost over the past fifty years—a staggering decrease that has resulted in a chronic shortage of beds for those who are most in need of them. Anyone who has tried to get someone they care about into a public treatment facility knows how hard it can be to do so. Even if Seung-Hui Cho had been admitted for extended treatment, it's unlikely that he would have been able to get intensive help for long.

Those who suggest that teachers and counselors alone need to solve the problem of troubled students sometimes assume that if the intervention occurs in an educational setting it will be less risky. It is not. In fact, I would suggest that the reverse is true. Deeply disturbed students often seem to be particularly antagonistic towards authority.

The fact that some students come to college ill equipped to handle more self-directed learning is well documented, but a multifaceted, national effort to instruct faculty how to teach the struggling student isn't under way. Instead, colleges and universities determine for themselves how much training, if any, faculty need. I don't mean to suggest that all faculty members need to have the same degree of training. Training needs to be customized to acknowledge that those who, for example, work exclusively with graduate students on research projects have different needs from those who teach huge introductory sections of undergraduates. But almost all faculty members could stand to learn more about teaching and about those whom we teach.

There is no doubt that we also need to address the issue of advising because it is one of the major factors that make a large institution feel more like a small liberal arts college by bringing students closer to faculty members. Advising should be a fundamental component of higher education, and it should be rewarded. Teaching and advising must not only be a part of the tenure packets of instructional faculty but also be a central component of their post-tenure careers.

As educators and as parents, we know that there are critical issues that need to be addressed to help our young people navigate their way through a world which is changing faster than it ever has in history. The tragedy of Virginia Tech was a tragedy of lost potential. All thirty-two of those killed would each have impacted the lives of countless others.

In his wonderful story *A Christmas Carol,* Charles Dickens wrote of two children he calls Ignorance and Want, who appear to Ebeneezer Scrooge when he is journeying through time with the Ghost of Christmas Present. The Ghost warns Scrooge saying, "This boy is Ignorance. This girl is Want. Beware them both, and all of their degree, but most of all beware this boy, for on his brow I see that written which is Doom, unless the writing be erased."

Attacks like the one on Virginia Tech haunt us, but they shouldn't paralyze us or make us lose faith in young people. Finding ways to make sure that we don't lose what is most precious to us will be one of the biggest challenges we have faced in decades, but it's a challenge we have the potential to overcome if we work together. The ghosts of the past do not have to be the ghosts of the future.

9.
Writers and
Writing

E VER SINCE the shootings at Virginia Tech, writing has become my most reliable method of communication. Speech is tricky, not just because my tongue is less agile than it used to be, but also because I worry about responding to a question like "How's it going?" If I were to answer honestly, it could be embarrassing. Sometimes I hear myself even before I utter a word, playing my phrases back the way you do when you listen to a bad recording of your voice. There are times when my spoken voice sounds nothing like me. I hear it engage students in discussion in the classroom as it tries and fails to sound teacherly. The voice on the page is more recognizable. Though the written voice still surprises me—shocks me sometimes, in fact—it has an honesty that the other one lacks.

On the page, you can allow experience to express itself through the lens of reflection. You have a semblance of control because you can always tear it to shreds or press the delete key. You can mull things over, take things back, scratch out and revise—something you can never really do after words have been spoken. The page allows for a pact of privacy—you don't have to show anyone what you've written. It's just you and a piece of paper (or the screen), the ultimate confidante. That is why diaries and journals comfort us. They are one of the few things that can be utterly our own. Although writing can never completely succeed in closing the gap between experience and expression, it can be a sublime approximation; the attempt itself allows us to take up temporary residence in the realm of enlightenment.

Some of those drawn to artistic expression are those whose own silence is burdensome to them. Written-down suffering is said by some to mitigate the experience of suffering, rather like an aspirin mitigates a headache—healthier to weep on the page than in the flesh. Creative writing, which yokes experience to imagination in radical ways, is sometimes promoted as a cure-all for those who may feel alienated from others or from themselves. Writers become Word Wizards, Practitioners of the Art of the Imagination. Writers can defeat time itself, redefining experience as they record it. If you are a writer working within the genres of poetry, fiction, playwriting, and creative nonfiction, you can imagine yourself in any role you choose. You can be the hero or the villain; you can make others speak in exactly the way you want them to. You can dress and undress them, love or leave them. You can admit at last who it is you want to be even as you mourn the fact of who you actually are.

Some students make the assumption that this is a discipline that doesn't require discipline from them. In this deceptively accessible field where imagination is celebrated, youngsters are encouraged to write—as indeed they should be. In fact, if you have ever entered a creative writing classroom of elementary or middle-school students you can find them engaged with material in remarkable ways. When children write creatively, they are much better than adults at discarding their assumptions about logic and reality. Stars can be peppermints, trees can laugh. As writer-educators such as Georgia Heard emphasize, children and creativity must go together. It is a way for young people to begin to discover who they are, where they are, when they are, how they are, and why they are the way they are. The creative writing classroom at any level is often a place of unrivaled joy because it is a place where students' voices matter. As teachers, we listen to them in that sacred space where the imagination holds sway. We rejoice with them when they find the perfect image or the telling phrase. Their creativity is premised on the notion that the writing classroom is safe—that they can explore whichever subject they wish with as much imagination as they desire. In a culture that places emphasis on standardized testing, it is one of the places where students don't have to focus upon getting the answer right because the answer is theirs not ours, and the "rightness" of it is how well they manage to convey it to us.

Writing classrooms, and creative writing classrooms in particular, are not breeding grounds for deviancy, they are learning centers for the imagination, where diversity can be celebrated in ways it cannot be to the same extent in other settings. Few questions or assertions are off limits, and what students tell us can disclose a lot about their lives and their assumptions.

I have been asked fairly frequently why it was that only Seung-Hui Cho's English professors and instructors seemed to be aware that he was an unusually quiet student while those in other disciplines didn't appear to notice him, even though he would have taken a variety of other classes. The answers reveal a lot about the nature of education at large state institutions where interaction between faculty and students can be limited. The relatively small class size in most writing classes—creative writing, literature, business and technical writing, and composition—means that students *can* be noticed. It is much more difficult to do this in large lecture classes. In addition, the nature of the assignments in creative writing allows students to express themselves much more freely than in other courses. The pedagogical approach in writing and literature is often based on newer models where interaction is a critical component of the learning process. Looking at the ways in which writing enables students to discover things about themselves and the world helps us understand why creative writing is fast becoming one of the most popular majors and minors, and the nexus of a battle between free speech and censorship, individual privacy and collective security. Before we impose strict censorship on student writers, it's important to understand what we may be losing if we do so.

WHILE A graduate student in the University of Arkansas' Creative Writing program, I served as codirector of Writers in the Schools. Funded by the University of Arkansas in Fayetteville and the National Endowment for the Arts, the program was overseen by the late James T. Whitehead, the six-foot-six, larger-than-life novelist and poet who flung himself into teaching the way a quarterback flings himself into a bowl game, and who inspired many of us to be as passionate about teaching as he was. Teams of graduate students were sent out all over Arkansas to teach K–12 students about the joys of creative writing. Writers in the Schools programs like this one have thrived over the past few decades, and it is one of the reasons so many students fall in love with writing.

On one particular occasion I was with my poetry partner in a small town in a remote area of the state. As a woman of color I was always aware of the fact that predominantly white rural areas in Arkansas could present me with challenges, but the teachers made us feel welcome, and I wasn't concerned. We began as usual by finding out about the assumptions the children brought to poetry. It has to rhyme, children often tell you, saddened by the fact that this means, for them, it's a medium fraught with danger. We try to dismiss assumptions like these, letting children know that poetry can indeed rhyme but it can also do other things—that it isn't a straitjacket but a vehicle for exploring subjects they may never have explored before.

Several classes had been grouped together, so there must have been close to a hundred elementary school students sitting cross-legged on the floor around us, gazing up as we talked with them about poetry. We were accustomed to such audiences. My poetry partner and I had our trusty menu of exercises to choose from: *Write about your quiet place. If the sea were suddenly made of chocolate what would happen? If you were a spoon what would it feel like? What do stars dream of?* We told them where we were from, my partner having been born in Arkansas, while I had traveled all the way over from England where my black Jamaican father had met and married my white English mother. I may even have shown them a photo of my father and mother—I can't remember. If I did, they would have been struck by my father's face—his very dark complexion and his wonderfully sensitive eyes.

Suddenly the hand of a little blond boy sitting at our feet shot up. He told us he wanted to let us know something. It was clear he was very excited about what he had to say. He pumped his arm and wiggled his fingers the way children do when they make an urgent request to go to the bathroom. It wasn't unusual for an elementary student to be desperate to share some idea he may have had about a poem, and we had already noticed that this student seemed to be particularly active. I thought I saw the teachers who stood at the edge of the circle of students stiffen a little. No doubt this was a child who could get worked up easily. I called on the boy to speak.

"Do you *know,*" he shouted out, placing exaggerated emphasis on his words and taking breaths midsentence the way children do, "Do you *know* in *this* town we're *all KKK*?" He beamed at us, totally unaware of the implications of his assertion. His teachers froze.

It was a tricky moment, not least because I had lived in Arkansas long enough to suspect that he was at least partially correct. It must have been 1983 or 1984, and it was quite possible that the Klan had a significant following in that particular region. I took a deep breath and said something like "Well, that's an interesting statement, though of course that's not really true anymore, is it? Because we're here now." The boy seemed to accept the logic of my argument. He grinned broadly and returned to his writing. Meanwhile, the teachers looked as if they were about to hemorrhage. One or two attempted a denial, scolding the student for his impropriety, but we quickly waved this off. I believe it was then that I asked the children to try to impersonate my British accent: "Bath," I said. "Tomato." They cracked up as they tried in vain to sound British.

Later, the teachers tried to apologize—one said we should not, on any account, believe what the boy had told us. We assured her it was fine and that we hadn't taken offense. We hadn't, and it was.

As it turned out, this particular two-day visit was one of the most memorable we had. The students were wonderful, the teachers receptive. Poetry and stories became a way of introducing children to the rich diversity of experience.

I tell this story because it seems to me that it says something about the nature of the writing classroom—that it is a spontaneous, unpredictable environment, one for which you can only do so much planning because it relies upon response to succeed. If you take offense too easily in situations like this, students—some of whom may be desperate to express themselves—retreat into silence. Finding ways to open up the dialogue so that people will actually talk to each other is crucial in education. It is an opportunity to address issues such as diversity in innovative ways, to impress upon young people that voices of difference can be exciting and informative. The focus should be on response not delivery. The students have an opportunity to introduce themselves to us and to each other. For this reason, writing classes *must* be small.

Disquieting stories about the size of writing classes circulate among English faculty: At one institution composition classes are said to resemble large lecture classes; at another university more and more students are encouraged to opt out of writing-intensive classes so that money can be saved. There is little doubt that at some schools budget cuts have resulted in larger classes. This translates into less focused time per student, less opportunity for faculty to get to know those they teach. At Virginia Tech, there are students who tell me they have not written a paper in years—that their high school experience consisted of objective testing and OpScan sheets. If they don't have intensive writing experiences in college, they may never have them.

Of course, even for those with high school writing experience, things tend to shift. Beginning writing students may not necessarily be encouraged to edit themselves with rigor, and often they are not ready to do so, especially if they are writing creatively. Too much editing can paralyze a young writer. At the college level, however, the situation can quickly turn challenging if a student is too insistent about his or her own creative excellence, or if a student has already determined she or he has nothing to learn before entering the writing classroom. At its best, creative writing is a discipline that obliges us to look and listen more intently than we ever have before; at its worst, creative writing can be a form of uncritical self-indulgence.

THE SHOOTING rampage of Barry Loukaitis in 1996 in Moses Lake, Washington, and its connection to a novel by Stephen King have been well documented. As Katherine Newman writes in her book *Rampage:*

> In fact, his actions were organized and rehearsed, according to police detectives, because Loukaitis was acting out the plot from one of his favorite novels: Stephen King's 1977 book, *Rage,* which police detectives found on Loukaitis's bedside table. In the novel, a teen holds his algebra class hostage with a revolver, kills a teacher, and talks about killing a popular student. During Loukaitis's shooting spree, classmates reported that he turned to one of them and said, "This sure beats algebra doesn't it?"—a direct quote from the book.[1]

In 1999, Stephen King removed his novel *Rage* from bookstores, explaining in interviews that he had written it during a difficult period of his life, and that he wished it had never been published. After the Virginia Tech shootings in 2007, King was questioned by reporters who wanted to know if he felt that writing could be a catalyst for violent action:

> I've thought about it, of course. Certainly in this sensitized day and age, my own college writing—including a short story called "Cain Rose Up" and the novel *Rage*—would have raised red flags, and I'm certain someone would have tabbed me as mentally ill because of them. . . . For most creative people, the imagination serves as an excretory channel for violence: We visualize what we will never actually do. . . . Cho doesn't strike me as in the least creative, however. Dude was crazy. . . . He may have been inspired by Columbine, but only because he was too dim to think up such a scenario on his own.[2]

In the same interview, King describes another student he knew called "George," who, he says, seemed much more likely to "blow" because of his enraged stories about flaying, dismemberment, and revenge, and the desire he expressed "to get back at THEM." It was George's quietness—the contrast between his character and his writing and his sense of victimhood—that alarmed King.

It is naive to expect that violence can be prevalent in one sphere (popular culture) and absent in another (the culture of the school). But the penalties for it in one can be nonexistent, while the penalties for it in another can be extreme. Some students are confused and angered by this double standard. People in the entertainment industry can make a fortune by depicting brutality; and writers can gain literary stature in part because of their unflinching and persuasive portrayals of extreme violence. Violence has almost become a "genre" in its own right—garnering the kind of praise from critics that was formerly reserved for the subtle depiction of relationships. Stephen King is, in my opinion, a writer of enormous talent, whose skills are often underestimated by people in academe. Some of his descriptions are as powerful as any we are likely to read. It would be a shame if college-age students were not permitted to study his work.

But it is worth asking why it is that violence has become such a dominant theme in American literature, movies, and video games, and whether, like the bully on the playground, it has shoved aside other themes that may have an even more important role to play in a student's intellectual development.

The obsession with violence in American society poses particular problems for women, in part because so many depictions of violence in the media celebrate (and reward, in the case of first-person shooter video games) a supercharged stereotypical masculinity, one that often involves young female victims who are depicted being raped or slaughtered by domineering male characters. Most English teachers are women; most teachers of writing are women, too. This means that female teachers are on the front line of this debate, whether we want to be or not. Men's voices have tended to dominate this discussion, which is surprising given the makeup of the teaching profession. The voices of women such as Catherine Itzin, the author of *Pornography: Women, Violence, and Civil Liberties,* have not been heard as often as they should have been.

Writers warn about the horror that will follow if they are asked to moderate their depiction of violence. If limitations are placed on the imagination in this way, what is likely to follow? Will portrayals of miscegenation be outlawed by societies that value racial purity? Will we be forced to black out lovemaking scenes lest they harm the values of the young? Will writers be obliged to pen moral treatises rather than novels, making sure that the good guys win and the bad guys are punished in portrayals that make a mockery of what it means to live in a flawed, untidy, often brutal society? Rather like the NRA, whose position is that any compromise about gun rights will inevitably lead to the abolition of the Second Amendment, some writers are adamant that there should not be any censorship whatsoever because it would inevitably lead to further encroachments on the First Amendment. I realize that comparing those who support the freedoms guaranteed by the Second Amendment to those who support the freedoms guaranteed by the First is likely to be offensive to both sides. Being a supporter of the First Amendment myself, however, that fact alone doesn't really bother me. What does bother me is the ease with which some writers assume that an obsessive depiction of excessive violence *never* creates an environment that countenances, encourages, or inspires violence. Why has the American fascination with violence become a fetish? Does the repeated depiction of rape and murder shape young people's attitudes towards those crimes, as an increasing body of scientific evidence suggests it does, or are they always completely impervious to its influence?

In 1993, the American Psychological Association's commission on violence concluded that aggressive attitudes and behavior correlate with exposure to violence in the media. Professor Elizabeth Newson, whose 1994 report describing the effects of excessively violent media on the young was signed by twenty-five psychologists and pediatricians, likens exposure to media violence to child abuse. Such assertions are controversial, not just because of their implications for free speech and their similarity to claims made by right-wing conservatives about the dangers of a liberal education, but also because of the impact they could have on the profit margins of many corporations. Meanwhile, educators, parents, and students can find themselves in the middle of an untenable situation.

There is no doubt that writing can be a cathartic exercise, so it isn't any wonder that those who may be in the greatest pain find refuge in it. Students sometimes write in hopes of finding affirmation, consolation, or even salvation. After all, the page doesn't yell at you; it seems in its white placidity to be a place of infinite patience. The page's limitless understanding is a gift for young writers, but it can become a liability for those who genuinely wish to engage with an audience. For writers, even when they are engaged in writing, the most solitary of art forms, have to imagine the page as their audience, an audience that answers back. They have to listen to a multitude of voices, not just their own voices playing slight variations of the same tune louder and louder in their heads. Writing is a sanctuary but it is also a taskmaster. And for those who come to writing without self-discipline, it can become the best friend who lets you down.

If writing is pursued with any degree of seriousness it isn't merely self-expression, it is communicable, reflective expression, a process of relentless interrogation. Unfortunately, those who are most severely damaged or disturbed may be the ones who are most likely to be attracted by it and least likely to succeed at it. This phenomenon isn't one that is examined much because those who care about teaching and writing prefer to focus on students' limitless potential. It's easier, therefore, to assume that all young people are equally prepared for the demands of artistic engagement. In an ideal world, that would be true, but in reality, this may not be the case. If writing can be a healing process for those who are willing to ask questions of themselves, it can be torture for those who aren't, especially if it is ever coupled with rejection.

To someone as egotistical, insecure, hypersensitive, damaged, and enraged as Seung-Hui Cho, rejection must have been the ultimate transgression. Writing can heal us, yes, but writing can also make us bleed. Even for those who, like Hart Crane, Sylvia Plath, Anne Sexton, and Randall Jarrell, charted a route to exquisite beauty in their work, writing did not cure what ailed them. In fact, because it can allow you access into the deeper recesses of the imagination, writing can be an agonizing process. All of these writers committed suicide, in spite of the light they shone upon the world. Turning that light upon their own particular darkness proved impossible.

Because writing gives students permission to say what they may not have said before (to begin a paragraph with "because," for example) it has enormous appeal, particularly for those who may feel that their voices have been silenced in the past. This is one of the reasons teaching writing can be especially labor intensive. Anyone who has taught creative writing for any length of time has worked with a number of students who are lonely or depressed. When we look around at the community of writing practitioners we see people who seem to have more than their fair share of angst, hang-ups, insecurities, depression, and paranoia. It is certainly an exaggeration to suggest that all writers are troubled, but it is true that writers seem to be more in touch with their personal demons, less afraid to explore a wide range of emotions in their work. For some young and some professional writers, writing is a way to make sense of a world that often seems brutal or nonsensical, a way to say, "My voice matters. *Please* listen to it."

Creative writing isn't simply about self-expression; it's about craft and hard work. It's about reading as much as possible, observing life in ways you may never have observed it before, and questioning your assumptions. Ironically, some of those who are most excited about creative writing don't really intend to explore life, they wish instead to bury themselves in the writing experience. For them becoming a Writer may be more important than the writing process. It is seen as a glamorous profession with a tradition that celebrates rebel-writers like Ernest Hemingway and Frank O'Hara, e. e. cummings (who thumbed his nose at punctuation, regular syntax, and capital letters), the Beats (Kerouac and Ginsberg, in particular), and black activist writers. There is a belief among some young writers that one of the most attractive aspects of writing is its rebelliousness: You don't do what society expects you to do and thus you redefine society by rewriting it. You can wander unfettered around the country like Jack Kerouac desiring everything and sampling most of it, or write in a frenzy like Rimbaud. You can howl with Allen Ginsberg and focus exclusively upon yourself. It is a life especially attractive to young men who yearn for freedom from responsibility. The only obligation is to one's art, and one's art is an expression of oneself, which makes writing a process akin to looking in the mirror commenting on your own reflection, warts and all. But the writing process itself can be underestimated by students who seek to emulate what they see as a "writerly" way of life. They write obsessively about themselves, partly because they are desperate to be heard. This does *not* mean that these students are deeply disturbed. In fact, only in very rare cases is that true. A significant number of students I have taught whose work is the most accomplished and resonant have suffered from a range of emotional problems, in part because of their acute sensitivity. We must not turn students like these away from writing. In fact, for their sake and for art's sake, we have an obligation to do the opposite. But we cannot automatically make the assumption that all students are equally prepared to make the same journeys at the same time. And when they don't seem to be doing so, we have to find effective ways to respond.

Poet Monica Barron's thoughtful essay "Creative Writing Class as Crucible," posted to *Academe*, the bimonthly online magazine of the American Association of University Professors, highlights the difficulty we often have as writers and teachers attempting to navigate through students' work. During one semester Barron seemed to be receiving a lot of writing about "serial killers, rapists, slashers, and murderers." In fact, there were so many examples that she gathered them into a file marked "suspects"—a file she asked a friend to come and retrieve should she wind up dead: "Some of the writing was simply over-the-top work of young men who didn't write very well (it wasn't the women writing this stuff). Some of it wasn't."[3]

Classrooms are an extension of the culture not its antidote, and some of the young people who are accustomed to consuming excessive violence in the TV shows and movies they watch, in the books they read, and in the games they play are not shy of reproducing it in their own writing. But as Chris M. Anson depicts in an imagined conversation between characters called "Everything" and "Nothing" in a piece in the same issue of *Academe* called "What's Writing Got to Do with Campus Terrorism?" wholesale surveillance and monitoring of students in creative writing classes could create an environment of sustained panic.[4] The truth is, if teachers raised the alarm every time a student handed in a piece of writing that featured violence, most school campuses would be swathed in flashing blue lights several times a week, counseling centers would be even more overcrowded than they already are, and police officers would be placed on permanent overtime.

Fortunately, most of what the writing teachers receive, even when it contains explicit violence, is *not* a prelude to actual violence. The difficulty comes in trying to identify writing which *may* indicate that a student is a threat to him- or herself or others. An experienced teacher usually has a pretty good idea if there is something seriously amiss, but it is possible to be mistaken. Educators and administrators are justifiably reluctant to sully a student's reputation by accusing him or her of something as heinous as wanting to harm other people. In addition, the word *student* carries with it certain assumptions. Students are in the process of becoming adults. Even if they are adults, the word *student* admits that they are not yet fully formed.

Some student papers, stories, essays, and poems are filled with sadistic images, depraved characters, the *N* word, curse words, and excessive violence, but in my experience almost all of the examples of this type of writing come from students who are compassionate, intelligent, serious writers committed to a realistic portrayal of the societies in which they live. Students point to Norman Mailer, Truman Capote, Elmore Leonard, and John Edgar Wideman, whose stark depictions capture the essence of human experience. Realism and verisimilitude are part and parcel of the college-level writing experience. Writing, like other art forms, is often deliberately provocative.

The relationship between a writer's character and his or her art is sometimes assumed to be transparent when it is, in reality, resistant to interpretation. Even Nobel Prize–winning authors can run afoul of readers and critics if a direct connection is made between the morality espoused in a work of fiction and the author's own ethics. The South African writer J. M. Coetzee endured a firestorm of protest when his novel *Disgrace* was published in 1999, a few years before he won the Nobel Prize for Literature. It depicts the rape of a white woman by black African intruders. Some critics, including Nobel Prize–winning author Nadine Gordimer, herself South African, felt that the book pointed to Coetzee's own racist assumptions. On the other hand, many writers would take issue with the idea that there is a traceable connection between a writer's character and his art, especially when that work of art is imaginary. If handling controversial issues poses problems for Nobel Prize winners, it's no surprise that the intentions of neophyte writers can also be misread.

ACCORDING TO the Association of Writers and Writing Programs (AWP), creative writing is fast becoming the most popular subject in the humanities. It has joined forces with composition studies, professional and business writing, and communication to become a large-scale phenomenon that marks a resurgence of interest in the field of writing. In 1975, there were 80 degree-conferring creative writing programs in the United States; in 2004, there were 720—a nearly tenfold increase.[5] But this doesn't even begin to capture the popularity of the discipline because many students take creative writing classes that are not necessarily included under the umbrella of an officially established creative writing program. In high school, students often cite creative writing as their favorite subject. Partly as a result of innovative programs such as Writers in the Schools, students are exposed early on to the joys of poetry, fiction, playwriting, and creative nonfiction. By the time they get to college, many of them wish to pursue creative writing as a major, a minor, or a concentration. Many more of them decide to do so later on in their college careers. Employers value communication skills—written and spoken—which has helped make writing even more popular. All over the United States, students are writing essays, stories, and poems, which are remarkably eloquent, passionate, revealing, profound, and beautiful. Some of this material does, by necessity, contain violence.

The assumption that a writer's work is always a form of autobiography conflicts with the assumption of many writers of fiction who hold that writing is almost never "true." Almost every text-book on fiction writing begins with a statement about the relation-ship between fiction and truth, and the need for a writer to develop an ability to "lie" well—to persuade readers that what he or she is saying is true. This means that the gap between reader and writer can be considerable, and that it is a writer's job to persuade the reader that what he or she says could be plausible or "true." When a stu-dent in poet Monica Barron's class was asked about writing of his that featured a serial killer, for example, he did not seem to under-stand what was meant by audience or the term *genre fiction.* It was therefore very difficult for Barron to know if he was merely writing within a particular convention or writing in a way that would be de-scribed as "ideation" by threat assessment specialists. In many ways, she was asking how much of this is yours, and how much is bor-rowed from other writers.

Some student-writers use writing as a kind of weapon—a way to intimidate and provoke. After all, there are entire schools of artists who have done just that. Students point to satirical precedent if they are called upon to describe what it is they have done in a piece of work. Seung-Hui Cho compared the work he produced in Professor Giovanni's class to that of Jonathan Swift who authored "A Modest Proposal." In Seung-Hui Cho's case, it seemed to be impossible for him to avoid telling some part of the truth about who he was, but he also seemed incapable of detecting or appreciating irony in his own work, even though he recognized it in the work of others. This sin-gularity of vision is dangerous for obvious reasons, but it is also typ-ical of young writers who have not read much or thought deeply about their own assumptions.

So how should teachers react when they are confronted with something that purports to be fiction or some form of creative writ-ing that also contains what may be threatening material? After the tragedy at Virginia Tech, many schools are likely to err on the side of caution by removing the student from class, possibly suspending or expelling him, even at the risk of legal action.

IN FEBRUARY 2008, Stephen Daniel Barber, a student at the University of Virginia at Wise, a satellite branch of the University of Virginia, made headlines when the story he wrote for his creative writing class alarmed his instructor and classmates. According to an article in the March 8, 2008, issue of the *Roanoke Times:*

> Barber summarized his story as being about "a crazy drug addict who ponders killing a professor, decides not to, then considers suicide . . . the character doesn't actually do anything other than think."
>
> The story is written in first person. At one point the narrator describes how news of Seung-Hui Cho's rampage at Virginia Tech causes him to sleep with a gun under his pillow. The professor who the narrator briefly contemplates killing is named "Mr. Christopher."
>
> According to a report by campus police Sgt. Randy Wyatt, the story alarmed Scalia and the students.
>
> "In the writing, he mentioned suicide, harming others, possessing a gun on campus, and other points that were alarming," Wyatt wrote.[6]

The name of the professor who taught the course was Christopher Scalia, one of the reasons the story, in which the narrator contemplates killing a "Mr. Christopher," alarmed those who read it. Christopher Scalia happens to be the son of the Supreme Court Justice Antonin Scalia. Wise County Commonwealth's attorney Ron Elkins was quoted as saying that the tone of the composition was worrying: "If I were his professor, I would interpret that [the story] as a potential threat," Elkins said.

Barber, an Iraq vet with a 3.9 GPA, was adamant that the story was fiction, something he claims to have told his professor. The day after he turned in his paper Barber was confronted by police. When it was discovered that he had three guns in his car—a loaded .45-caliber automatic pistol, a loaded .22-caliber rifle, and an empty 9 mm pistol—he was temporarily detained in a mental institution, released, and then expelled. According to this article and subsequent ones, Barber told reporters he planned to sue the university or re-enlist. It is not clear at the time of this writing which of these options he chose.[7]

In Barber's case, there is no doubt that using the first name of his professor in the story, even though it is a popular name, furthered the suspicion that the story was autobiographical. Christopher Scalia's parentage made authorities even more concerned about a potential threat to security. Given his high-profile father, the instructor would be seen as a potential target for an attack. As soon as weapons were discovered in Barber's car, it was impossible for the school to dismiss the incident. I should add that it is not uncommon for students in Virginia to own guns, and that many have concealed carry permits. It is likely, therefore, that it was the cumulative effect of these discoveries that led to Barber's expulsion.

We know that there are times when what we write about draws heavily upon our own biographies and desires. Pretending that it doesn't and claiming that no teacher has the right to report anyone who produces disturbing writing is ridiculous. But it is dangerous to assume that all those who produce writing that contains violence are themselves potential perpetrators of violence. If we believe that, we would have to incarcerate everyone from Stephen King to the Coen brothers, along with the writers of *The Sopranos, Deadwood,* and *CSI,* to name just a few. Ideally, each case involving writing should be judged on its own merits, so that we don't suspend or expel students for having vivid imaginations and a passion for verisimilitude.

We should be mindful of the fact that the most reassuring, non-violent portrayals in the past have often masked an obscene brutality. The pen is capable of ferreting out hypocrisy and exposing cruelty, and the portrayal must be married with a raw and sometimes shocking honesty if it's to be effective. Not depicting violence at all could be as dangerous as glorifying and exploiting it.

Although I have serious reservations about the trend to glorify violence, and although I hope that writers will begin to question the ways in which an obsession with violence manifests itself in contemporary literature and film, we need to be wary of penalizing students who are trying to capture the world as it has been presented to them.

School shootings place teachers and students directly in the line of fire in all kinds of ways. Teachers of creative writing and composition become especially vulnerable. We need to be supportive of those teachers who try to intercede *and* those students who are wrongfully accused. Organizations like the Modern Language Association (MLA), AWP, the National Council of Teachers of English (NCTE), and the Conference on College Composition and Communication (CCCC) must be key players in this debate. The national PTA organization, state legislators, and boards of trustees must also play a pivotal role, along with experts in security and mental health. I am worried about proposed solutions that are premised on the idea that the classroom is a contained space. It is not. Behaving as though it is places people in jeopardy.

WHILE I was serving as chair of the English department at Virginia Tech, I was contacted in March 2005 by an attorney who asked me if I would be willing to write to a young African American man who had been convicted of homicide. The young man was a poet, he was in despair, and he did not want to agree to a plea bargain agreement. If he accepted, he could avoid execution and instead spend the rest of his life in prison. The attorney said that this young man, who was only eighteen years old, had been—clichéd though it sounds—in the wrong place at the wrong time, manipulated and duped by older, hardened criminals. But he was passionate about writing and trying to find solace in poetry. His lawyer was hoping I could say something to encourage the young man because it would mean more if it came from someone who wrote poetry. He said he believed that his client's life was worth saving.

Initially, I didn't want to respond. I thought about the families of the people who had suffered because of him, and imagined how I would feel were I one of them. Trying to help this young African American man wasn't something I felt I should have been asked to do. Besides, if I said the wrong thing and he turned down the plea bargain and chose death instead, I knew I would feel responsible. I have to admit that I thought fleetingly about the headline, "English Professor Tutors Killer," which made me distinctly uncomfortable. The irony of this given what happened later is searing.

I asked the lawyer—an earnest, thoughtful man, who was desperate to save his client from execution—to give me a little time to think it over. He agreed, relieved that I hadn't turned him down outright. In fact, his relief was so obvious that it made me feel even guiltier than I had before. In the end I said yes because my reasons for declining all sounded like excuses.

So I wrote to the young man, trying to find words that would convey to him that solace could be found in poetry. I had said similar things to other students before and would say similar things again, later that year, when I met with Seung-Hui Cho. I wanted to give him some sense of how writing could save your life, if you let it. But I was afraid that what I told him would sound empty. Although I had known despair, I had also been blessed with the tools to hack my way out of it. There was no optimistic scenario for this young man. Even if he avoided death row, every door he looked at from that time onward would be locked.

As I now reread the letter I wrote, I see so many things I could have said better. But I am also trying to accept that you do the best you can at the time, and that, if this isn't sufficient, you must learn to forgive yourself. This is an excerpt from my note to him:

I know that you are facing a very difficult decision and that there must be many things swirling around in your head right now. Sometimes it's hard to know what to do, so I am sending these words to let you know that there is still beauty and there is still wonder in the world, and that poetry has the power to comfort us, if we allow it to do so.

There is an ancient Indian saying that I try to live by: "Everything not given is lost." In other words, if we don't learn to give things away, if we don't learn to share who we are, then there is nothing but sadness and loss. So these words are my small gift to you. Remember, too, that you have something to give to the world—something that will be lost if you decide not to stay with us. There are things you will be able to say in your poetry, things that may be far more important than you know. Your words could make us understand who you are and what you see, and why things were said or done. How many hundreds of poems will not be written if you are not here to write them? A word has the power to change the world. It can be uttered from anywhere at anytime by anyone. It could be uttered by you one day.

I do not know you, so I cannot know the fear you must feel as you think about your future. But I do know that you love poetry, and that your writing shows that you have a spirit that is alive and full. So, as one writer to another, I want to share with you words from a poem by a famous African American poet, Gwendolyn Brooks. It is a beautiful poem— a plea to young people not to die because there are things of glory left to see. I don't have the whole poem in my head, so I'll try to send you a copy through Mr. ____ so that you can read the whole thing.

You are only eighteen. There is still so much for you to know, so many questions to ask, so many journeys to take. . . . You can take journeys in the pages of books; you can discover new

*lands in the miracle of words. I promise that's true. If you
are willing to ask the hard questions, you can find answers
that can make you free. It takes courage to believe in this.*

*Here is my wish for you: May you find joy in small things;
may you find hope on the edge of tragedy; may you find
gentleness where you least expect to find it; and may you find
peace in the shining light of your poems.*

I sent him some poems and his lawyer told me he would deliver
them and the letter to the young man. Later on I learned that he had
opted to live and had accepted the plea bargain in the end. The
lawyer wrote to me some time after that and told me that one of the
young man's poems had been accepted for publication. I don't fool
myself into believing that it was a letter from me that made the difference, especially as there was so much I was incapable of knowing
about him. If anyone did make a difference it was his extraordinary
and dedicated lawyer, who refused to give up on someone he believed had potential.

These days I, too, am writing my way out of the darkness—
slowly and clumsily, feeling my way towards what are often dead
ends, making a mess of chapters, having to begin all over again, embarrassed and lost. I find a word or a phrase and hold it up to the
light only to discover it is hopelessly flawed. The writing process has
become for me a process akin to grieving because it is the stubborn-
ness of it that bludgeons you, the need to keep returning to the same
travesty. What people like to call "the healing process" doesn't live
up to its billing. Instead, it is an entry into different configurations of
pain, a series of accommodations and reconciliations. I take the hard,
knotty tumor of the word *grief* and chisel away at it until it attains its
own stark beauty. Then I put it on—an encumbrance to be worn
around the neck, one whose weight, I hope, will not prevent me
from ever standing upright again.

10.
Armed and Dangerous

IN A photo in the April 30, 2007, issue of *Time* magazine, Seung-Hui Cho points his gun at the camera. His eyes can be seen above the barrel of the gun, but it appears to be the gun itself doing the seeing—its single mechanical eye as steady as vengeance. Because of the angle of the camera the gun is enormous, its barrel a black hole of annihilation. Cho is already dressed for the role of killer. Everything in his pose says he is ready; nothing in this stark visual depiction is superfluous. Cho has already located his target—us. He will not deviate from his script until the anticipated climax occurs. He has found his voice at last, and it's ready to blast 174 bullets into our consciousness at the speed of a typical semiautomatic—almost at the speed of sound. The perspective is forced because the image compels the viewer to assume the role of victim.

In another photo, Cho is seen pointing a gun to his head. The expression on his face isn't that of a typical victim. Suicide is his choice—a final act of defiance that will allow him to exit on his own terms in his own time. He is both murderer and victim in this photo, but Cho the murderer has the upper hand. His mouth is clenched, and his black clothes and gloved hand signify his role as executioner and add to the ritualistic aspects of the drama he is creating. Cho's video clips, photos, and writing constitute obvious attempts at propaganda. He is intent upon promoting the idea of Cho as Avenger; he wants us to be cowed by his power, but this can only be achieved if he has a weapon large enough to intimidate us. Assiduously, he is converting himself into an icon—something others can emulate, just as he emulated Eric Harris and Dylan Klebold. He knows he will be famous; he knows there will be blood.

The videos and still photos demonstrate that Cho knew how to manipulate symbols and manufacture menace. Cho's pose was deliberate; it was meant to show that he was undergoing a metamorphosis, consciously trying to make himself a larger-than-life killing machine. Like his eyes, the camera becomes both mirror and window—a way of seeing the world but only within the confines of his own distorted reflection. Cho has pushed everyone else out of the way to make room for his own bloated ego, but he has to try hard because even he suspects that all this may be pointless—that, in fact, his despair may be more potent than his rage. He needs to pump himself up with props. His only trustworthy allies by this time are his guns. He has invested himself in the notion that his .22 Walther and 9 mm Glock will transform him from a stuttering, uninspired student-writer into a martyr. He has to convince himself that guns have the power to erase humiliation. From the age of three onward, Cho's profound inability to relate to others had been observed by his family. But it was the Columbine shootings that provided him with a template. In Columbine, he located a dramatic climax grandiose enough to satisfy his need for vindication and for vengeance. In his violent take on the American Dream he, the character "Seung Cho," aka "Ismail Ax," was invincible.

School shooters Eric Harris, Dylan Klebold, Kip Kinkel, and

others share a number of characteristics with Seung-Hui Cho, even though they were much younger than he was. Like Cho, these young men read from a script that was premised upon cultural assumptions about masculinity and violence.

Kip Kinkel carried out an attack at Oregon's Thurston High School seventeen hours after he'd murdered his parents. Before he killed his mother, he shouted out to her that he loved her. Then he shot her in the back of the head with his 9 mm Glock. Like Seung-Hui Cho, Kinkel had a sister who was extremely successful, whom he seemed to envy and resent. In May 1998, Kinkel was fifteen years old and plagued by voices telling him to kill. He had previously been caught at school with a loaded weapon, but this had not triggered the usual investigation, in part because his parents were both teachers and well respected in their community. Although Kinkel's obsession with guns and explosives had worried his parents for years, they were in denial about the extent of his illness, preferring instead to assume that he would (absurd as this sounds) use his talents to become some kind of bomb expert, or that he would simply grow out of his fascination with guns, bombs, and knives.

At one point in his journal Kinkel wrote, "I feel like everyone is against me, but no one ever makes fun of me, mainly because they think I am a psycho." Elsewhere he confided, "All I want is something small. Nothing big. I just want to be happy. . . . Why did God want me to be in complete misery?"[1] There is an odd juxtaposition between the voice of the calculating psychopath and the voice of the child, just as there is in Cho's video diatribes and in some of his writing. He is victim and perpetrator, innocent child and bloodthirsty villain, and there is no sustained attempt made to recognize this discrepancy, let alone reconcile it.

For those addicted to drama, guns offer a grand finale. For the severely disturbed and/or delusional, guns can be a way to silence external and internal demons.

In FBI analyses of school shootings, and in publications like

Deadly Lessons: Understanding Lethal School Violence by the National Research Council and Institute of Medicine, there are a number of indicators that suggest a student is contemplating an attack. Not surprisingly, foremost among them is a history of mental illness, a preoccupation with suicide, and a fascination with violence. The connection between mental illness and violence is hotly disputed by many psychologists and psychiatrists, who emphasize that those who are mentally ill are no more likely to commit acts of violence than those who are not. The other factor that seems to be important in a number of school shootings is bullying, and there are certainly some instances where this seems to have fueled attacks. In *Bowling for Columbine*, Michael Moore attributes violence in the United States solely to the availability of guns. His thesis is simple and emphatic: Remove guns from the hands of students, and remove ammunition from places like Wal-Mart, and school violence will diminish. Although the picture is more complex than this thesis suggests, there is no doubt that guns, mental illness, and a predisposition among some young people to violence combine to make a lethal cocktail. But not all attacks are reliant solely upon guns.

Most attacks on schools are not spontaneous. They are planned for weeks, months, even years, which means that students have time to acquire things like bomb-making manuals (one of the favorites for school shooters is *The Anarchist's Cookbook*), or join online conversations about how to make effective bombs. Dozens of homemade bombs were to be the primary means of slaughter at Columbine High School, and Kinkel laid explosive booby traps at his home after he had murdered his parents. Guns are still the weapon of choice for most school shooters, but because the scale of the devastation is particularly important to some of them, bombs are also very appealing. Nevertheless, it is rare to have a school rampage that does not feature guns as the primary weapons, and this allure for these students should not be underestimated. Seung-Hui Cho found in the gun exactly the kind of weapon he needed. It was lethal, efficient, reliable, menacing, unambiguous, and macho. In the end, this seems to have been precisely how Cho wanted to see himself.

TWO YEARS before the tragedy, when it was accidentally discovered that a student at Virginia Tech was carrying a concealed weapon on campus, guns were officially banned at the university. (The student was not intending to use the weapon to perpetrate a crime; he had a concealed carry permit and hadn't realized he had violated any regulations by bringing his gun to campus.) The fallout from the ban had been significant. Some gun rights activists were furious and disputed the right of the university to ban weapons if someone had a concealed carry permit. The Panel Report recommended that the state attorney general's office clarify the policy with regard to guns on campus because a number of Virginia colleges and universities were not clear about what they were permitted to do. Virginia code isn't helpful when it comes to this issue, and two bills to give college governing boards the authority to regulate guns on campus died during the 2005 session. In real terms, the issue may be moot. There are no magnetometers and no searches conducted at Virginia Tech, so there is no way to know whether or not a student is bringing a concealed weapon to campus, unless you come upon it by chance. Today, a perpetrator can smuggle weapons onto the campus as easily as Cho did on 4/16.

Since the tragedy, university spokesperson Larry Hincker, whose job it was to announce this policy to the public, has become a prime target of gun rights advocates on the Web. For some of the most ardent supporters of gun rights, Hincker and the administration were to blame for what happened because the prohibition prevented students from defending themselves when Cho attacked. Had students been permitted to carry firearms, they argue, this tragedy could have been prevented, or at least the death count could have been reduced. Those on the left immediately dismiss this argument—something I did at first.

While the Panel Report found no instances "in which a shooter in campus homicides had been shot or scared off by a student or faculty member with a weapon,"[2] in fact, there have been several where this has happened, one of them only a few miles away from Virginia Tech.

In 2002, a Nigerian graduate student, Peter Odighizuwa, shot three and wounded three others at the Appalachian School of Law in Grundy, Virginia. Although there are different accounts of the event, it seems that Odighizuwa, forty-three, was apprehended and subdued by students, two of whom retrieved personal weapons from their cars. In another case, Luke Woodham, the 1997 Pearl, Mississippi, school shooter, was apprehended by assistant principal Joel Myrick who held a gun to Woodham's neck detaining him until law enforcement arrived. Had Myrick not done so, sixteen-year-old Woodham would have escaped, quite possibly adding to his total of two killed and seven injured at the school. (Prior to his rampage, Woodham had committed matricide.) An avowed Satanist, Luke Woodham was not judged to be insane.

These examples and others like them are rare. The idea that it will always be possible to wait for law enforcement or security to arrive is the position of most school districts. There are drills for students and faculty, and emergency response plans that often include lockdowns. But controversy remains about the effectiveness of such procedures. What if perpetrators have planted devices in various locations that prohibit law enforcement from acting swiftly? The four-hour nightmare of Columbine was partly due to this strategy.[3] Given the fact that security and law enforcement often arrive too late to prevent an attack, it should not be surprising that some teachers, especially if they are far away from law enforcement, wish to arm themselves.

In August 2008, the *Houston Chronicle* reported that teachers in the tiny school district of Harrold, Texas, were allowed to carry pistols if they received training. The location (150 miles northwest of

Fort Worth and a thirty-minute drive from the sheriff's office) is remote, and the school board felt it would be difficult for law enforcement to respond quickly should there be an outbreak of violence.
The policy has caused consternation among educators. Some security
experts have expressed concern that more guns on campus means
that there is a much greater risk of injury to students. It is not clear
how the firearms will be stored to guarantee that they will not be
stolen, for example, nor is it clear if the training teachers have received will be sufficient to enable them to respond effectively in a
crisis situation.

At Virginia Tech, a perceived lack of security has resulted in the
formation of Students for Concealed Carry on Campus (SCCC), a
fairly robust special interest group who, supported by the NRA,
lobby for the right to carry concealed weapons if they have a valid
permit. The Panel Report includes an informative article by Jennifer Epstein, originally published on Inside Higher Education, about
whether or not students should be permitted to carry arms.[4] Epstein
highlights some of the dangers of adding firearms to a student population, some of whom are irresponsible when it comes to alcohol
and drugs. Accidents with firearms have resulted in deaths and injuries, particularly in fraternity houses. In one case, at Oregon State
in Corvallis, two dozen guns were found in a frat house, most of
them in insecure places. Of course not all students are irresponsible,
but carelessness with firearms could pose a major problem. I should
add that there are campuses that permit students to carry firearms if
they have concealed carry permits, and, so far at least, they appear to
be as safe as other campuses.

If communities cannot be rid of guns, we need to offer a far
greater degree of protection to faculty, staff, and students. The challenge is daunting for a university the size of Virginia Tech, whose
campus police force can only be in a limited number of places at
once. Although I have serious reservations about allowing any more
armed students on campus than we currently have (some members of

Virginia Tech's ROTC occasionally carry weapons, though all receive rigorous training), it is important to acknowledge that students' concerns are not unfounded. Classrooms are vulnerable just as local communities are vulnerable. Pretending they are not and telling young people not to worry it will never happen again is, sadly, a promise no one can make.

In 2008, a visit by the owner of the online company that sold a weapon to Seung-Hui Cho only helped deepen the divide between those who support concealed carry and those who are against it. To mark the one-year anniversary of the shootings, students were asked by the SCCC to wear empty holsters to campus to show their support of their right to carry firearms. Some did so, generating classroom discussion—and concern. But it was a visit by Eric Thompson of TGSCOM Inc. that proved to be more controversial.

Thompson was invited by the SCCC to speak in a series of discussions they had planned called "Firearms Education Week." (Thompson's online company sold a .22 Walther to Cho and, coincidentally, provided Steve Kazmierczak, the Northern Illinois shooter who killed five students and himself during an attack on Valentine's Day 2008, with two 9 mm magazines and a holster.) When Thompson came to campus, he was armed with a special offer: a sizable discount on gun purchases for all Virginia Tech students. Thompson wanted to do whatever he could to help us recover from the tragedy, he claimed, and he was prepared to sell his guns to students at cost to prevent further loss of life. He felt this was the least he could do for us.

AFTER SPENDING nearly three decades of my life in the South, I have come to believe that a solution that involves gun prohibition is one that would never work. This leaves us with a very difficult challenge. Given the number of weapons in the United States, is it possible to keep guns out of the hands of children, the mentally ill, and those with criminal records? Currently, the answer on all three counts is no. Although some states have closed loopholes that allow people to purchase weapons legally, there are still many states (Virginia is one) where it is very easy, under certain circumstances, to obtain weapons without undergoing a background check. Weapons don't need to be registered in Virginia, and it's perfectly legal to get a gun from a friend or an acquaintance, or to buy one at a gun show, where no background check is required.

According to most estimates, there are 90 firearms for every 100 people in the United States for a total of 250 to 270 million. Many people own multiple weapons (most of those I know who own guns own several), but a significant proportion of American households have no guns at all. Overall, however, the rate of ownership is higher than anywhere else in the world. (Yemen has the next highest rate, 61 firearms per 100; after that comes Finland at 56.)[5] Although some towns, cities, districts, campuses, and other public areas have restrictions on gun ownership, these prohibitions have recently been challenged in the Supreme Court. In June 2008, the Court ruled in a 5–4 decision in favor of an individual's right to own guns for self-defense and hunting, overturning the District of Columbia's thirty-two-year-old ban on firearms. Numerous lawsuits against other cities, such as San Francisco and Chicago, will no doubt follow. The assumption that prevails in some parts of Europe—that there will always be law enforcement nearby so armed intervention can be handled by trained personnel rather than by citizens—doesn't necessarily hold true in countries where either the government itself is corrupt or unstable, or geography means that people may need to defend themselves. According to a recent *USA Today* poll, more than 83 percent of Americans believe they have the right to bear arms. Any attempt to relieve people of weapons in the United States is likely, therefore, to be undemocratic.

In the case of the six-year-old at Buell Elementary in Flint, Michigan, who shot and killed his first-grade classmate, Kayla Rolland, in February 2000 with a .32-caliber handgun, the boy found the weapon on his uncle's bed. The gun was used during drug deals. The little boy and his mother were staying with the boy's uncle because they had been evicted from their home. The boy said he had not expected the little girl he shot to die, sounding like the six-year-old he was. Incredibly, after the shooting, some people lobbied for the execution of the boy for his crime. (The Supreme Court, again in a 5–4 ruling, has abolished juvenile executions, ruling that it is unconstitutional to sentence anyone to death who committed a crime when he or she was under eighteen.)

It's not simply a question of carelessness on the part of some gun owners; it's also a question of how difficult it is to keep track of weapons in the United States. Increasingly, people are acquiring arsenals. A few guns lost or taken may or may not be noticed. When thirteen-year-old Mitchell Johnson and eleven-year-old Andrew Golden attacked Westside Middle School near Jonesboro, Arkansas, in 1998, one of the weapons they used was a semiautomatic rifle they'd stolen from Andrew's grandfather's cache. They also grabbed weapons belonging to Andrew's father—a .38-caliber derringer, a .38-caliber snub-nose, and a .357 Magnum.[6]

According to most polls, the majority of Americans believe that keeping guns out of the hands of children, the mentally ill, and criminals is essential if we are to protect our communities. In spite of this, as Virginia has proven since 4/16, it can be exceptionally difficult to pass even the most commonsense gun control legislation. The aggressive pose adopted by Charlton Heston at NRA conventions is still fresh in politicians' memories. At the 130th NRA Convention in 2001, Heston, as he had done the previous year, held a weapon aloft (this time, a musket from the American Revolution) and declared that he had only five words for us: "From my cold, dead hands," a saying that was greeted with wild applause. The cry has resonated for years, especially among politicians who are indebted to the NRA for their contributions to its campaigns, and was a declaration of war by people who are as fiercely protective of their Second Amendment rights as pro-lifers are of the rights of an unborn fetus. As he brandished his weapon, Charlton Heston demonstrated his appreciation of the power of symbolism and the significance of ritual. The man who had played Moses and Ben-Hur knew how important it was to exude power during the climax of his speech. Visually, the weapon was designed to instill fear and guarantee dominance—much like the waving of the tribal spear. The tableau—he held the pose for some time—was supposed to silence opposition, and, in spite of all the parodies that followed, it was remarkably effective.

After the Virginia Tech tragedy, cautious state politicians didn't want to mention the word *gun.* For this reason, they paid a lot of lip service to mental health reform and campus security—issues that suddenly caused them sleepless nights. Although comprehensive legislation has been introduced by Governor Kaine to address some of the severe problems Virginia has relative to mental health, both mental health care and campus security are in dire need of a much greater infusion of funds. Neither is likely to get them given the current budget shortfalls.

A few of the more courageous members of Virginia's General Assembly dared to work with some of the victims' families to introduce legislation that would make it harder for mentally unstable people to purchase guns. Governor Kaine introduced a bill in Virginia that would oblige those who sold guns at gun shows to conduct a background check on purchasers. Currently, no such check is in place. Many people, including many moderate gun owners, agree that gun show purchases *should* come under the same jurisdiction as purchases made at other venues, but gun rights advocates mounted a fierce campaign. Politicians who have benefited from the support of the NRA were terrified of offending their powerful and generous ally. They looked at people like Michael Bloomberg, the mayor of New York City, and learned an important lesson: If you spoke out against the proliferation of guns you faced an avalanche of protest by extremists determined to beat you into submission. Many politicians, even if they were genuinely concerned about this issue, remained silent. And thus it was that the proposal to require background checks at gun shows wilted and eventually died in the Virginia General Assembly when two Democrats, Senator Roscoe Reynolds of Henry County and Senator John Edwards of Roanoke (not to be confused with the former vice presidential candidate), joined with Republicans on the State Courts of Justice Committee and voted to reject it. That was in late January 2008, and by then, images of the Tech slaughter were already fading fast.

When Seung-Hui Cho purchased his guns, he did not acknowledge that he'd been ordered to receive outpatient treatment. Even if he had, there is some dispute about whether or not, at that time, he would have been prohibited from procuring a weapon. Since then, the loophole has been closed. Those who are involuntarily committed cannot now legally purchase a weapon through a registered vendor. State legislators are gambling on the fact that these same people won't realize they can easily purchase firearms at gun shows.

In Virginia, buying a gun is a piece of cake. If you order it online first, you can pick it up at a convenient location. For Seung-Hui Cho, that was J-N-D Pawnbrokers, situated literally across the street from the main, tree-lined mall entrance to the campus. It probably took Cho about ten seconds to get from the edge of campus to the door of the pawnbrokers. He waited the required thirty days before obtaining the Glock 19. The Glock—the more powerful of the two pistols used by Seung-Hui Cho—can be bought for about $500 from any online dealership. It's considered one of the most reliable guns on the market. With a lightweight frame composed of a dense polymer, and with numerous safety features, it is often used by law enforcement. Both the Glock and the .22 Walther are semiautomatic. You can't fire continuously with a pull of the trigger as you can with fully automatic weapons—you have to pull the trigger each time. But this can be accomplished very quickly. Semiautomatics make it possible to shoot without having to reload until the magazine is empty. In Seung-Hui Cho's case, the magazines he purchased contained both ten and fifteen rounds. According to the Panel Report, Cho purchased some of his ammunition on eBay, some from Wal-Mart, and some from Dick's Sporting Goods stores. When it comes to buying ammo, there is a plethora of family-oriented outlets from which to choose.

IF ALL of the attacks on schools we have suffered since the 1990s had been perpetrated by terrorists from other countries we would be in a much better state of preparedness. We would recognize at once that something needs to be done to address the issue, for school shootings are a form of domestic terrorism. But because the perpetrators are homegrown, there is a tendency to think of them in the same way as we think of "domestic violence," to perceive them as being less threatening.

The statistics can be comforting. After all, according to the April 30, 2007, issue of *Time* magazine, students in 2005 had one chance in two million of dying violently in school. Overall, violent crime is trending downward. Mass killings are less than a quarter of 1 percent of U.S. homicides, which run at around 11,920 deaths per year, or 10.08 deaths for every 100,000 people. Although this is far higher than the homicide rate in France (4.93 deaths per 100,000) or England and Wales (0.31 deaths per 100,000) or even Switzerland (6.4 deaths per 100,000), it could be worse.[7] The United States makes over $533 million from gun sales. It could be argued, therefore, that there is an economic advantage to gun proliferation (as long as you don't try to subtract health care costs from that total). But as Lieutenant Colonel Dave Grossman suggests in *On Killing: The Psychological Cost of Learning to Kill in War and Society,* the statistics on aggravated assault both here and in Europe are indeed cause for concern. The trend towards fewer attacks, often cited as an indication that we're much safer than we used to be, may not, in fact, be reliable, especially when improvements in our ability to save lives are taken into account.

For the most part, it is as easy for students to kill on our campuses as it was in 1999 when Harris and Klebold terrorized Columbine High School. Since the early nineties, there has been an effort to create a reliable "profile" of school shooters. But experts, including FBI profiler Mary Ellen O'Toole, warn that it's impossible to come up with a list of red flags to identify school shooters.[8] It may be more helpful instead to examine factors *peculiar to the environment that exists in schools and colleges* that threaten campus safety. I have included factors relevant to both K–12 and higher education because I believe that examining them in isolation is misleading. Typically lists of risk factors include such things as gun accessibility, mental illness, pop culture's glorification of violence, and bullying. But I believe there are additional cultural factors to consider. I have included them in the list below because, combined with those commonly cited, they have the potential to contribute to education's perfect storm:

1. A shortage of teachers and resources in K–12[9]
2. A lack of treatment facilities and services for mentally ill students of all ages[10]
3. The accessibility of guns and bomb-making equipment and manuals
4. The prevalence of mental illness and suicide in the student population[11]
5. A "nonteacherly focus" in higher education*
6. A pop culture that routinely exposes children and youth to excessive violence

---

*By this I mean both the shift in focus in higher education from students to revenue raising and the lack of emphasis on training faculty to teach students with differing needs.

7. A growing divide that separates youth culture from adult culture[12]

8. The prevalence of bullying in K–12 (often called "harassment" when it affects the adult community)[13]

9. A rise in alcoholism, drug abuse, and prescription medication abuse in student populations[14]

10. Open campuses with relatively little security or security funding

Additional factors such as the dramatic rise in the suicide rate among teenagers should also raise red flags.[15] I do not wish to suggest that this list is comprehensive. It is not. But I am concerned that lists such as these sometimes fail to take into account the culture that exists in K–16, and the crisis we are facing as we witness an exodus of teachers *and* funds from the education system, the most critical cultural infrastructure of all.

In the October 16, 2006, issue of the *Chicago Sun-Times,* Bill Dedman described what happened in Alaska when Evan Ramsey decided to punish fellow students and his principal:

In their own words, the boys who have killed in America's schools offer a simple suggestion to prevent it from happening again: Listen to us.

"I told everyone what I was going to do," said Evan Ramsey, 16, who killed his principal and a student in remote Bethel, Alaska, in 1997. He told so many students about his hit list that his friends crowded the library balcony to watch. One boy brought a camera. "You're not supposed to be up here," one girl told another. "You're on the list."

Instead of being appalled by his plans to murder teachers and students, Ramsey's friends "crowded the library balcony to watch," one of them hoping to record the attack for posterity. It is estimated that there were roughly twenty students up on the balcony, all of whom had come to witness the slaughter the way fans come to see a football game. It is the girl's statement at the end of the quote that is, perhaps, the most disturbing of all. Her schoolmate was scheduled for slaughter but somehow she didn't understand the victim's role she was supposed to play.

These student-shooters are not in hiding; they are out in the open. Other kinds of threatening behavior are being mimicked, sometimes by young people who have no idea that the climate has changed and that "pranks" will now be read as threats.

In August 2008, two eighteen-year-olds from Southwest Virginia, who claimed to have been inspired by the movie *The Dark Knight*, left joker calling cards at various businesses in their community, including a Kmart and a Dairy Queen. They had scrawled vague threats on the cards. It was meant as a joke, they said, and was never intended to hurt anyone.[16] Nobody laughed. The two young men were originally charged with conspiracy to commit an act of terrorism. No doubt those receiving the cards would recall that, in the recent blockbuster movie (which, incidentally, attracted the largest audience in a single day in movie history), the cards were delivered by a sociopath addicted to killing. But how would two teens know that the rules had changed? After all, adults manufacture terror all the time and feed it to the young for entertainment. Why shouldn't the young manufacture it for themselves and feed it to us for a laugh? Recently the charges against the teens have been significantly reduced, and it looks likely that all charges will eventually be dismissed if there are no further violations in the next twelve months. The case was covered by the media, which means that the boys' prank is likely to shadow them for years.

The dominant characters to emerge in American entertainment are involved in an elemental struggle, but it's not necessarily a struggle against an identifiable evil. In fact, the hero himself may be the most evil character of all. If there is a genuine hero, his triumph is usually short-lived; humiliation constantly resurrects itself. We see it in the derisive, humiliating laughter of the Joker in *The Dark Knight,* and we see it in the return of insatiable killers like Freddy Krueger *(Nightmare on Elm Street)* and Jason Vorhees *(Friday the 13th).* Even more troubling because of its verisimilitude is Gus Van Sant's 2003 critically acclaimed movie, *Elephant,* with its chilling reenactment of the kind of killing spree Harris and Klebold undertook at Columbine, a spree that ends midkill. Nowadays, rampage movies are all the rage. One way or another, there will be blood. Even when this phrase is not assigned to the title of the movie, it will function as the dramatic climax of a story, just as it does in real-life school shootings.

No matter how many times it is replayed, reimagined, and revisited, violence doesn't lose its grip on the world of entertainment, as long as it's ramped up a notch. It isn't necessarily caused by anything—in fact, it's often more effective if causality cannot be traced because gratuitous violence endows perpetrators with far more power. There are no keys to unlock the minds of these killers, no clues to be followed, except those that lead you astray. For those who come into contact with these rampage killers, love at first sight is replaced by death at first sight. Viral and predatory violence—to borrow some of the last words spoken on screen by Heath Ledger's Joker—seems these days to "complete us."

Like a typical contemporary antihero, Seung-Hui Cho didn't need wisdom for a successful attack, or courage, or even a lot of money; what he needed was stealth, a constancy of purpose, a lot of ammo, and two reliable weapons. Two guns made him, in a sense, two men—all the more likely that he could outstrip the tally achieved by Harris and Klebold.

Cho was in eighth grade when he began fantasizing about a day when he could silence other people for good. In a process of depersonalization, Cho obliterated his own humanity, mechanizing himself to such an extent that he appeared to some of his victims to be nonhuman, a kind of automaton. To those who saw him in Norris Hall, he didn't seem filled with despair or rage. In fact, it was his calmness that was most horrifying, his ability to distance himself from the act of killing. In the past, he'd worn sunglasses to signal his difference and conceal his expression. He could hide and be exposed simultaneously by drawing attention to himself as a person of difference. They made him an enigma, endowed with a kind of power, but they also increased his isolation. He didn't want to be isolated at all—at least not in 2005 when he made overtures to women, sought counseling, and spoke about his own torment in his writing. He wanted to be a successful, romantic figure, an anguished writer. He wanted to write like Shakespeare and make women love him for it. On the whiteboard outside one young woman's dorm room, Cho wrote lines from Shakespeare's *Romeo and Juliet*. This was passion in extremis, the kind of passion he had written about in his novel. It was centered on idealized, unattainable beauty, agonizing insecurity, and an immature possessiveness:

> *By a name*
> *I know not how to tell thee who I am*
> *My name, dear saint is hateful to myself*
> *Because it is an enemy to thee*
>
> *Had I it written, I would tear the word* [17]

This was Cho the hyperbolic, would-be lover, the young man who is said to have written lines from the song "Shine" by Collective Soul on the walls of his dorm room, lines that echoed his desire to learn to speak and to be loved. He was asserting his identity, forcing everyone to sit up and take notice of him at last. Listen to me, he was saying, and listen well.

Cho understood the power of words and ideas because he selected a quote in which words were destroyed. The quote is confessional and intimate; it casts the female he is pursuing in the role of auditor. Obsessed with his inability to speak and write as well as he wanted, he wished to destroy his very name. He saw the object of his affection in idealized, romanticized terms, hence his choice to quote from *Romeo and Juliet,* the ultimate adolescent tragedy of star-crossed, archetypal lovers whose deaths define their families and live on forever in the imaginations of those around them. As usual Cho was writing about himself; as is typical of stalkers, he was the object of his own affection.

Seung-Hui Cho wasn't someone who had learned to share much of anything—not his thoughts, not his companionship, and not the women he adored from afar. Almost all of the debates he had were with himself. In Gollum-like dialogues, he anticipates and refutes arguments, but the argument inevitably comes down in favor of Cho. He may have thought he'd found the perfect refuge for his angst and fury on the page, but the page was as merciless as humanity, and he was rejected there as well. Although police have disputed the fact that Seung-Hui Cho was a "stalker" in the legal sense, he watched young women, showed up in disguise at the dorm room door of one of them, and sent instant messages that concerned them so much that two young women called the police in December 2005. Some now believe there may have been a link between the double homicide he committed more than two hours before he started shooting in Norris Hall—that it was possible he was looking for one of the young women he had bothered previously.

Like someone writing a horror story, Seung-Hui Cho crafted his attack so that the suspense would build. Like other school shooters who thought of their shooting rampages in terms of performances, he had completed a dress rehearsal, chaining the doors of Norris on one occasion, according to some reports. He would have known that the first murders would create a frenzy of activity, all of which centered on him—though no one would know his identity at the time. He would have known that a dramatic climax is dependent on suspense. It was the order of the slaughter, of course, that was so horrifying—the fact that he ended with suicide and didn't begin with it, the fact that he was number 33 rather than number 1. As methodical a person as he was, Seung-Hui Cho would have understood why order is capable of trumping everything else in the end.

GIRLS ARE often targeted for slaughter, and an attack is often a reaction to some slight, some form of humiliation the perpetrator believes he or she has suffered. In the case of girls and women who shoot schoolchildren, as Brenda Spencer did in 1979, blaming her attack on the fact that it was "just Monday," attacks can be accompanied by allegations of sexual abuse. It is not clear whether or not Brenda Spencer was repeatedly beaten and sexually abused as she claimed in 2001 during her parole review.[18] Sex, vengeance, and violence are swirled together. If perpetrators get pleasure from inflicting pain, the sexual and dramatic climax of their rampage is synchronous.

Rampages by men are hardly a new phenomenon. A number of scholars, researchers, and security experts have cited other cultures where there is an expectation that, every so often, a man may go completely berserk and embark upon a killing spree. In *Guys and Guns Amok: Domestic Terrorism and School Shootings from the Oklahoma City Bombing to the Virginia Tech Massacre*, Douglas Kellner cites MIT psychologist Steven Pinker's research and situates some of the most shocking examples of violence within the context of what he sees as a "crisis of masculinity." By examining the media spectacle and the male gun fetish, Kellner uncovers the hypocrisy inherent in our response to rampages. But it is the following quote from Pinker, cited in Kellner's text, that I found particularly haunting. In *How the Mind Works*, Pinker writes about the rampage phenomenon as it manifests itself in ancient cultures: "Amok is a Malay word for the homicidal sprees occasionally undertaken by lonely Indochinese men who have suffered a loss of love, a loss of memory, or a loss of face."

The amok man is patently out of his mind, an automaton oblivious to his surroundings and unreachable by appeals or threats. But his rampage is preceded by lengthy brooding over failure and is carefully planned as a means of deliverance from an unbearable situation. The amok state is chillingly cognitive. It is triggered not by a stimulus, not by a tumor, not by a random spurt of brain chemicals, but by an idea.[19]

Cho has sometimes been characterized by the media as stupid. There is at least one account, however, of his mathematical excellence from a classmate of his in high school, and he graduated from high school as an honors student with a 3.5 grade point average. Business Information Systems, Cho's original major, boasts a strong program at Virginia Tech. Even though creative writing was challenging for him because of the obstacles he faced with language and his emotional immaturity, he was, in my opinion, a person of keen intelligence who was driven by ideas. In fact, it was his cerebral quality that made the anger in his poetry more unsettling. In his work, he wasn't simply "losing it" the way students sometimes do when they can no longer control their emotions; he was a student pondering his own anger, cognizant of the fact that it existed. There was an oddly dispassionate quality to his passion, an ability to become a kind of impenetrable wall, something he achieved through his silence (both pose and affliction, or so it seemed to me) and his reflective sunglasses.

When an autopsy was performed on Seung-Hui Cho there was no evidence found of chemicals or drugs in his body. Nor were there any brain tumors that could have accounted for his behavior—as was the case with Charles Whitman, the 1966 University of Texas–Austin Tower sniper, who was found to be suffering from a glioblastoma, and who requested in his suicide note that an autopsy be performed to try to find out why he was being tormented by homicidal thoughts. The lack of artificial or biological stimuli that could help explain what happened was disturbing because it meant that, like the trigger for the amok man's rampage, the cause of Cho's rampage could not be easily identified.

According to Pinker, the amok man feels he has nothing to lose because he has been humiliated and because he is not a "Big Man." He kills others, even though it may mean he himself is killed. When I lived in Sierra Leone, the term *Big Man* was commonly used to describe those leaders who wielded dictatorial power. One of the so-called Big Men local to the Northern Province where I lived was a paramount chief. One day, he buried alive two animals and a little boy so that he could increase his own potency, an "idea" that may have more relevance than we like to admit in contemporary Western societies.

In the *Diagnostic and Statistical Manual of Mental Disorders,* the Intermittent Explosive Disorder (IED) is comparable to the amok man's condition. This is the disorder suffered by those who experience road rage or who commit domestic abuse. It is manifested mostly in young males.[20] Narcissistic Personality Disorder (NPD) also captures some of the common traits of school shooters. We know that Seung-Hui Cho had been diagnosed in middle school with chronic depression and selective mutism, but although his behavior and actions are similar to those exhibited by people suffering from NPD and IED, only a mental health professional working with Cho could have made an accurate diagnosis. If we assume for a moment that the "amok man" exists, however, and that an *idea* can be the catalyst for a rampage, this would suggest that rampages can be counteracted by ideas, too. It therefore becomes even more important to find ways to engage youths predisposed to violence. Sadly, it is unlikely that schools will ever have the resources to do this on a large scale, which is one of the reasons that the roles of parents, guardians, friends, siblings, and mentors become so important in the lives of young people.

The death toll is still relatively low for school shootings—in part, because a sizable number of attacks have been averted by the vigilance of law enforcement, the courage of parents and students, particularly female students, and the dedication of teachers. In many cases, intervention comes in time. People report their concerns and law enforcement reacts quickly. But those who dream of slaughter in our schools are dreaming big. If the attacks on Columbine and Virginia Tech had utilized all the ammunition the perpetrators had in their possession, if all the bombs there had detonated successfully, and if there had not been a remarkably swift response time by law enforcement at Virginia Tech after Seung-Hui Cho had begun his shooting rampage in Norris Hall, the death toll for these two attacks alone could have been in the hundreds.

Columbine shooters Harris and Klebold were not relying solely on the guns they carried, nor were they planning to kill as few as they did. The fact that they "only" managed to kill thirteen and wound twenty-four was a mistake; they had dreamed of killing five hundred. In fact, their first killing spree was an appetizer, a prelude for what would come next, for the two boys had planned to explode a number of bombs—one in the cafeteria/library, others jerry-rigged to their cars. It was sheer luck that most of them failed to detonate.

Similarly, Seung-Hui Cho had 203 live rounds left when he took his own life. Like the Columbine shooters he modeled himself after, he could have killed many more. Arkansas school shooters Andrew Golden and Mitchell Johnson, who set off an alarm so that students and teachers would flee, then positioned themselves on a hill so that they could gun them down in the playground, had over 1,000 rounds of ammo left when they were apprehended. Though these shooters may be relatively few in number, the weapons to which they have access mean that the damage they inflict can be grotesquely disproportionate to their numbers.

As the authors of *Rampage* point out, most of the school attacks that are foiled appear to be the result of the actions of girls who have learned that an attack is imminent.[21] The notorious "Trench Coat Mafia" attack planned for New Bedford High School in Massachusetts—an attack that was supposed to surpass Columbine—was to include guns, snipers, and bombs, and was to be videotaped for posterity. It was foiled by a girl, Amylee Bowman. It can be difficult to get accurate data about foiled attacks, but, of those Newman and her coauthors have studied, a pattern emerges:

> Whereas all of the would-be shooters were boys, in seven of the nine cases, those who spoke out were girls. In two cases the tipsters are identified only as "classmates" or "fellow students." The data indicate only one boy—a young man who had been threatened by a lone attacker at Mills High School in Millbrae, California—coming forward. Every other case where we have information on the gender of the tipster, it is a girl. We believe this is an important finding—although with such a thin database, it can hardly be considered conclusive.[22]

Why are girls willing to break the code of silence and alert people to a potential attack? In part, Newman and her coauthors conclude, it is due to the strength of their social ties; Amylee Bowman felt close to a teacher she was afraid would be targeted. It is encouraging to know that there are young women who will go up against a group as strong as New Bedford's Trench Coat Mafia, a group that espoused Nazi ideology. Ironically, girls—those who would often be considered by the shooters to be the weakest of all—proved to be the ones with the power to thwart them. But it is asking a lot of students to take this risk, and many are afraid to come forward. Finding better ways to prevent attacks on schools before they evolve into full-grown plots is vital.

In his controversial book *On Killing: The Psychological Cost of Learning to Kill in War and Society,* Lieutenant Colonel Dave Grossman claims that the media portrayal of killing—particularly first-person-shooter games but also contemporary horror movies and excessively violent literature—replicates conditioning techniques used by the military. He claims that the media barrage on young minds mirrors the type of desensitization, Pavlovian conditioning, and denial defense mechanisms used to dramatically increase the firing rates in war. Grossman was amazed to find that the nonfiring rate during combat had been remarkably low before the military interceded with special training programs that employ techniques very similar to those utilized in first-person-shooter games:

> In World War II, 75–80 percent of riflemen did not fire their weapons at an exposed enemy, even to save their lives and the lives of their friends. In previous wars nonfiring rates were similar.
>
> In Vietnam the nonfiring rate was close to 5 percent.[23]

Grossman's central claim is that certain kinds of programming and brainwashing techniques are remarkably successful in creating a more lethal soldier, and that similar techniques have been imported into American and Western popular cultures. Grossman charts the recent dramatic increase in aggravated assault in the United States, the United Kingdom, New Zealand, Scandinavia, and other European countries. He draws upon his own military experience as well as his multiyear investigation of conditioning and desensitization. Although he believes that, from a military point of view, this kind of programming can be important when war is waged, he sees its indiscriminate application on the young, in first-person-shooter video games in particular, as extremely dangerous—so dangerous, in fact, that he thinks it threatens the fabric of society. School shootings to Grossman are a manifestation of the altered psychology of conditioned youth. In spite of the controversy surrounding Grossman's conclusions, claiming that all these attacks on schools and universities are aberrations ignores an obvious trend.

In the days following the tragedy, John Derbyshire, *National Review* Online's conservative radio talk show host, was one of the most vocal critics of students and faculty who were gunned down in Norris Hall. He asserted that the victims should have defended themselves. He asked why no one had jumped Seung-Hui Cho, especially as Cho wasn't "some Rambo, hosing the place down with automatic weapons." In fact, as even Derbyshire himself admitted later, many people trapped in Norris reacted heroically. Some of the victims barred doors, rushed students to safety, even charged the shooter. For Derbyshire (who appears to believe he would have been faster than a speeding bullet had he encountered Cho) the insults were designed to humiliate. Indeed, Derbyshire was doing to the victims precisely what many school shooters claim has been done to them — deliberately emasculating them in a public forum, calling them weak, dismissing their humanity. In too many cases to document, name-calling, particularly names that undermine a boy's macho image or suggest that he is not a full-blooded heterosexual male, can cause lasting damage, and is often cited by school shooters as the primary reason for their rampage. Derbyshire knew he would be touching a nerve, which was why he said what he did in this context. Derbyshire's rampage was verbal, but it still had the capacity to hurt.

If we give our children cigarettes, some of them are likely to get cancer. When we give out guns like candy, some young people and those who are mentally unstable will inevitably get their hands on them to injure other people. The NRA's notorious mantra "Guns don't kill people, people kill people" is deliberately misleading. People kill people with guns. They do it with other things, too, but denying that they use guns to kill is ridiculous. But assuming it will be easy to alter America's fascination with firearms is equally absurd. The right to bear arms is a right many Americans would die for, in much the same way as the British or the French would fight to retain the right of free speech or health care.

At Virginia Tech, as at other institutions, we have spent hundreds of hours trying to make sure that our classrooms have decent ventilation and adequate technology. But the personnel and funds we need to make the buildings secure are harder to acquire. Schools need to think much more creatively about how to address these issues during a time of dwindling budgets. Can we afford to continue to gamble on the fact that our classrooms will not prove tempting to an increasing number of homegrown killers and determined terrorists?

There are too many young men like Harris, Klebold, Cho, and Kinkel, who are alienated from their communities and unable or unwilling to find a way to reenter them. A few of them are dreaming about ways to wreak havoc upon their classmates. They have the skill and the will to do it, and we are providing them with the tools to make it happen on a grand scale. If we don't make a concerted effort to address the root causes of this problem, some of these would-be student-shooters are likely to see their biggest dreams come true.

It is time to remove the guns from Seung-Hui Cho's cold, dead hands for good.

Part Three

DIALOGUE

11.
Testimony

I F YOU don't tell the truth, the whole truth, and nothing but the truth about your own life, someone may claim they have the right to tell it for you.

In August 2008, I learned that the Virginia Tech tragedy had been metamorphosed into a "verbatim play" at the Edinburgh Festival. A friend told me her family had seen the play, which was called *The Boy from Centreville,* and featured Seung-Hui Cho's own words and the words of others with whom he had come into contact.

The *Telegraph* enthused:

Top marks go to students from Central drama school who, together with the input of a number of Theatre de Complicite stalwarts, including director Catherine Alexander, have put together a compelling devised show about last year's Virginia Tech massacre.

The physicality—and video imagery—is superb. What's even more impressive is the way first-hand testimony is woven into an exploration that lets no one off the hook: not the impassive killer, Seung-Hui Cho; nor the authorities; nor well-meaning arts students with their blind faith in the civilising force of theatre.[1]

Cited by reviewers as an example of "pure theatre," which linked graphic documentary to suspense, the "docu-drama" was devised by Catherine Alexander and students from the Central School of Speech and Drama in the United Kingdom. The "first-hand testimony" is, according to some who have seen it, what endows the play with a feeling of authenticity.

For the most part, the reviews suggest that the play was more than a collage of horror, and that the Christ-like imagery in the play was appropriate rather than offensive. Some of those who saw the play and who posted reviews online found it beautiful and resonant; others were taken aback by the depiction of Cho as Christ on a crucifix—a role he usurped for himself in his video diatribe.[2]

In the "verbatim" format used by the creators of *The Boy from Centreville,* people's own words were spoken by "characters" chosen to depict them, characters who were shaped by the creators' notions of what happened. According to the reviews, *The Boy from Centreville* includes the frantic 911 call a female student made under the desk as Cho was in the middle of his rampage. This part is said to be especially realistic.

At the end of the docudrama, Cho mimes the gunning down of students and faculty to drumbeats and music. Those who crafted this production found an ending that would have been deeply gratifying to him—a recapitulation of the grand finale he chose for himself, played out at one of the greatest international drama festivals in the world. Quite literally, it fused slaughter to artistic expression and made all the world his stage.

I have written to the Central School of Speech and Drama requesting a copy of the play. It is not clear yet whether I will be permitted to read it. My inquiries seem to have taken the director by surprise, perhaps because we were thought of as characters rather than human beings whose words could—in theory at least—contradict the ones that were borrowed.

The director has informed me that sharing the play with me could violate the privacy agreement she has with those who agreed to have their words utilized. Some of them, she tells me, were only willing to do so anonymously. (Once again, I am confounded by issues of other people's privacy, although my own privacy—along with that of others involved in the tragedy—appears to have been violated.) It seems that the list of people with whom the director has to consult is more extensive with every e-mail—actors, the dramaturges, the designers. She says she has ethical responsibilities to consider in a collective effort like this one before she shares the play with me. I agree that this is the case, and that these responsibilities may be more far-reaching than she supposed. She assures me there were people from Virginia Tech who came to see the play and liked it. She doesn't tell me who they are.

If indeed I am a ghostly, reconfigured character in *The Boy from Centreville* (according to my colleague's family, there is a black woman in the play who tutors Seung-Hui Cho and who they assumed was meant to represent me), I wonder what I am saying in this "verbatim" play, where kidnapped words have fused reality to performance.

According to some of the reviews, the play positions itself within the context of Edgar's lines in Shakespeare's *King Lear:* "The weight of this sad time we must obey / Speak what we feel, not what we ought to say," and is thus fused to a tradition of revenge tragedies that Cho himself found compelling. Cho spoke what he felt, too. Sadly, as his video testimony demonstrates, the words he used were not ones he "ought" to have said.

Much as I would like to do so, I cannot claim that only those who have experienced a tragedy have the right to speak about it. There are times when those on the outside of an event will be able to view it with clarity, and times when those on the inside will be able to do so. I am annoyed with myself for not being able, initially at least, to assume innocence on the part of those who wrote and performed *The Boy from Centreville.* It would have been less painful had they remained silent. Yet I, too, am writing a version of the truth—assuming that I know more about it because I happened to live through it, even though experience doesn't always result in insight, and the mirrors we hold up to the world are often distorted by our own reflections.

If I ever meet those who participated in *The Boy from Centreville,* I hope I will find a way to speak honestly with them. Afterwards, less wary than before, perhaps we will see each other more clearly. However hard people try they cannot tell the whole truth. Location determines perspective. Even the most authentic stories we tell are no more than heartfelt approximations.

I WAS surprised at first when I received them—official-looking envelopes, with a seal on the top left-hand corner of each envelope. Their authors testified to their own innocence; they offered me encouragement before they appealed for help; they told me they could see that I was in pain and that I needed to know that they were praying for me. The tone was never penitent because they were never guilty—the correspondents from state penitentiaries, the inmates who wrote to me.

I can't recall how many letters I received from prisoners over the next few months. It was hard to keep track of everything. They'd seen me on TV and wanted to make a sworn testimony (via correspondence) that they had been wrongly accused. One, who extolled his virtues at great length, seemed to desire a long-distance relationship.

I was embarrassed at first that my pain had been so visible. It bothered me to think about the number of hands that would have opened these letters, how many eyes perused them before they were mailed. I didn't know what the protocol was in situations like this.

Did someone check the letters first to make sure there was nothing weird in them? Did the prison make a copy for its files? How many letters per week could an inmate write?

And then, as the novelty wore off, it seemed to be as much about offering comfort as it was about proclaiming innocence. There was something touching about some of the letters, as if it were possible they meant what they said. I suspected my sorrow was tricking me into sentimentality. I wanted the world to be kind again so I searched for tenderness everywhere.

Sometimes there was a lot of God in their sentences: They were praying for me, they said, they knew that God would find a way to help me. My correspondents knew about regret and guilt, despair and alienation. One claimed he knew exactly how I felt. Larry and I decided I had been selected because they assumed that if I'd agreed to tutor Seung-Hui Cho I'd advocate for anyone.

As I read those letters from men in penitentiaries, the permanence of my new identity made itself apparent. Until then, I fancied I could always wipe the slate clean and start again somewhere else—Outer Mongolia, maybe, or Papua New Guinea? But these letters from prisons told me the situation was irreversible. From some people's perspectives, I would be imprisoned in a cell with Seung-Hui Cho forever.

Dr. Elisabeth Kübler-Ross's five stages of grief—denial, anger, bargaining, depression, acceptance—outlined in *On Death and Dying*, are not really stages at all. They form a kind of soup. The ingredients are often related to these five, but altered in some significant fashion. Disbelief, for example, is connected to denial, but it's not quite the same thing. Denial suggests a deliberate turning away from facts we refuse to acknowledge, whereas disbelief suggests that we acknowledge the horror but can't find a way to accommodate it in our imaginations. Unlike Kübler-Ross's use of the term *denial*, disbelief isn't really a stage—not for me, at least. I don't graduate from it into some other state. I simply force disbelief into the background so that it's possible to function. There is always the vain hope that I'll awake to the fact that this was only a nightmare after all. It's what makes the transition between sleeping and waking one of the most painful transitions of all because, for a few seconds after the alarm goes off, I forget that the waking world has coupled with a nightmare. Then memory assaults me once again, persuades me it would have been better never to have had those moments of respite.

Anger isn't simply anger, either. If it were, it would be easier to deal with because, as soon as you realize that justice is never guaranteed, the anger would be more likely to dissipate. Instead, anger is replaced by an elemental fury that has little to do with justice and everything to do with pain. It is primitive and incontrovertible; it obliges me to rail against ghosts.

I am puzzled by the bargaining stage because I have yet to experience it, and it sounds gentler than the other stages. But I never imagined that there was a way to appeal suffering. You just have to endure, that's all. I learned this as a child, and it was a lesson confirmed in adulthood. You cannot bargain your way out of suffering. Those exchanges are always illusory.

Depression isn't a stage at all. It's a state of mind that all sane people, at various points in their lives, inhabit. But it is acceptance that is, perhaps, the most dangerous stage of all because, like Janus, it has two faces. There is a beneficial acceptance that involves struggle and reconciliation. This is a process the terminally ill often experience as they begin to realize that death is inevitable, and that the time they have left is precious. But there is also a blind acceptance, a process that encourages us to accept suffering without making a sincere attempt to marry it to the learning process. It is this kind of acceptance that teachers, parents, and students need to actively resist.

THE INTERVIEWS I gave over one and a half days following the attack resulted in an avalanche of correspondence and phone calls — thousands of them, from people all over the country. Many were generous words of encouragement; others demonstrated that a similar tragedy could easily have happened elsewhere, and was likely to happen again. In one e-mail, letter, or call after another, strangers told me about their own experiences of trying to get help for those in need. I had not realized until then that the problem was so pervasive. Because their voices helped shape this book, I am including brief summaries of typical testimonies I received. Each one points to the urgency of the problem. Where necessary I have changed minor details to protect people's identities. The gist of their accounts, however, remains.

There were notes from parents who wrote heartbreaking accounts of how they had been trying for years to get long-term, intensive assistance for their children. They told of their struggles with bureaucracy, and of the stigma and cost attached to mental illness. A father told me he had tried everything, but it had proven impossible to get his son committed, even though he desperately needed to be. The chronic shortage of long-term care facilities meant that his pleas were ignored.

There was the note from a teacher in Texas who wrote of her time serving as chair of an English department. A student in the class of a young instructor seemed highly unstable. When she reported his erratic and possibly threatening behavior to a counselor, the counselor was able to persuade the student to drop out of school for a while so that he could focus on getting the intensive care that he needed. This should have been a story with a happy ending. Unfortunately, the professor wrote that the counselor was later replaced *because* of the efforts he had made to protect the student and the instructor. He was seen by the administration as being too proactive in his intervention.

A professor from the Midwest, who was struggling to deal with a student stalker, described his efforts to get an appropriate response from his university's administration. His former creative writing student had graduated, which made the situation even trickier. Unfortunately, the professor learned that unless he was physically attacked by the student (who had been hospitalized for mental illness, had attacked someone with a knife, and had spent time in prison for shooting someone) he could not get a restraining order.

A liberal arts professor from Georgia wrote that she had experienced threatening and disturbing behavior by students. She saw it as being symptomatic of a pattern of violent behavior by alienated young men in our nation. She identified it as an urgent national problem.

A note from a psychiatric nurse highlighted the obstacles that exist when you attempt to get help. Like other health professionals who contacted me, the nurse wrote that she remembered when it was relatively easy to get a temporary detention order for people who desperately needed it—something she said was no longer true.

A teacher from Maryland wrote that she is working with "fragile children," and that she understands the enormous challenges of trying to be responsive. I found this description accurate. Some of the most vulnerable students seem to have labels plastered all over them: *Fragile. Breaks easily. Handle with care.*

Several faculty members at Virginia Tech and other local schools spoke with reporters in the months following the tragedy, or wrote thoughtful editorials about their experiences with troubled students. Still others reminded readers that mental illness and violence rarely go hand in hand. They warned that difference can sometimes be wrongly perceived, especially if people are unfamiliar with certain conditions from which others suffer. Autism can be confused with misanthropic behavior, for example, with tragic results. A colleague in the English department advised us to prepare for a wave of autistic students who would soon be entering college, with high IQs and differing needs. Finding ways to be responsive to these new members of our community is essential. I try to listen with care, knowing how much I have to learn.

There are some positive developments on the horizon. For example, the omnibus mental health bills introduced around the first anniversary of the mass shootings at Tech is a step in the right direction. In theory, these should result in increased access to mental health services in Virginia. But the recession and the grim economic outlook for the next few years are having a devastating effect on funding. In October 2008, Governor Kaine announced a $2.5 billion shortfall for Virginia's two-year budget. Nearly six hundred state workers are being laid off, and cuts of 6 to 8 percent in education have already been imposed. More are expected to follow. Everyone will be asked to make sacrifices, and it's unlikely that even the most concerned governor will be able to keep all of his promises.

So, as the state and the country struggle to deal with unprecedented economic challenges, I try to carry the words of these parents, teachers, health workers, and students in my head. They urge me to speak; they remind me of the consequences of silence.

SOME WOUNDS are unlikely ever to heal.

An incident in September 1999 shows how fractured a community can become after it has been brutalized. At that time, a few months after the attack on Columbine, fifteen trees were planted in memory of the dead, including two in memory of the shooters. According to news reports, in what must have been an extraordinary exhibition of fury, a group of about forty parents and community members stormed the area designated as a prayer park during a memorial service, tacked up notices that read "Unrepentant murderers" on two of the trees, and proceeded to chop them down. In a violent testimony to their own outrage, the parents and other members of the community wanted their voices to be heard. It is likely that they felt that their suffering outdid any desire to memorialize the shooters. So they simply tore down the trees that represented those they thought should be silenced forever.

There was swift condemnation. Some were particularly distressed that the young people at Westfield Community Church, who had led the effort to memorialize the dead, were subjected to this kind of fury. Commentators penned editorials berating the parents and community members for the attack on the prayer park. People urged the pro-testers to forgive the two shooters and let the community heal.

At Virginia Tech, Seung-Hui Cho's name was left off of memori-als, and the Hokie stone meant to represent him was repeatedly re-moved from the impromptu mourning site. I understand what it's like to want to pray for someone in dire need of prayer. I wanted to leave a flower on Seung-Hui Cho's stone because I believe that he, too, was victimized by his own illness; instead, because the stone had been removed by someone who was offended by it, I carried the flower home with me. But this was a small thing to endure—far less painful than the suffering of those who yearn to mourn in peace at their relatives' or friends' memorials.

Shouldn't victims' loved ones have the right, if they so choose, to pay their respects to their loved ones without the constant re-minder of the fact that they were murdered? If the shooters came from outside the community, if they hadn't been students, it is un-likely that they would be memorialized at the same location. Cus-tomarily we ensure some degree of separation between murderers and their victims. Those of us who wish to pray for the perpetrators can carry those prayers to another site. The shadows of the gunmen don't need to follow their victims to the grave.

But a form of reconciliation may be possible even under the most terrible of circumstances. The attack by a lone gunman on an Amish schoolhouse in Lancaster County, Pennsylvania, took place in October 2006. Five little girls ranging in age from seven to thir-teen were killed, and five others were wounded. One of the victim's injuries were so severe that she is permanently disabled. In response, however, many members of the Amish community reached out to the family of the killer and attended his funeral.

Although there were some commentators who felt that forgive-ness on the part of the Amish without remorse on the part of the killer was ill advised, most people were humbled by the community's quiet resignation in the face of incomparable loss. Perhaps it was

also their separation from the surrounding community and their intense privacy that helped them through this process. Because their
faith is so strong, they knew that their little girls were already with
God. The person who murdered them, on the other hand, would be
held accountable for what he had done.

In the days that followed 4/16 I received thousands of e-mails and
dozens of letters and phone calls that were designed not necessarily
to inform me of something but to comfort me instead. Many were
sent by people from various faiths. Some of the letters, e-mails, and
phone calls touched me deeply. There was an e-mail from a colleague
of mine, Joan, who reminded me to ask myself not just "What more
might I have done?" but instead to follow up with this corollary:
"Do I believe I did all I could?"

There were e-mails and letters from people in the United Kingdom and Sierra Leone. For some reason, the notes from people in
the United Kingdom, even from total strangers, were ones I was
never concerned about opening. I had the sense, I suppose, that they
would be measured and sensible, practical and compassionate, and
they were.

An e-mail from a friend in Sierra Leone helped put things in perspective. She reminded me that I was alive, which meant, she told
me, that things were fine. And although this sentiment may sound
callous to people in wealthier parts of the world, it was an accurate
evaluation from someone who lives in a place where survival is often
the sole measure of good fortune.

E-mails, letters, and cards from former students made me understand again how our students can teach us if we let them. "Don't be
discouraged," one of them writes, in an effort to comfort me, "the
odds were against you." Another tells me that I helped inspire him
to become a teacher when I taught him thirteen years before. He
says he is passing on his love of reading to his children.

One of the shortest e-mails I received was from a colleague in the English department—someone I have come to admire even more during adversity. The last two sentences are the ones that touched me the most: "Let me help you carry this horrible burden. That goes for tomorrow and twenty years from now."

We are repositories, conduits. Other people's stories inspire our commitment. Compassion breeds compassion. Burdens can be shared.

IN THE period that followed the tragedy, Seung-Hui Cho squatted in my imagination. A vortex swirled around him. Cho constituted the steady, unblinking eye of the storm. I hovered on the periphery of the vortex, just beyond its outer bands. It could open up at any time and devour me if I didn't tread with care.

On the periphery, time was erratic. Sometimes it behaved chronologically. On other occasions—often when I least expected it—time was disobedient, careening back to April 16 where it adopted a pose of temporary paralysis, mouth agape—as if past, present, and future were a single interminable howl.

When I dared to enter the vortex, mostly during nightmares when my guard was down, it was always chilly and badly lit. Cho's face was shocking: He had cried—or blasted—his eyes away. All that was left was an empty, featureless face. He could not look at the sky—too blue. A mirror of ice was positioned under his feet. He cut it out—a shard of the sky to treasure forever—then realized too late that he'd cut out the ground from under him.

During these torturous months, King Lear, the disappointed and delusional old man, was a loyal companion. His insanity, mirrored in the storm on the heath and harnessed to iambic pentameter, confirmed that the whole world had gone mad. Like an obedient daughter, I strove to believe that tragedy could be lyrical. The outcome would not be filled with corpses. Few people seemed to notice that I entered the classroom drenched from the storm and stuttering.

Sometimes, even when I was far away from Norris Hall, I would hear Cho's alliterative silence emanating from the ground, disembodied and disinterred, distraught and disingenuous. I wondered if I had forgotten to let him know that writing was not about knowing things for certain but about knowing nothing with certainty. Questions ricocheted from memory to mouth: *What else did I forget? Who or what else will not forgive me?*

I became suspicious of tidiness, afraid that this was what I was doing by writing, tidying things up, gluing a bow to the lid of catastrophe while the question marks march off into the distance—*left-right, wrong-right, left-right, oversight*—an army of shuffling interrogatives in danger of tripping over themselves.

In the aftermath, perspective itself became a variation on the theme of subterfuge. I found the third-person, ultralimited point of view—*He killed them all (they know not why he did)*—and the first person singularly confessional—*I taught the young (once upon a time).* The first person was as much of a bully as the third. Trauma and paralysis were bedfellows who snored loudly in my ear.

In September 2008, seventeen months after Cho's guns transformed the campus, I skated on the deceptively calm surface of Robert Frost's poetry. In my class The Form and Theory of Poetry (as if things were fully formed rather than fragmented, as if theory endowed artistic expression with orderliness) we read Frost's famous poem "Home Burial."

I realized too late that I should not have chosen this poem, located as it was in close proximity to where I had been hiding. In it, the horrors of grief were dramatically rendered in a conversation between a mother and a father mourning the death of their child. But after we had studied the poem, I was determined to learn Frost's blank verse poem by heart, if I could bear it. I would carry it around in my head, turn it over, look at it from different angles, and try to reconcile two startlingly different points of view. If I were lucky, I could begin to dismantle the scaffolding of pain on which my existence seemed now to be precariously balanced.

In Frost's poem, the couple recites lines to each other across the barbed wire of gender. The husband pleads with the wife to share her grief with him, but the wife finds the husband's interrogation suffocating. Drawn to the burial site of her child—a family plot that can be viewed from the upstairs window of their home—she lives inside elegy, defined by the parameters of her child's grave.

Woven into the poem is a sense of betrayal. The husband feels betrayed because his wife is inconsolable. His love for her is great, it seems, but much to his dismay, it compensates for nothing. The wife feels betrayed by her husband's seemingly indifferent reaction to the child's death. The fact that he dug the grave himself appalls her. The bluntness of the spade he used is an image that haunts her. For her, the juxtaposition between the ordinariness of things and the extraordinary nature of the tragedy makes life intolerable. It's not that she can't bear to remember her dead child, it's that she can't bear the fact that her husband does *not* appear to remember him.

Grief is greedy. Its dominant theme—the primacy of memorial—cannot countenance forgetfulness. That is why, if life is to progress into the future tense, grief has to be coaxed to a place of reconciliation. The fulcrum of the tragedy is the couple's inability to clearly articulate their own points of view. In a poem composed almost entirely of dialogue, the man and the woman speak at cross-purposes, engaged in a form of dialogue that is messy and tangential, confessional and oblique. Pain distorts expression; words are misinterpreted. For the husband in Frost's poem, who had taken it upon himself to bury their child, it's possible that manual labor was the only method he had to assuage his grief, but he does not say this to his wife. How could he? How do you find words large enough to house such a weighty offering?

The end of the poem does not provide us with neat closure. The wife is seen opening the door ready to flee, while the husband, in a fit of chauvinism motivated by panic, threatens to bring her back—by force if necessary—if she dares to leave. Caught in an emotional storm, forced to repeat the same frenetic waltz over and over again, the grieving husband and wife spin around on the rim of their baby's grave, damaged and bereft.

Frost's poem is a testament to the potency of pain. It's about how we are conditioned to locate ourselves in a particular place when grief is thrust upon us. It reminds us that communication is the only avenue to redemption. As King Lear himself learned, if we enter dialogue wearing too much armor we will be incapable of hearing other voices. Our own voice will jangle in our heads; our own perspective, when heard as an incessant solo voice, unmitigated by the suffering of others, will terminate in madness.

I realized that the title of the poem didn't simply refer to a homemade burial site but to the burial of one's entire home in the pit of grief. It wasn't a foolish poem to select only a year and a half after the shootings; it was a poem I was meant to read again. And although I taught it poorly (in class, trying to explicate Frost's lines, I avoided key points—so help me God, I taught like an old fool), reading it reminded me of how grief had tricked me into blindness.

These are my small epiphanies. All along, the public has been playing the role of the husband in "Home Burial," insisting on knowing everything. But in the sorority of mourners there is a special language that resists being spoken. It is the only authentic language, and its syntax is suffering. Verbs in this language are headstones: *to suffer, to lose, to mourn, to bury.* It is a strong-stressed language made up of Anglo-Saxon, spadelike idioms that labor to bury you alive. Bridging that chasm between speaker and auditor is a lifelong quest for all those who wish to fathom experience. We want to say to those who ask the questions, and who formulate for themselves the quick answers, "You know nothing unless you are a character in this drama." But this is a foolish thing to say. For how can we reasonably expect others to know what we ourselves can only feel?

All along in my particular story, my husband has been playing the role of the quiet knight. I don't care if this sounds sappy because it is the truth. But blinded by my own tears, I have not seen him often enough, sitting on the window ledge, looking out with me onto the site of horror: Virginia Tech, our home, where we met and married for better or for worse, in the chapel on the edge of the Drillfield, a few hundred yards away from Norris Hall—which means, of course, that the campus is a site that can be translated back into joy. It is where we fell in love, and where we still love each other. And if we should decide to leave this place, we will make the journey together, bracing against each other when the storm swirls, accepting the fact that there will be times when words cannot begin to do justice to the lives we lead.

All along, resurrection was possible. Gradually, something was rising up to overtake the horror. Each day, a little more surfaces. The sound of Cho's guns is being drowned out by the lively voices of students hurrying across campus to learn.

At one point in Robert Frost's "Home Burial," the husband at last sees what the wife was gazing at from the window. He understands that she has been staring at the grave of their child. He tells her that he sees it, though she had been sure he would never have the capacity to do so. And though the poem travels from there into a deep resentment, we encounter this opportunity for compassion—a moment of potential illumination when something good could have happened had the parties been able to hear each other.

We pause with the poet to witness this extraordinary moment. Frost has dared to tell the truth about grief. He hasn't resolved anything; he has simply shown it as it is.

Other views are possible. If I dare to open my eyes, I have the capacity to see more than a grave.

12.
Translating
Race

WHEN MY father passed away in 1961, a white English doctor broke the news to my white English mother. He told her that her husband had died, adding that she would be much better off without him. My father was black, you see, and from the doctor's point of view, this one characteristic eclipsed all others.

My mother was almost penniless when my father died. She was left to care for three small children ranging in age from two to seven at a time when the sight of biracial children was offensive to some Londoners. But what did it matter if some damn fool told her that the man she loved was worthless? My mother would not countenance this kind of racism. She loved my father with an ardor that even death could not extinguish. The paltry prejudice she encountered, therefore, did nothing to decrease her adoration for her late husband; in fact, it may well have stoked it. She despised the dull-witted doctor for his inability to appreciate genius. She knew exactly what her husband was: He was Namba Roy, Jamaican artist, writer, and sculptor, the boy who couldn't afford to remain at school after he reached the age of eight. (My mother had a superior education, having left school at thirteen.) In her opinion, my father was, quite simply, magnificent. She identified with him and with her children to such an extent that she spoke in the first-person plural when she referred to "colored" people—presumably because she knew in her heart that she was an honorary black.

I have often thought about what the doctor told my mother that day. As I grew up and learned more about who my father had been— his paintings and sculptures that sang of Africa and of his Jamaican Maroon roots, his novels that were a poor man's courageous attempt to journey back to his island home—I am struck by how ingrained racial prejudice still is. Lodged deep inside a person's imagination, crouching next to fear, it functions as a kind of cataract, infecting clear-sightedness with haze and shadow.

Although more than four decades have passed since my mother became a widow, the tragedy at Virginia Tech reminded me that the change in racial attitudes has been less dramatic than we like to believe.

As soon as the shooter was identified as an "Asian male," other people of Asian descent became targets. Instead of serving as an opportunity for us to learn more about the pressing issues that face Asian American communities—the stigma attached to mental illness or the pressures on those who are often called "the model minority," for example—there was a tendency to make simplistic assumptions about race. To some, the name and features of Seung-Hui Cho triggered paranoia, the fear that an "alien" being had infiltrated our community.

On April 16, in response to the announcement that the perpetrator was an Asian male, the Asian American Journalists Association (AAJA) issued this plea:

> As coverage of the Virginia Tech shooting continues to unfold, AAJA urges all media to avoid using racial identifiers unless there is a compelling or germane reason. There is no evidence at this early point that the race or ethnicity of the

suspected gunman has anything to do with the incident, and to include such mention serves only to unfairly portray an entire people.

The effect of mentioning race can be powerfully harmful. It can subject people to unfair treatment based simply on skin color and heritage.[1]

The AAJA's plea went largely unheeded, especially when it was discovered that Cho had lived in isolation on campus, deliberately excluding himself from the community.

Korean-born SuChin Pak, writing for MTV.com, captured the feelings engendered by the continual emphasis placed on Cho's status as a "Korean national":

When we are continuously bombarded with media headlines or sound bites that use the words "Virginia Tech Massacre" and "Korean National," a subtle connection is made. The assumption is made that somehow Cho's place of birth, his immigrant status, has something to do with the massacre. It doesn't matter if the rest of an article goes on to talk about Cho's schizophrenia or troubled past or gun control or violent movies, the implication is there. Cho is a foreigner, let's get that straight from the beginning, let's make sure that's part of the conversation.[2]

It is easy for those who have never experienced racism to assume that this degree of sensitivity is unwarranted. But Cho's "foreignness," his marked difference, instilled fear in some of those who heard the description "Asian male," and then the name Cho Seung-Hui. The videos and photos he produced confirmed the worst fears. This wasn't the innocent-looking, wide-eyed boyish face in the school photograph, but the face of an armed assassin. Here was the epitome of Otherness. This alien killer "Cho Seung-Hui" didn't sound or look like a typical American—didn't even put his first name first.

The situation was potentially explosive, and it was fed both by those intent upon promoting racial tension, and by those who failed to understand that continually identifying a killer in terms of his ethnicity could lead people to conclude that all those of Asian descent were suspect. The fact that his ethnicity was mentioned over and over again suggested that it could be construed as a clue to his perverse behavior, or as something we needed to purge.

It is impossible to examine the role played by race and ethnicity in the tragedy without mentioning the eight letters that have come to epitomize the complex relationship between Cho's racial identity and public concern about coordinated terrorist attacks by "foreigners" living in the United States. The terms "Ismail Ax" and "A. Ishmael" were both used by Cho—the former was written in red ink on Cho's arm and found after he committed suicide, the latter was the name he adopted when he addressed his package to NBC. Both the Muslim spelling of the name ("Ismail") and the Judeo-Christian spelling ("Ishmael") continue to generate intense speculation. Some of the most ardent commentators claim it indicates that Cho was a Muslim fundamentalist with terrorist leanings. Some see it as evidence that he was a member of a Korean jihad.[3] The fact that April 16, 2007, was Holocaust Memorial Day also suggested to some observers that Cho's attack was anti-Semitic in nature, though according to investigators there is no evidence that Cho deliberately targeted a particular racial or ethnic group. The only connection between the Holocaust and the attack seems to be coincidental: Dr. Liviu Librescu, the heroic professor who braced himself against the classroom door so that his students could leap from the second-floor windows to safety, was a Holocaust survivor.

The resonance of the names "Ismail" and "Ishmael" is not confined to religious texts. Ishmael Bush is an ax-carrying and ultimately enlightened character in James Fenimore Cooper's novel *The Prairie*; a noble character in the novel *Ishmael* by E. D. E. N. Southworth; and, of course, the mysterious narrator in Melville's *Moby-Dick*, to name just a few. The fact that Cho was an English major was frequently mentioned as evidence the name was a literary allusion rather than a religious one. Some related it to video games or movie characters; others claimed it was an anagram. But it was the name's religious connotations and its connections to Islam that resulted in the greatest controversy.

With a scarcity of clues about Cho's identity and motivation, people drew their own conclusions. The name "Ismail Ax" served as one of the few indicators of who Cho was. It's likely he intended it to be cryptic, that he assumed it would generate a mountain of speculation. Diligent about erasing information about himself, Cho deleted the files from his Virginia Tech e-mail account, wiped his hard drive, and disposed of his cell phone, but chose to recast himself as Ismail Ax and A. Ishmael—names he seems to have felt embodied his new persona.[4]

"Ismail" has been connected by bloggers and others to a "Virginia jihad network" (aka the "paintball jihad network") and to two of its members in particular, Yong Ki Kwon and Randall Todd Royer. Yong Ki Kwon, a naturalized South Korean engineering student from Fairfax who graduated from Virginia Tech, was among those convicted of conspiracy to commit acts of terrorism in November 2003. Kwon, who was sentenced to eleven years and six months in prison, has testified against a number of others in the Virginia jihad accused of conspiracy to commit terrorism. These include Ali Al-Timimi, an American Islamic scholar sentenced to life in prison in April 2005. Another member of the group, a white American, Randall Todd Royer, was convicted of conspiracy to engage in jihad in 2004. According to news reports, Royer was known by the name "Ismail." Investigators have not suggested, however, that Cho met or corresponded with Kwon, Royer, or any other members of the northern Virginia group. (Kwon graduated before Cho arrived at Virginia Tech.) Moreover, some commentators, notably the Middle East expert Milton Viorst, point to flaws in the investigative process of the Virginia jihad network as it pertained to the prosecution of Ali Al-Timimi.[5]

Suspicion that Cho and Yong Ki Kwon could have been in

league with each other has been fueled by the fact that both students were Koreans living in Northern Virginia and both attended Virginia Tech, though at different times. The extensive media coverage of a Virginia jihad network suggested to some observers that Cho could have been connected to it in some way, and they therefore searched for mention of this in the Panel Report.[6] But the assumption that Cho's ethnicity and the adoption of the name "Ismail" are enough to prove he was part of such a network is ill-advised.

Sadly, the silence emanating from the Virginia Tech administration, coupled with the fact that law enforcement did not follow up on some important leads in the investigation, has left some people with questions not only about Cho's allegiances but about the possibility that, in the years before the tragedy, more was known about potential threats to the campus than was made clear in the Panel Report.[7]

As we search for answers to questions that could have grave repercussions on race relations, it is helpful to bear in mind that Cho was unbalanced, and that any clues we may find, especially those he deliberately left us, are unlikely to reveal the full story.

WHEN WE talk about school shooters like Kip Kinkel, Michael Carneal, or Luke Woodham—all white males—we don't usually refer to their race or ethnicity, even though it could be argued that being a young white male is one of the characteristics commonly found among school shooters.[8] Typically in cases involving criminal activity, race is used to initially identify a suspect but discarded after the suspect's identity is known. Even in the most outrageous of crimes, the perpetrator's race is seen as incidental if he is white. It wasn't "Anglo-American (or white American) Timothy McVeigh," it was simply "Timothy McVeigh." Contrast this with the phrases used most often to describe Cho: "South Korean Cho Seung-Hui," "Korean national Seung-Hui Cho," "Immigrant Cho." This terminology wasn't necessarily attributable to racism; sometimes it was a way of abrogating responsibility. If Cho was identified as Korean he could be seen as the foreign trespasser who didn't belong here in the first place. He wasn't one of us after all. It was comforting because it suggested (especially if you erased other school shootings from memory) that the problem was fundamentally un-American.

Because it was important to find a "difference" on which to hang Cho's rampage, prejudice wasn't confined to racism. When rumors began to circulate in blogs and in the media that Cho was "on the autistic spectrum"—a "diagnosis" that was suspect at best—autistics and their families were well aware of the danger inherent in this claim. They were concerned that autism would be forever linked with his name and, by extension, to violence.

It is important to remember that, in many cases, it has been a school shooter's perceived normalcy that has persuaded teachers and administrators to ignore signs of trouble. In Cho's case, however, it is possible that some of those who tried to communicate with him were mindful of the fact that they knew little about Korean culture. Insisting on speech could be construed as aggressive. In other words, cultural assumptions could have had both an obvious and a subtle role to play in how Cho was treated. It's likely there were questions that were not asked, answers he was not urged to give in some of his classes because people didn't know what to make of him.

When I make presentations on diversity, one of the things I often point out is that in academia people of color are less likely to be informed of mistakes they may have made but more likely to be punished for them. Because of this, when the punishment is meted out, people of color are justifiably upset because they have been given little or no prior warning of what is about to happen. Some of those in supervisory positions in schools around the country have admitted to me that they feel reluctant to give honest feedback to people of color lest they be accused of racism. I think it's possible that, in Cho's case, a similar kind of reticence may have been at work throughout his life—an assumption that questions should not be asked in case they caused offense. It would help explain why he was able to navigate through the world so stealthily, even though he seemed to be trying to call attention to himself in whatever way he could. I remember his startled expression when I would ask him questions—as if, after twenty years of silence, it hadn't occurred to him that anyone would be interested in what he had to say. I may not have been willing to venture so far into his silence had we not shared an immigrant's heritage. Because there were things he had experienced that I had experienced myself, it was possible to begin to speak across our differences. Difficult as it was to try to communicate with him, it was made a little easier by the fact that we both knew what it was like to be identified in purely racial terms by people who were unsympathetic to your racial heritage. But I am reluctant to suggest that I understood him more than others, or that I had a clear sense of who he was. All I got were glimpses, and these were rare.

The backlash against Asian American students was not as severe as I feared it would be. I am not suggesting that the tragedy did not affect many in the Asian American and Korean communities. The backlash was real. But the swiftness of the recovery said a lot about the resilience of Asian Americans in this country.

One reason racism didn't further inflame a tragic situation was the reaction of the people of South Korea, who reached out to the Tech community and demonstrated how dismayed they were by what Seung-Hui Cho had done. It was impossible for racists to claim that Koreans were predisposed to "evil" when Koreans were grieving with us.

Another factor that served to quell extreme reaction was related to imagery. This time, it was the beautiful faces of Cho's victims—African American, Middle Eastern, Jewish, Anglo-American, Asian, Hispanic, French Canadian, South American, and mixed race—that testified to the universal nature of the catastrophe. The multiracial and international aspects of the educational enterprise in America were there for all to see. As we gazed at their smiling faces (victims' photos were included on everything from the opening dedication of the Panel Report to the memorial segments in the media) we couldn't help but appreciate the enormity of what had been lost. Racial diversity itself became the most effective antidote to racism. Cho's hate-filled words were diluted by those he imagined he could silence forever. Because the violation was felt deeply by people from many different countries it leapt over racial and ethnic divisions and could not easily be translated into caricature. Without caricature, it is impossible to effectively promulgate racism.

Racism also didn't take hold on campus because a new generation of young people recognized the attack for what it was: a random assault on a community by an individual rather than a manifestation of some kind of ethnic predisposition towards violence. Although it is discouraging to see how easily today's students self-segregate along racial lines, there is also a remarkable tolerance among people under twenty-five, many of whom have come to accept that racial difference is not a sole defining characteristic. Virginia Tech students were often circumspect and mature in their responses to what happened. Most of them did not attribute Cho's actions to anything other than his own frame of mind.

Although racism was, sadly, a part of the reaction to Cho's rampage, the relative lack of extreme repercussions was one of the more encouraging outcomes of this tragedy. It suggests that, in spite of the challenges we face as a multiracial community, many of us have the ability to see each other as multifaceted human beings—something Cho in the last years of his life was not able to do. His self-imposed isolation seemed to be at the heart of his psychopathology. He divested himself of his ethnic community, divorcing himself from his own rich culture.

When I worked with Cho, some of his assumptions seemed at times to be both racist and misogynistic. He tended in his writing to turn people into stereotypes. His bitterness, combined with what appears now to have been severe mental illness, distorted his vision to such an extent that it blinded him to humanity's potential.

Pekka-Eric Auvinen, the eighteen-year-old school shooter who attacked his school in Tuusula, Finland, in November 2007 killing eight people, summed up this attitude in three words that were emblazoned on the front of the T-shirt he wore on his YouTube video: *Humanity is overrated.* When Cho called his fellow college students "brats," even though he himself had relied entirely on the financial support of his family, he was unable to appreciate the irony of this characterization. By the time he purchased his weapons, he had entered fully into an allegorical narrative. Inside the persona of Cho the Avenger he could absolve himself of blame: I am unhappy; you are different from me; therefore, you are the cause of my unhappiness. This kind of faulty reasoning led a mentally ill, frantically lonely person to conclude that he had every right to seek redress. The happier the students around him were as graduation approached, the more keenly he must have felt his own unhappiness and isolation. His rampage was an act of madness, but it was also inspired by envy. Those who claim that he should be seen exclusively as an innocent victim (something that is unlikely to have been proposed had he, say, been a member of the KKK or an avowed neo-Nazi) presume that volition and misanthropy never join hands with instability, but perhaps there are times when they do. And if we don't recognize that hatred was also a part of Cho's worldview, we make a risky assumption, and, in my opinion, a flawed one: that his attitude towards others was irrelevant, subsumed utterly by his illness, and that this was the only thing that needed to be addressed.

IN SOME postings I read, the fact that three of the people involved in alerting the administration to Seung-Hui Cho's problems (Nikki Giovanni, Fred D'Aguiar, and myself) were faculty of color was cited as evidence that Virginia Tech was a racist institution that routinely ignored the voices of black people.

The black professors who sounded the alarm, Drs. Roy and Giovanni, were ignored in a way they wouldn't have been if they had been white women sounding the alarm about a dangerously unstable black boy. Had the mental health professionals directed by the court to evaluate his mental state done their jobs properly, this entire tragedy could have been averted. In the final analysis, nobody noticed this boy for who he was — an innocent victim of mental illness that was stereotyped to death.[9]

It's certainly true that the university has an uneven track record when it comes to diversity. But would things really have been different had those who reported their concerns been white?

In fact, some of them were. Lisa Norris, for example, an instructor in the English department, reported her concerns to the college.[10] What about the claim that had Cho been black, the reaction would have been much swifter? In my experience, the race of a troubled student at Virginia Tech did not result in a more urgent response, in part because the same conditions existed, regardless of color: a rigid adherence to privacy laws exerted a stranglehold on the system. The system itself didn't discriminate — all students and all faculty, whatever their race, were equally ill served by it.

I have to admit I have found it more challenging to talk about racism after the shootings. When the student described in a previous chapter — "Student A" — posts his scathing attacks online, employing racial epithets as often as he sees fit, the main reaction I have is one of weariness. In my own fiction and poetry, if I have to capture a scene involving, say, a racist encounter, I have not shirked from using pejorative terms racists use. How else would I achieve verisimilitude or emphasize how harmful these words can be? I believe that banning such terms from literature or from other kinds of artistic portrayals would not only deprive us of works of genuine merit but also be unenforceable in a free society. Yet I find myself unwilling to include the word in my description of Student A's writing, in part because I refuse to repeat words from pieces designed to wound rather than enlighten. I am reluctant to call upon a word that ricochets across the racial landscape like a bullet. The six-letter word for African Americans, used as a weapon by thousands of white people for far too long, hurls me up against things I'm tired of remembering. I find it deeply upsetting because I know that it is directed at me and mine, and that it takes so much energy to deflect it. I yearn for a time when I will not have to explain why language like this is so injurious to those at whom it is lobbed. I am reminded of one of the notes I received not long after the shootings.

The anonymous note sent on a white postcard was unexpected because it accused me of racism against Asians. The first sentence was in quotes, perhaps because the writer wished me to imagine it being spoken out loud: "Go back to your home." In the next sentence, the writer claimed I was not qualified "to teach college level students," that elementary students would be better able to appreciate my skills. I assumed this was meant as an insult, but I have great respect for elementary school teachers, a respect fueled by the extraordinary skills my mother displayed when she taught her elementary school students in South London, so the insult was ineffective.

It was the next sentence that puzzled me the most:

"Your bias [sic] just like the rest of Blacks in America; towards the Asian American."

There was insufficient space on the back of the postcard to contain the author's fury. I was addressed as "Prf? LUCINDA ROY." Above my name was a statement saying how glad the writer was that she or he didn't send a son to the school. I assumed this was a reference to Virginia Tech. In parentheses is the phrase "confidential or non confidential" included, perhaps, out of a desire to cover all bases. It reminded me of a story I heard in London years ago about a Nigerian man who had attended a British university. On all of his subsequent mailings he referred to himself in this way: his name first, followed by "B.A. (failed)."

I decided that the postcard was less accusatory than the notes I received that accused me of being too sympathetic to Cho because, the writers mistakenly assume, I am Korean. It was much less menacing than the note cards I received from someone who objected to my skin color and threatened to travel to Virginia to kill me. But it saddened me that people have so much ready-made anger to unleash upon the world. It is meant to wound; it is usually a form of yelling. I am sorry that the writer assumed I was prejudiced against Asian Americans. In fact, the opposite is true. I am proud that some people think I look Asian. It makes me feel connected to a magnificent, diverse continent. My Jamaican heritage makes it likely that there is African-Anglo-Asian blood in my veins. Why would I be ashamed of any of these racial identities whcn each one has its own richness?

The racist utilizes a rhetorical device known as *synecdoche* in which a part of the body stands for the whole person. (Think "red neck," for example.) It is an efficient and potentially dangerous device because it enables the racist to diminish the racial object by assuming that skin color and/or racial features determine one's identity. Having been born in London at a time when being biracial was still relatively unusual, I grew accustomed to being seen as an anomaly. Nowadays, though racism certainly hasn't disappeared, being black or mixed race is less likely to cause consternation. About a year ago when we asked Larry's nephew what things were like at school, he reassured us that racism wasn't what it used to be. No need to worry about him, he told us. All the girls thought it was just fine for a guy to be black. "Being black isn't like it was in your day, Uncle Larry," he said, with mischief in his eyes. We had to laugh at what he was implying, even though there were some troubling implications to that statement. Growing up in the sixties in London it was a different story, and I became used to dodging racial slurs like "wogs," "monkeys," "coons," "golliwogs," and "nig-nogs," a term the headmistress of my primary school mistakenly used once when my mother and I were nearby.

Racism is ubiquitous. I have experienced it on all three continents where I have lived. In the United States, small rural towns are reputed to be especially hostile to difference. Though the hostility isn't nearly as pronounced in college towns that attract racial and ethnic minorities, people of color have to adjust to the demands of predominantly white towns in rural Southwest Virginia. Blacksburg, though its name suggests otherwise, can present racial and ethnic minorities with certain challenges.

When my husband arrived in Blacksburg in 1977 to enroll at Virginia Tech, his mother looked around for other African Americans. Having been recruited from Germanna Community College as part of a new Engineering Technology program designed to attract minorities, Larry didn't know what to expect. After his parents dropped him off at his dorm, his mother insisted that his father drive around the block until they spotted another black person. Round and round they drove, as Larry's father became increasingly impatient, and Larry's mother increasingly anxious. They were unable to spot a single black person anywhere in the vicinity. Had Larry's parents realized that this first venture into Southwest Virginia would mark the beginning of a thirty-five-year sojourn for their son, they would have been even more alarmed.

Not enough Latinos, precious few African Americans, and even fewer Native Americans are making it into higher education. There is little doubt that, in the absence of well-conceived pipeline programs that incorporate early intervention strategies to prepare younger students for higher education, and without innovative recruitment strategies, many colleges and universities in the United States will be predominantly white, Asian American, and international, which means that the tension is likely to grow. In the future, mothers who bring their African American children to campus will still be driving around the block looking for signs that things have changed.

Whenever I talk with young people about race and racism, I am reminded of a course I taught on the literature of the civil rights movement. The class was made up of an even number of high-achieving and at-risk students. I was hoping that, if we could get students engaged in the material, they would be more likely to remain at Virginia Tech and graduate on schedule. The teaching assistant for the class was of Asian heritage, and there I was with my Anglo-Jamaican-ness, so we were thoroughly multiracial.

At one point, a group of African American students was chatting with me about new technology. I asked them why they weren't using the computer labs throughout campus. Their answer stunned me: "We thought the computers were for the white students," they said. Their comment spoke volumes about the lack of access they assumed they had to educational opportunities and was something I endeavored to bear in mind as I taught.

In an effort to include mature voices in the course on the civil rights movement, I posted a request online, asking if anyone in the community wanted to join us for open discussions. The first person who happened to see the posting several days before the class began was a white woman living in West Virginia. Her name was Joan Browning. She asked if it would be okay for her to join our class discussions. She was interested in the civil rights movement, she wrote, and mentioned that she herself had been a Freedom Rider.

Every day during class that summer Joan joined us online. She spoke with students about fear and the power it has to hold you back. She described what it had been like for her back then—a young white woman no older than they were who risked her life to proclaim that racial inequality was unacceptable.

When I held a reception in my home for the class, Joan showed up at the door. I had invited her, but I never expected her to travel all the way from her home in West Virginia to be with us.

Like Joan, my mother often had to take matters into her own hands. She carried a lethal weapon, for example, the only one she could afford. My mother's weapon of choice—the pepper shaker she would stuff in her pocket whenever we went out—was not especially intimidating. As I grew older, I wondered how she would manage to get an attacker to stand still while she shook it into his eyes. (The pepper didn't come out very fast, so they would both need to be patient.) Attackers may not be overcome by the little white woman with the plastic pepper shaker, but they would at least be well seasoned.

Whenever I think about these two courageous white women who had the courage to embrace difference, I am reminded that race does not have to imprison us inside our own separate cells. Asian, African, Anglo—we must attempt to translate each other. We will get the translation wrong at times, but the effort—as long as we do it without reservation—will make us strong. And that is the task: to give all young people the opportunity to learn these multiple languages, to invite them to share in the splendor of dialogue.

13.
Parents and Children

M Y MOTHER preferred trees to certain kinds of people. Increasingly as I get older, I have to admit that I occasionally understand her preference.

Trees were central in my mother's imagination because of their innocence and endurance. It didn't matter what they were, she loved them all: oak trees, elm trees, weeping willows—for which she had a particular affinity. Apart from the little children whom she taught, she didn't believe there was much that was innocent in the world, but she believed in the innocence of trees. On Clapham Common in South London, she would dance around with us on the Wiggly-Waggly Way, a path she had christened that ran through a small wooded area of the common, skirting the edge of the South Circular Road. When she read the chapters with the sentient tree character, Treebeard, the ancient Ent in *Lord of the Rings*, her eyes filled with tears, so moved was she by J. R. R. Tolkien's obvious passion for trees. According to Tolkien's story, the Ents had been unable to speak until the Elves had taught them how to do so. For a woman who had always felt a special communion with trees, the idea that speech could be elicited from them by Elves would have confirmed everything she suspected. I now realize that my mother was a kind of "tree whisperer." One of the sorrows I have is that she never lived to see Peter Jackson's brilliant trilogy. I know she would have watched it over and over, oohing and aahing as John Rhys-Davies's booming Welsh voice spoke to the little hobbits. She would have cheered out loud when the Ents—enraged by the fact that the old trees, their brothers and sisters, had been decimated—charged into battle.

When I was roughly seventeen, I wrote a poem for children about a giant who protects the forest against marauders. I composed it coming home on the 137 bus, which made it a kind of poem-in-transit. The poem was written in fourteeners, fourteen syllables in each line. The lines galloped along like a horse, beginning: "Far away where rivers run and winter flowers bloom / A giant hides in banishment for sins his race has done." My mother asked me to make a copy of the poem, which I did in my careful though inconsistent script. She folded it up and carried it in her pocket. She was the first fan of my writing, and, though she was frequently my only fan, her solitary status did not in any way dampen her belief in my genius. She always told me—a little Jamaican British girl with broken front teeth, nearsightedness to the point of blindness, raggedy clothes, and a school uniform that was spotted and stained— that what I said mattered.

She did the same thing for her elementary school students, persuading every one of her seven-year-olds in classes of over thirty-five students that they could and *would* learn to read. Every one of them did. Like Tolkien's Elves, my mother taught her own "Entings" how to speak. When I gained entry into King's College, London, she was the first to applaud, and her applause was always the loudest and the longest. She laughed all the time, many times a day, because in spite of the suffering she endured, she appreciated the absurdities of existence.

She taught me that things invisible could be even more comforting than things seen. In spite of how poor we were, the world she helped me to create for myself was a joyful one, a place where fear takes cover.

In the nineties, I was involved in a project that brought Virginia Tech students and older African Americans together. The African Americans were alumni of the Christiansburg Institute, a local technical school that, prior to desegregation, had provided education to black students. Some of the students told me how much it meant to them to interact with people who were their grandparents' age but who weren't their professors. One young African American student was particularly enthusiastic, commenting on how much she yearned for some kind of ongoing dialogue with older people outside of the academy. In general, however, the opportunities afforded to students to engage in intergenerational dialogue with those who were not faculty members were few and far between.

Child development specialists, educators, and social commentators have frequently pointed out that young people thirst for the wisdom offered by an older generation. The child development specialist Dorothy H. Cohen summed up the situation in this way:

> In former times and less complex societies, children could find their way into the adult world by watching workers and perhaps giving them a hand; by lingering at the general store long enough to chat with, and overhear conversations of, adults . . . by sharing and participating in the tasks of family and community that were necessary to survival. They were in, and of, the adult world, while yet sensing themselves apart as children.[1]

In conferences with students, I am saddened to learn that the work they are showing me has rarely been shared with their parents. When I ask them why not, they are taken aback by the question. But it strikes me as unfortunate that it is often the teacher of writing, even more than the parent, who communicates with students about things that matter deeply to them. Why is it that parents often seem to have no idea what their children believe in, yearn for, are fearful of and passionate about? Why do students often know relatively little about their parents? Why are we not talking to each other more often and about subjects that matter? If we as parents had to write character studies of our children, what critical pieces of information would we omit?

Some young people don't hear voices from an older generation at all. American culture has an unhealthy obsession with youth, in large part because such a focus is profitable. We know that old notions of community are difficult to establish in a culture where people move an average of eight or nine times in their lives. This lack of stable, nurturing communities that foster interaction with older people can mean that a young person may have little guidance from anyone, particularly when she or he makes the transition to college.

In Peter Wallenstein's book *Virginia Tech, Land-Grant University, 1872–1997*, there is a revealing description of what life used to be like on campus during the term of John McLaren McBryde, who served as president of the school from 1891 to 1907. Some parents took the idea of in loco parentis literally:

> Anxious that their sons would be all right, they conceived the school small enough that McBryde could know, and look after, all his charges. One letter said, "My boy is coming to your college today. Please give him a sunny room on the second floor and help him choose a good roommate." Another urged McBryde, "My two boys left this morning for your college. Charles is a husky boy and will get along. William is in poor health. Please see that he wears his hat and coat when the weather is bad."[2]

Even at the turn of the century, when enrollment at VPI (Virginia Polytechnic Institute) numbered in the hundreds, it would have been difficult for McBryde to assume the kind of parental role being described here. Today, it would be preposterous to expect it of anyone at an institution the size of Virginia Tech.

Yet in part due to aggressive marketing campaigns by schools, many parents are wooed by large universities that claim students are assured of a "small college feel." The lack of supervision is a distinct advantage for students who make friends relatively easy and are proactive about their education; they revel in their newfound freedom. But for others, a large campus environment can be a recipe for disaster.

According to the Panel Report, Seung-Hui Cho had been warned by his counselor that a school the size of Virginia Tech wasn't a good fit for him.[3] He had struggled to communicate throughout his middle school and high school years, and his school counselor urged him to select a smaller college closer to home. Nevertheless, Seung-Hui Cho decided to attend Virginia Tech. He was an adult; it was his prerogative to do so. He was going to a place where he knew no one. He ended his counseling sessions when he was in the eleventh grade. He was not on any medication, and there would be no special accommodations for him because no one at Virginia Tech had been told about his selective mutism. Although his family tried to keep in close touch with him, valiantly making the eight-hour journey there and back from northern Virginia every weekend during his first semester, it would have been difficult for them to get a clear sense of how he was coping. Like many parents, they relied upon their son's own accounts of how he was faring, and let him know that they were there for him if he needed it. Right up until the mass shootings on April 16, the Cho family called their son every Sunday.

But even the most diligent parents often struggle to communicate effectively with their children. The old-style "generation gap" has morphed into something more complex, in part because it involves the insertion of technologies we haven't had to cope with before, in part because of the aggressive co-opting of youth by corporate

America. There is so much static it can be hard for us to hear each other across the generational divide. Many of our kids, for good or ill, have been leased to special interest groups—the cell phone companies, the malls, the video game industry. Because Virginia Tech is a City of Youth, this trend is easily observable. It means that, even though the relationship may look quite good on the surface, parents and children may know remarkably little about each other. Some K–12 and college-age students have turned down the volume all the way on their parents, as Seung-Hui Cho appears to have done.

Unlike a number of other school shooters, Cho is not thought to have had coconspirators. But in middle school and high school shootings where children are much younger and more likely to confide in others, the picture can be very different. Children search for role models. As school shootings demonstrate, they can find them in the worst possible places. In *Rampage*, the sociologist Katherine Newman and her coauthors point out that shooters are often "joiners" whose efforts at belonging have been rebuffed. Far from the "loners" often depicted by the media, they want acceptance so much that they decide in desperation to kill others to make sure they can't have it either.

One of the critical questions for parents is this: *How involved should I be in my child's education?* "Helicopter parents" is a negative term used in higher education to describe parents who "hover" over their offspring. Stories on CNN and in parenting magazines warn of the dangers of being overprotective—how it can hinder a young person's maturation and lead to chronic dependency.[4] Overprotective parents have indeed turned dependency into a cottage industry, and there seem to be an increasing number of "children" approaching middle age bent on making sure that the nest is never empty. The College Board website even invites parents to take a quiz so they can measure (and presumably moderate) their own helicoptering tendencies. On the other hand, helicopters are also used for rescue efforts. They can swoop down in minutes to pick up victims.

They can be lifesavers at times, and currently the role of parents of college-age students is being reevaluated by education specialists. Some experts now assert that the positive effects of the so-called helicopter parent may outweigh the negative. Hopefully, this trend will continue as a growing number of colleges and universities begin to see their relationship with parents more in terms of partnership than exclusion.

Parents play a key role when it comes to identifying and responding to the problems of troubled or deeply disturbed students. The vast majority, if given the opportunity, do whatever they can to assist their children. If the "child" is an adult, however, the issue is more complicated.

Virginia Tech interpreted the Family Educational Rights and Privacy Act (FERPA) very narrowly. Skadden, Arps, the law firm that provided advice for the review panel, included a summary in the appendix of the Panel Report, clarifying some of the rules relating to FERPA. The most significant among them pertains to the disclosure of information: "Under FERPA, schools may release any and all information to parents, without the consent of the eligible student, if the student is a dependent for tax purposes under the IRS rules." For years, faculty and staff at Virginia Tech have been instructed not to disclose confidential information to parents, and there is confusion about this among faculty and staff at other institutions. If students feel that their right to privacy has been jeopardized, they may challenge this protocol in court. Moreover, this revised interpretation of FERPA may not be in line with a school's existing policies, so parents may want to discuss these issues with their college-age children.

Students and parents bear a responsibility to inform colleges of pertinent issues relating to a student's education. When this critical information is lacking, the results can be tragic.

Open communication is the best defense we have against attacks on schools by students, but it is also the best way we have to get to know our children. Some parents are uncomfortable speaking about ethics and morality, but the assumption that moral instruction is a key component of American education is, alas, not always accurate. Even if a valiant effort is made in schools to teach ethics, unless those lessons are reinforced in the home they are unlikely to be absorbed.

IT IS never easy to begin a conversation across a generational divide, especially if a parent has never embarked on this kind of journey before. As a teacher of poetry, fiction, and creative nonfiction, I have found that one of the easiest ways to initiate meaningful dialogue is through writing—not because it is a more formal process, but because it aids in reflection and often elicits authentic responses. Writing isn't necessarily autobiographical, but it does reveal something about what we have experienced, what we assume, and what we know about the world.

Over the past three decades, young people whom I have taught have frequently told me about their hopes and fears. They have written inspiring poems about love and moving poems about despair; their stories have revealed their varied perspectives. I have been struck by the fact that some of the conversations they are eager to have with teachers of writing are conversations it would benefit them to have with their parents or guardians.

It is my responsibility to encourage students to ask hard questions of their writing and their perceptions. But some students are telling their parents too little and their teachers too much. If, in addition to the work they do for us, students were to write for their parents the saga of their own biographies, what would these reveal? How would such a gift be received? Were parents to assign creative writing exercises to their children, and if children returned the favor, they would likely learn a lot about each other. If they wrote poems and stories together, there are all kinds of new, cross-generational conversations they could have. Keeping a shared diary with a child— a place where parent and child are permitted to record their thoughts without fear of repercussions—can enable open communication. Treating each other to "get-to-know-me" sessions, in which a favorite song, movie, or book is shared, can also help us become better acquainted. Poems and stories by professional writers can act as catalysts for dialogue. Writing itself, because it is such an intimate, reflective process, grants us unusual access into our own and others' imaginations; it facilitates an objectivity that can be lacking if dialogue is spoken rather than written. If as parents we had to write essays in which we described our children's imaginations, what would these tell us about them and about us? How well acquainted are we with the dream-visions of those we love?

In almost every case, young people wish to speak, but some of them seem to have no idea how to enter into dialogue with their parents. But it's difficult to know our children in the present if we don't take the time to find out who they want to be in the future, or who they thought they were in the past. How can we tell them to embark on a journey towards, say, accounting if we don't know that the destination they dream of, the only one that matters to them, is in digital art or the study of history? How will they know us as individuals if the only role we permit ourselves is a guarded one grounded solely in the unwavering reinforcement of authority?

Students reveal themselves in astonishing ways when they write. It is tragic if we end up thinking, "If only I had known this or that about my child, I would have been a better parent." It's sad, too, if children live with these same regrets about their parents. Parents should address drugs and alcohol, smoking and sex with their children, but it can be just as important to find out who your child hopes to be, and what he or she believes in. Entering each other's worlds should be an exploratory journey that can lead to a deepening of mutual respect.

In 2004, when I was asked to write a short essay for the introduction to the English department's custom composition text, I described how I approach the writing process. It seems relevant now as I think about the demands placed on us by writing, and the power it has to give us access into each other's worlds:

> We come to texts, whatever form they take, with the most liberating and dangerous tool of all: our own perspectives. In order to be successful communicators, we have to acknowledge our assumptions when we read, interrogate our assumptions when we write, and revise our assumptions when we speak.[5]

Real dialogue, whether written or spoken, is always a process of reevaluation. Our assumptions about each other can prevent us from fully engaging across a generational divide that can be traversed more easily than we sometimes imagine.

In spite of all the demands of parenting, there is one sure method of discovering a young person's voice, and that involves finding ways to learn and laugh together. This one parenting skill supersedes all others. It is what my mother did for me. Her contagious sense of humor and her insatiable intellectual curiosity allowed me to thrive.

One of the most important lessons my mother, the elementary schoolteacher, taught me was this: never forget that there is an endless forest of children waiting to learn. She was absolutely right.

14.
The
Anniversary

I T IS April 16, 2008, the one-year anniversary of the Virginia Tech shootings. We have gathered on the Drillfield, the large expanse of green that constitutes the heart of the campus.

The center of the field is treeless. In spite of the tireless efforts of landscaping crews, a few footpaths have been carved out by the feet of students who insist on taking shortcuts to class. After the attack, white canopies were erected on the Drillfield so that mourners, even when it rained, could pay their respects at the huge bulletin boards on which a community had traced its grief. We wrote messages to each other and to the dead with thick black markers.

From the well of the Drillfield, I can gaze up towards Burruss Hall, look slightly to the right and catch a glimpse of Norris Hall, which has housed offices and labs since the shootings.

I occasionally think of E. A. Robinson's poem "Reuben Bright" when I look at Norris Hall. It tells the story of a simple butcher who obeyed the rules and tried to live honestly in the world, but who was thrown into despair by the death of his beloved wife. Each of the sonnet's fourteen lines is written in iambic pentameter. Robinson forces his character forward to his terrible climax. In the final line, Reuben Bright tears down the slaughterhouse. The butcher's loss is absolute, but at times the iambic rhythm (*ba-boom, ba-boom*) almost seems to mock his pain, its rhythm mimicking a heartbeat, intimating a kind of order that no longer exists. Reuben the butcher, accustomed to slaughter, rails against the finality of death. Having lost his wife, the butcher recognizes at last the ramifications of the verb *to kill.*

At Virginia Tech we have decided not to tear down the slaughterhouse, opting instead for a careful reconstruction. A committee composed of some of the victims' families and members of the VT community recommended that it house centers of healing—one focused on student engagement and another on peace studies and the prevention of violence. The effort to transform loss into something hopeful is a way for Virginia Tech to come to terms with the future. It is a worthy focus—more sincere than the "Invent the future" slogan Virginia Tech asked us to adopt in the aftermath of the shootings.

People place flowers at the door of Norris Hall, and I try not to see the blossoms as metaphors for cut and dying beauty. I try to see them instead for what they are—gestures of compassion.

When I was a student in the Creative Writing program at the University of Arkansas, one of my teachers was John Clellon Holmes. Author of the novels *Go* and *The Horn,* he was a chronicler of the Beat movement. In some ways, as many have observed, he seemed like the odd person out in that group. He didn't write on taped-together reams of teletype paper like Jack Kerouac, or possess Kerouac's ability to yoke experience to spontaneous prose. Instead, John seemed to stand at the edge of this great circle of blazing energy that was Kerouac and Neal Cassady and Ginsberg, marveling at the conflagration while taking careful notes. He has been characterized by some as a hanger-on, a relatively conventional figure among a group of writers who harnessed rebellion to art. John recorded the route taken by the Beat Generation, and mourned its passing with a steadfastness as bright as Kerouac's falling candles of heaven. In his essay "This Is the Beat Generation," published in the *New York Times Magazine* in 1952, he wrote:

> The wild boys of today are not lost. Their flushed, often scoffing, always intent faces elude the word, and it would sound phony to them. For this generation conspicuously lacks that eloquent air of bereavement which made so many of the exploits of the Lost Generation symbolic actions.

In the 1980s, John seemed to me to be an infinitely patient, gentle man, who smoked too much when it was still something you could do in your office with impunity, and listened to the strains of things past. He was part of a tight group of men who defined the University of Arkansas' Creative Writing program at that time—Jim Whitehead, Miller Williams, Bill Harrison, and John. They knew what kind of program they wanted to establish, and they were fiercely protective of it. They nurtured talented writers like John Dufresne, Steve Yarbrough, Donald "Skip" Hays, Lee Martin, C. D. Wright, Leon Stokesbury, and Barry Hannah, who helped make the program famous.

Each year as it neared the anniversary of Kerouac's death, John grew more depressed. The program knew that his period of mourning was coming; it was built into the schedule. As the date neared, John would withdraw to spend time with his wife and to mourn in private, unable by that time to teach at all. I was in my twenties when I was there, and it puzzled me why someone would permit himself to be so overcome by grief even though the tragedy had happened many years before. But now, on this one-year anniversary of the tragedy at Virignia Tech, I remember John's face, and I begin to see things that only an intensification of loss, coupled with age, lets you see.

———

WE ARE gathered to remember our dead. In spite of the wild boys of the fifties who believed so fervently in the deification of self-expression, and who pranced and danced and juggled with knives, this ceremony in April 2008 is still an eloquent bereavement.

The service is being broadcast by CNN and by the local TV stations; there is coverage on NPR. A live broadcast of a tribute to the dead.

Each year the coverage will likely diminish, either because people will want to see this as a mere aberration or because, one day soon, a greater, more terrible shadow will rise to eclipse this one. We will shake our heads and ask ourselves again, *What could we have done to prevent this?* We will hold each other closely and wait for the shaking to pass.

Unlike a year ago when the wind was bitter and snow flurries turned April into winter, this day proclaims spring. The sky is a warm blue, the grass a welcome green; heavy blossoms explode on flowering dogwoods and cherry trees. Everything seems rounded into bud and blossom—no sharp angles anywhere. As is customary in April, spring's kindly curvature envelops southwestern Virginia. This is the season's blessing in the New River Valley—a time of fecundity and promise. The black ribbon of mourning overlaid by the VT logo seems at first to be anomalous on a day like this. Burruss Hall with its Hokie-stone facade is as imposing as ever. We look much like we used to look in our previous life.

After the media storm abated, we gathered our belongings and resumed our journeys. A new influx of students—the largest class in history—joined us. They are undaunted by what happened, and their lack of experience not only dilutes our own grief, it distinguishes us from one another, as though we speak different dialects. I think of another poem, this one by the British poet T. S. Eliot, in which he describes how the three magi felt when they returned home to their own lands fundamentally changed by the miraculous birth they had witnessed. The magi cannot adjust to an old routine. They have become out of place with their own settings and circumstance; they long for death so that they can reside with their savior.

In Tech's revived world of renewed and manufactured energy, those of us still grieving drag unwieldy sacks behind us. We search for places to stow our memories. Today, we have the right to ask each other to share these burdens without embarrassing anyone. Most of the people gathered here today dare to speak honestly to one another. The anniversary, terrible though it is, is welcome in some ways. On the one day of the year when sorrow is sanctioned, we don't need to offer excuses for our expressions.

In his poem "For the Anniversary of My Death," W. S. Merwin points out something that cannot be appreciated until after the fact: Each year we pass the anniversary of our deaths with no way of knowing that we do so. In 2006, April 16 had been unremarkable; we passed the day as we usually did in springtime.

This morning the crater of the Drillfield is awash with orange and maroon. President Steger and Governor Kaine speak of remembrance and renewal. I try to listen but I find myself drawn to the undertow, as if we are all whirling in an eddy and being sucked down into a vortex. And indeed the Drillfield dips in the center like a shallow, asymmetrical bowl made by an amateur potter. There is a two-second delay before the words reach the speakers at the back of the crowd, an effect that forces the governor and the president to navigate among their own echoes. We hear the two leaders, then hear them cloned, as if their exact counterparts are standing on the other side of the Drillfield relaying a message they've sent to themselves. From their positions near the memorial circle lined with engraved stones, their voices return to them like boomerangs.

They read aloud the names of the thirty-two who were killed.

We are reminded of what they might have done had they lived—worked among the poor, furthered cultural understanding, championed discoveries, laughed, loved their families, made us stronger.

We disperse for a few hours, then gather again that evening for the candlelight vigil on the Drillfield. It was the photos of the vigil after the shootings last year that most of us remember—how thousands of candles flickered as we tried to grasp what had happened. Tonight, each of us is given a candle that has been thrust through a hole in the bottom of a red paper cup. The paper cup I am given has a Coca-Cola logo emblazoned upon it. Others, too, seem to be stamped with advertisements for Coke or Pepsi. American enterprise cannot be quelled by something as unprofitable as grief. I wonder if my cup was donated. I wish that the corporation had thought to cover its logo with our own logo of grief, the way people at other universities and other countries did when they mourned in unison with us. It would have been a fitting way to pay tribute to something more significant than money. But I decide that, instead of complaining about things I cannot change, it is better simply to take the cup which has been offered, just as the child nearby does, and hold up my embedded candle with the rest. It's dark now anyway, so what does it matter what's on the side of my flimsy cup—all that matters is what the candles symbolize tonight.

Larry and I watch as our candles' flickering lights join hands with the lights of thousands and thousands of others in our community. When we hold them up against the dark we are bobbing on an ocean of illumination. Something inside me opens up and tries to bloom. Its petals are small—nothing like the blooms on the Japanese cherry tree in our front yard that is only just beginning to unsheathe itself. And then the bugle sounds out taps.

And wouldn't you know that someone has thought to include a literal representation of what it means to reflect upon and echo others' voices. One of the bugle players has been stationed at the site of the thirty-two stones (always only thirty-two) while another has been stationed a few hundred yards away at the war memorial chapel to answer the call. The chapel, where so many people from our community have been honored before, is a place where tragedy is proverbial. The site of old loss is joined to the site of new loss, and the thread—the note that links them together—is the sound of light shimmering across the dark.

The student musicians play the familiar melody. Although there are no official lyrics, I was taught words to taps as a child in England. Those of us who are hinged to words in much the same way as we are hinged to suffering, hear them:

All is well, safely rest, the silent words assure each other, *God is nigh.*

The young students in military uniform play; we listen. Things lost can come back to us in another form. Translation and metamorphosis do not have to be brutal.

And thus, on this day one year later, I am persuaded that tragedy doesn't end with silence but with song. The beautiful faces of the beloved dead are resurrected. Our dead call to us; the survivors must respond. By their blessed light, we can learn to listen to each other all over again.

Epilogue

Y OU ARE not meant to say you are sorry after tragedies like this. People avoid doing so. And thus it is that the same fear that kept some people silent before the tragedy keeps people silent all over again.

I could not prevent the tragedy at Virginia Tech. Although I felt that Seung-Hui Cho was suicidal, I did not witness the full extent of his rage; he kept it hidden from me, or perhaps he didn't feel it when we were together, or perhaps it grew inside of him like a tumor until nothing was left.

I have friends who believe that Cho was a monster, and friends who believe that he was simply a very sick young man in need of help, a victim of his own illness. My conclusions are less cut-and-dried. I believe he was easily hurt, yearning for affirmation, desperately lonely, and severely mentally ill; I also believe that he was enraged and resentful, envious, narcissistic, and prejudiced. In the fall of 2005, however, he reached out for help. Back then, even he seemed to know that he was spiraling out of control.

There are more Chos, more Klebolds and Harrises, more Kinkels, and more Woodhams in our schools than people like to believe, just as there are in society as a whole. Schools don't act as filters against violence; in reality, they can be attractive sites for vengeance.

There have been some positive changes since the shootings. The university's internal committees have made dozens of recommendations about security infrastructure, communication, and technology to go along with the more than seventy recommendations in the Panel Report. Locks have been placed on classroom doors at Virginia Tech, though most teachers I know are reluctant to use them routinely because of the problem it poses with late arrivals. We now have a very efficient emergency notification system (e-mail, phones—cell and landlines) and a siren warning. New personnel have been hired in key student support positions and in the Virginia Tech Police Department. Tech employees have worked tirelessly to make sure that doors can no longer be chained shut. Instructors and students can now look up and see a brightly lit ticker that tells us what to do in an emergency. The other day my students told me they like the ticker because it displays the time.

One of the most encouraging reactions to the tragedy by the university was the creation of a new Center for Peace Studies and Violence Prevention headed by Professor Jerzy Nowak. (Professor Nowak's late wife, Jocelyne Couture-Nowak, a beloved instructor of French, was among those killed on April 16.) Students will soon be able to get an interdisciplinary minor in peace studies through the College of Liberal Arts and Human Sciences. The Norris Hall Taskforce also recommended to the administration that a Center for Student Engagement and Community Partnerships be created, a move that promises to expand student engagement with the community and greatly enrich the student experience. Both centers are to be housed in Norris Hall.

In April 2008, less than a year after the shootings, Governor Kaine signed omnibus mental health bills to reform and fund severely strained mental health services, adjust legal commitment criteria, and improve campus security.[1] The new legislation should result in a more coordinated and thoughtful response to troubled students, particularly as it relates to such things as the sharing of information, commitment criteria, student records, and parental notification. It was encouraging to see that funds were allocated to support this legislation in the budget, though it is well known that a far greater infusion of funds is needed. In the past few months, however, the economic situation has become dire. The burgeoning economic crisis and Virginia's $2.5 billion biennial budget shortfall threaten to undermine progress the governor and the state legislature have made. It will take courageous and visionary leadership to make sure that this does not happen.

The Virginia legislature failed to close the gun show loophole when two Democratic senators voted in favor of retaining it. Anyone eighteen years or older can purchase a gun at any gun show in Virginia without undergoing a background check. "Just say no to guns," we tell Virginia's children. "Please don't forget to leave your weapons in the parking lot when you drive to school during hunting season." The angry students who seem to be making increasingly frequent appearances in classrooms here and abroad continue to be shuffled through an unresponsive system. When it happens again, we will point at law enforcement, counselors, parents, and teachers who didn't seem to realize that a student was a ticking time bomb, or who, if they did see that there was a problem, were unable to deactivate him. The thorny cultural issues we need to address will be avoided.

There were eight years between Columbine and Virginia Tech. Eight long years to learn important lessons. Eight years during which time a young boy in Northern Virginia was fantasizing about two boys from Colorado whom he planned to outdo. We are betting the lives of our children on the fact that he was an exception.

Since the mass shootings at Virginia Tech, American schools and universities have been regularly attacked by students. Schools in half a dozen states have been targeted. The schools include Delaware State University in September 2007; a high school in Cleveland, Ohio, in October 2007; a technical school in Baton Rouge, Louisiana, a high school in Memphis, Tennessee, a junior high school in Oxnard, California, and Northern Illinois University, all in February 2008, a particularly bad month for school shootings. Finland, meanwhile, has seen two significant attacks: one at Jokela High School in Tuusula in November 2007, and another in Kauhajoki in September 2008.

The figures may not look too bad at first. Sporadic violence is, after all, to be expected. But other factors make the situation more volatile than it appears. In the United States, legislators who rail against these outbreaks of violence often do not admit, for example, that there is nowhere to send troubled students because most publicly funded psychiatric facilities have had their budgets slashed or have been closed down altogether. In July 2008, a mental health patient at Carilion Roanoke Memorial Hospital, having waited in an emergency room for nine hours following an evaluation, committed suicide.[2]

There is little mention in most reports that a number of attacks have been foiled due to the vigilance of teachers, parents, students, and law enforcement; little mention of the fact that some of the perpetrators had the capacity to slaughter hundreds rather than a handful but that they committed suicide, surrendered, or were captured before they could do more harm.

State and national boundaries are less relevant than they once were, and the problems we face here are being encountered elsewhere. We lag behind our students, first-generation "digital natives." We routinely underestimate the potency of technology, its ability to reshape attitudes and behavior. Our statistical data often reflect our provincialism. Attacks are rarely connected in meaningful ways, even though television, movies, and the Internet have enabled a kind of ideological miscegenation (for want of a better term) that has changed the cultural dynamic forever and is redefining national identity. Viruses go global swiftly. A young man in Finland can watch the videos posted by a young man in Virginia; a young man in Virginia can be inspired by two boys in Colorado. We look at the same footage within seconds of each other. Young people hear the same refrains, have similar dialogues, see and resee, read and reread what is fed to them and what they themselves produce, until these words and images become ingrained in their imaginations. Filters are passé, editors retro. Voices instilling hate and images inciting young people to commit violence proliferate. We countenance them because we value free expression. The challenge will be to discover how we can maintain this freedom without placing young people at risk.

On June 17, 2008, more than a year after the shootings at Virginia Tech, an $11 million settlement with twenty-eight of the victims' families was approved by a circuit court judge. The settlement included monetary compensation and medical benefits for eighteen of those who were injured. Two families did not file lawsuits, and two families were not satisfied with the settlement and so may continue negotiations.[3] As part of the agreement, families were permitted to have access to information about the tragedy, including meetings with the governor and university officials. There was no admission of liability by the Commonwealth of Virginia or by Virginia Tech.

On October 18 and 19, 2008, the members of the Policy Group, as part of the settlement agreement, met with victims' families. There were two separate meetings: one that lasted six hours was for those who were injured and their families; another that lasted eight hours was attended by the families of those killed.

Some family members remain dissatisfied with the information provided to them, especially, they say, since some of it conflicts with what they were told earlier. There are still nagging questions about the university's response to the double homicide, and about the timeline provided by the administration to the review panelists. In his October 19, 2008, article in the *Richmond Times-Dispatch*, David

Ress summed up the key points of difference. (The phrase "Massengill's investigation" relates to the investigation conducted by panelists serving on Governor Kaine's review panel chaired by Colonel Gerald Massengill):

- The half-hour-long interview with student Heather Haugh that led police to mistakenly pursue a "person of interest" off campus started 46 minutes later than officials told Massengill's investigation. . . .
- Tech's Policy Group, made up of top officials responding to the crisis, may not have known police had a lead about a person of interest who was off campus until as late as 9:25 A.M. Cho began shooting in Norris Hall about 9:40 A.M.
- Police never searched the rental van Cho drove. . . .[4]

The forty-six-minute time differential is of particular concern to victims' families because it suggests that there may not have been a "person of interest"—slain student Emily Hilscher's boyfriend—in the picture until much later. This means that, in the initial stages of the investigation on the morning of April 16, it is possible that no one had any idea who the killer was or where he might be, yet a warning was not issued to the campus. Tragically, Virginia Tech police chief Wendell Flinchum is quoted as saying he did not "mention any leads" to the Policy Group. "That seems to contradict Massengill's August 2007 state panel report. . . . That report said Flinchum began updating top Tech officials at 8:10, informing them of a probable suspect who was off campus."[5] According to Ress's article, the panelists did not see police notes for that day. It is unclear why this was the case, but Massengill has suggested that the focus of the report was on how emergency responders managed the crisis, particularly their response to the shootings in Norris Hall.

On November 22, 2008, Governor Kaine had a three-hour meeting with survivors and victims' families, who expressed concern about a number of unresolved issues. According to a report by David Ress in the *Richmond Times-Dispatch,* families want corrections to be made to the Panel Report so that it reflects what actually happened on April 16. They have also called for an investigation into the disappearance of Cho's records from the Cook Counseling Center. Governor Kaine, describing the meeting as "substantive," has pledged to look into their concerns.[6]

Sadly, President Steger and his key advisers have not helped their own case by remaining silent for so long. The only extended narrative provided by the Policy Group about what occurred on the morning of April 16 was the written statement read by David Ford. It is not surprising, therefore, that there appear to be discrepancies between this account of what happened and what actually took place. The university administration determined who would represent it and managed the documentation sent to the panel. The result was that key voices were sometimes missing.

I am hopeful that some of the questions can be resolved eventually. Many of the victims' families took it upon themselves to travel from a great distance to meet with the administration at Virginia Tech, even though, for some, it must have been extremely painful to set foot on campus. It was courageous of them to do so, and it speaks to the fact that they still have lingering doubts. It will never be possible to put all their questions to rest, but some of the most important of them can be resolved.

Through more open communication and a national commitment to education, it is possible to make this campus and others safer than they are currently. It's not too late to engage in meaningful dialogue.

WHEN I began thinking about the title for this book, I was saddened by how rarely the upper administration of Virginia Tech spoke to victims' families, and I was plagued by questions about Cho's volatile silence. As I wrote, I began to understand how pervasive silence is when it comes to issues relating to the well-being of the young in this country. It took a while to realize that, in my role as a teacher,

I was always more intimately connected to the title than I liked to believe. If I remained doggedly silent, how would I bear it if some other tragedy on the scale of the one we had endured (or even greater, perhaps) occurred in the United States or elsewhere? If I honestly believed that what we had witnessed was not an aberration but a mounting rage among a small minority of young people who see themselves as both victims and vigilantes, how could I refuse to speak?

The right to remain silent must be guaranteed because it functions as a servant of justice. It allows people—especially those who are most vulnerable to abuse—to gain access to assistance; it provides us space in which to reflect before we speak; it enables us to obtain legal counsel. But silence is being used too often these days by those in leadership positions who want to ignore critical questions. It is too easy to clam up, or to leave others to speak on your behalf and thus avoid personal risk. When silence is used as a substitute for leadership, communities are obliged to take on that risk themselves.

But speaking up is never easy; there is always a price to be paid. Reading about other school shootings and living so long inside the heads of angry young men has been challenging. I want to read happy books that have beginnings, middles, and ends that don't wound you. I want to laugh like I used to with people I love.

Often I think of the people of South Korea who have mourned with us, and I hope that, instead of dividing us from each other, this tragedy will bring Virginia Tech and South Korea much closer than before.

I think also of Seung-Hui Cho's family because their grief must be inconsolable. If there is too much disparity between the amount of compassion we need and the amount we receive, despair is often the result. I hope this isn't the case for his parents, and that they are able to find comfort in their courageous daughter, Sun-Kyung, who served as the family's translator when they tried to obtain help for their silent son. The statement Sun-Kyung issued is one I carry with me. She, too, is one of her brother's victims. She had to carry the burden of speech on behalf of everyone else; now she carries the burden of his furious silence. I hope she knows there are people who have made similar journeys and who pray that she finds peace.

To Seung-Hui Cho, I say this: I cannot allow the insanity of your attack to rob me of the right to forgive or the right to find joy. If I dwell with you in the dark there will be others I will not be able to see. Forgiveness was never yours to take away; it was mine to bestow. Those you attempted to silence are singing their redemptive lullabies. I hear them. They are beautiful. May you hear them, too, and find peace.

And to those whose loved ones were taken from them, and those severely injured in the attack, I say these three words, knowing that, however often I repeat them, they will never be enough: I am sorry.

EVEN THOUGH as a writer and a teacher I spend so much of my life living inside words, I have come to believe you can't write your way out of anything. I believe, rather, you write your way in.

I have written of the need to select new words to replace those that threatened to imprison me. But now that I've reached the end of this story, I understand that banishing those words altogether would be foolish. They will come back to haunt me if I don't reconcile myself with them as well.

Because of this, the six end-words Cho gave me (*Seung, sunglasses, sorrow, stone, silence,* and *guns*) shape these stanzas, and the six words I have claimed for myself (*students, teachers, beauty, voice, reconciliation,* and *peace*) are there, too, in various forms, in my sestina of necessary words. Perhaps less valiant and more tentative than I hoped it would be, it is the best I can do for now. Even grief can be a kind of gift.

End Words:
A Sestina

Spring or fall it's a solemn story: Seung—
hungry, chimerical, his sunglasses
winking in the room's pale light, his sorrow
sinking us both, as if our shoes are stone
tablets and the carpet is mud—waits. Silence
expands like a lung. Cho is under the gun.

Two years later, at the range, the gun
teaches a new lesson about holes. Seung
likes the histrionic bullets. Silent
behind his ostentatious sunglasses
he wills himself to turn soft flesh to stone.
He must kill soon. An unkempt sorrow

blooms, spreads its wings. He waits till sorrow
flies clean away. He's confident with guns—
spent years telling himself that sticks and stones

may break his bones but words can never . . . Seung
mutes the volume on the world, his sunglasses
doing with light what his sermonic silence

does with speech. The sovereignty of silence
hems him in. His catechism, sorrow,
sat between us when we met. His sunglasses
thrust me onto glass. He did not bring guns
with which to shoot me. I don't know why. Seung
brought me gifts instead: ponderous stones

to hang around my neck—a dull, whetstone
rosary. In April, pumping silence
full of expletives, the Riddle-Boy, Seung—
his own wounds now encrypted, his sorrow
gorged and frantic—brandished a pair of guns,
removed—forever—his sunglasses.

I was a teacher; now I wear sunglasses.
Sight is kinder on a dimmer switch. Headstones
bruise me. *(Sorrow, sorrow everywhere, only salt to drink.)* The gun
tells time—click-Glock, click-Glock. Kindly voices
give us CPR: "Sever horror from beauty,"
they warn.
                    By their laughter I know my students

hear the voices of an unarmed choir. We teach
peace in the stuttering light, reconcile silence
with the world's residual, clamorous beauty.

Recommended Texts and Resources

April 16th: Virginia Tech Remembers, by Roland Lazenby and Virginia Tech student journalists. New York: Plume/Penguin, 2007.

"The Bogeyboys," by Stephen King. Written soon after the attacks on Columbine, this keynote address deals with issues such as censorship and gun control. http://www.horrorking.com/interview7.html/.

"Cities in Crisis: A Special Analytic Report on High School Graduation," EPE Research Center, Christopher B. Swanson, director. A report prepared for America's Promise Alliance, April 1, 2008. http://www.americaspromise .org/APAPage.aspx?id=10354.

Deadly Lessons: Understanding Lethal School Violence, National Research Council and Institute of Medicine, Case Studies of School Violence Committee. Mark H. Moore, Carol V. Petrie, Anthony A. Braga, and Brenda L. McLaughlin, eds. Washington, D.C.: The National Academies Press, 2003.

Depression, a resource booklet revised in 2007 and available from the National Institute of Mental Health. Available in pdf format at http://www.nimh .nih.gov/.

Guys and Guns Amok: Domestic Terrorism and School Shootings from the Oklahoma City Bombing to the Virginia Tech Massacre, by Douglas Kellner. Boulder, CO: Paradigm Publishers, 2008.

KidsPeace Institute.com features resources for parents. http://www.kidspeace .org/healing.aspx?id=1464.

Mass Shootings at Virginia Tech: Report of the Review Panel, the official report commissioned by Governor Tim Kaine. It is available in full at http://www.vtreviewpanel.org/report/index.html.

On Killing: The Psychological Cost of Learning to Kill in War and Society, by Dave Grossman. New York: Little, Brown, 2006.

Rampage: The Social Roots of School Shootings, by Katherine Newman, Cybelle Fox, David J. Harding, Jal Mehta, and Wendy Roth. New York: Basic Books, 2004.

Rutherford Institute, website features descriptions of zero tolerance cases. http://www.rutherford.org/.

School Violence: Fears Versus Facts, by Dewey G. Cornell. Mahwah, NJ: Lawrence Erlbaum Associates, 2006.

There Is a Gunman on Campus: Tragedy and Terror at Virginia Tech, edited by Ben Agger and Timothy W. Luke. New York: Rowman and Littlefield, 2008.

Threat Assessment in Schools: A Guide to Managing Threatening Situations and to Creating Safe School Climates, U.S. Secret Service and U.S. Department of Education, 2004. Available in pdf format at the Department of Education website, http://www.ed.gov.

Notes

Prologue

1. Throughout the book, I refer to *Mass Shootings at Virginia Tech: Report of the Review Panel* as the Panel Report. This document has sometimes been referred to as the Panel Review, but this can lead to confusion because the term really refers to the review panel appointed by the governor, and the review process. The full report is available online at http://www.vtreviewpanel.org/report/index.html.
2. Reports about the number of injured vary. Some of those who received minor injuries were not initially included in the tally used by the media. I have therefore cited the numbers given in the Panel Report, which draw upon Virginia Tech's own records and take into account those students who sustained injury when they jumped from the second-floor classroom of Norris Hall.

Chapter 1

1. Shawna Morrison, "Tech police chief studying up on his job," *Roanoke Times,* December 21, 2006.
2. CNN.com, "Cho family statement," http://www.cnn.com/2007/US/04/20/shooting.family.statement/index.html.

Chapter 2

1. According to the Panel Report, Cho submitted work to a publisher in spring 2005: "The idea for a book sent to a New York publishing house is rejected. This seems to depress him, according to his family" (22).

Chapter 3

1. Panel Report, 23.
2. Ibid., 46.
3. Ibid., 2.
4. Ibid., 23.
5. Ibid.
6. Ibid., "Summary of Key Findings," 2.
7. Katherine Newman, Cybelle Fox, David J. Harding, Jal Mehta, and Wendy Roth, *Rampage: The Social Roots of School Shootings* (New York: Basic Books, 2004).
8. President George W. Bush, http://www.whitehouse.gov/news/releases/2007/04/20070417-1.html.

Chapter 4

1. CNN.com, "Killer's manifesto: 'You forced me into a corner,'" April 18, 2007, http://www.cnn.com/2007/US/04/18/vtech.shooting/index.html.
2. Ibid.
3. Daniel Marotta, "Media Backlash at Virginia Tech: Community Chafes at Media's Constant Coverage," April 19, 2008, http://abcnews.go.com/US/VATech/story?id=3059025&page=1/.
4. Tom Breen, "Few on campus blame Va Tech president," *USA Today,* August 31, 2007, http://www.usatoday.com/news/nation/2007-08-31-887467212_x.htm/.
5. Hank Kurz Jr. and Vicki Smith, "Va Tech president defends himself," *USA Today,* August 31, 2007, http://www.usatoday.com/news/topstories/2007-08-31-887467212_x.htm/.

Chapter 5

1. I am basing my account of what transpired at the Policy Group meeting on the material included in the Panel Report. In July 2008, twenty thousand pages of documents were released to reporters from the *Richmond Times-Dispatch,* who asked to review them under the Freedom of Information Act (FOIA). The release of information to victims' families was

one of the stipulations in the $11 million legal settlement between victims' families and Virginia Tech. This material was immediately reviewed by *Richmond Times-Dispatch* reporters David Ress, Carlos Santos, and Rex Bowman, and by a deputy news editor, John Hoke. According to a series of articles published in the *Richmond Times-Dispatch* from July through September 2008, some documents were missing from the first seven boxes of material reporters were permitted to review in the presence of a Virginia Tech official. According to Cheryl Magazine, the *Richmond Times-Dispatch* Sunday editor, who described the process in "Reporters dig deep into Tech massacre" on July 20, 2008: "The university told the reporters that exemptions to the FOIA allowed it to keep secret many of the most important documents surrounding the event, such as Tech President Charles W. Steger's e-mails and notes and Cho's school records." President Steger has not released his own notes on the grounds that they are covered by attorney-client privilege. See http://www.inrich.com/cva/ric/search.apx.-content-articles-RTD-2008-07-20-0073.html and http://www.inrich.com/cva/ric/search.apx.-content-articles-RTD-2008-07-20-0228.html.

2. The complete statement by Kay Heidbreder can be viewed at http://www.vtnews.vt.edu/documents/2007-05-21_Heidbreder.doc.
3. Panel Report, 81.
4. The Emergency Response Plan 2005 (ERP-2005) is not included as an appendix to the Panel Report, but, formerly, it could be accessed through the Virginia Tech website. The 2008 version of the emergency plan can be accessed at http://www.ehss.vt.edu/. All public institutions are required to devise an emergency response plan and to update it as necessary. At the time of the tragedy, ERP-2005 (minimally revised in November 2006) was the plan that would have been in effect. According to the Panel Report, "the university's ERP deals with preparedness and response to a variety of emergencies, but nothing specific to shootings. The version in effect on April 16 was about 2 years old" (16).
5. Panel Report, 81.
6. Ibid., 25.
7. David Ress, "Did Tech shootings spur idea to close?" *Richmond Times-Dispatch,* September 13, 2008, http://www.inrich.com/cva/ric/news.PrintView.-content-articles-RTD-2008-09-13-0122.html.
8. The Panel Report suggests that the VTPD "had the authority to send a message," but lacked "the technical means to do so," though it also makes clear that Chief Flinchum's role with regard to the Policy Group was advisory. (See Panel Report, 16.)
9. Panel Report, 81.
10. Ibid.

11. Patricia Mooney Nickel, "There Is an Unknown on Campus: From Normative to Performative Violence in Academia," in *There Is a Gunman on Campus: Tragedy and Terror at Virginia Tech,* ed. Ben Agger and Timothy W. Luke, 159–84 (New York: Rowman and Littlefield, 2008).

12. Panel Report, 82.

13. Ibid., 26. Police officers are not generally identified by name in the Panel Report, though Chief Wendell Flinchum is identified. Instead, they are referred to in terms of their units: the Virginia Tech Police Department (VTPD), the Blacksburg Police Department (BPD), etc. I have adhered to this protocol in this book.

14. Ibid., 82.

15. President Steger argued on a number of occasions that the tragedy could have been worse, saying, "The crime was unprecedented in its cunning and murderous results. And yet it happened here," continuing, "To say that something could have been prevented is certainly not to say that it would have been. Moreover, it's entirely possible that this tragedy, horrific as it is, could have been worse." See http://www.usatoday.com/news/nation/2007-08-29-887467212_x.htm.

16. David Ress, Carlos Santos, and Rex Bowman, "Tech release of records omits key materials," *Roanoke Times,* July 21, 2008.

Chapter 6

1. Newman et al., *Rampage,* 55.

2. MSNBC.com, "High school classmates say gunman was bullied," April 19, 2007, http://www.msnbc.msn.com/id/18169776/.

3. Panel Report, 42.

4. Vincent J. Bove, "Crisis of Leadership: A Response to the VT Panel Report," available at http://vincentbove.blogspot.com/. This is a comprehensive critique of the Panel Report. Although I do not agree with some of Bove's claims, he carefully reviewed the report and made apparent some of its inconsistencies.

5. In 2008, the university was ranked 42nd out of 662 universities nationwide in the annual NSF research enterprise survey. Budget cuts have severely impacted education funding in the twenty-first century, and Virginia Tech has not only been unable to rise higher than the top 40, it has often fallen out of the top 50. In 1996, Virginia Tech ranked 51st. In 2001, the year after President Steger came into office, the university ranked 49th. Individual departments have fared much better, however, with chemistry, geology, and some in engineering doing exceptionally well.

6. "Sports People: 'Not Serious Students,'" *New York Times,* July 3, 1987,

http://query.nytimes.com/gst/fullpage.html?res=9B0DE6DD133DF930A
35754C0A961948260.

7. "Whatever Happened to the Class of '69?" *Virginia Tech Alumni Association News,* Spring 2000.

Chapter 7

1. Panel Report, 2.
2. Ian Urbina and Manny Fernandez, "University Explains the Return of Troubled Student," *New York Times,* April 20, 2007, http://www
.nytimes.com/2007/04/20/us/20virginia.html?_r=1&scp=5&sq=
Virginia%20Tech%20+%20Chris%20Flynn&st=cse&oref=slogin/.
3. Panel Report, 23.
4. *Presidential Internal Review: Working Group Report on the Interface between Virginia Tech Counseling Services, Academic Affairs, Judicial Affairs, and the Legal System,* August 17, 2007, http://www.vtnews
.vt.edu/story.php?relyear=2007&itemno=459/.
5. Panel Report, 7.
6. Ibid., 14.

Chapter 8

1. Panel Report, 32.
2. Dewey G. Cornell, *School Violence: Fears Versus Facts* (Mahwah, NJ: Lawrence Erlbaum Associates, 2006), 11–13.
3. Panel Report, 39.
4. A diagnosis of autism was not made for Seung-Hui Cho, though it has been linked to his name intermittently in the media. In *Newsweek* (April 30, 2007, "Special Report") Cho's pastor was quoted as saying "I felt him a little autistic and advised his mother to take him to hospital." The Panel Report refers to autism in the mental health history section (p. 35), saying that the relationship between selective mutism and autism is "unclear," a statement that could, unfortunately, engender fear in people who are unfamiliar with autism. Autistic students who are academically qualified to attend college are usually mainstreamed in the United States. There is *no* evidence to suggest that autistic students are more prone to violence than nonautistic students.
5. The Rutherford Institute reports the case of the chicken finger in "Tracking and Fighting Zero Tolerance," 10/27/03: "*Kissinger v. Jonesboro School District* (AR): Eight-year-old Christopher Kissinger was suspended for pointing a chicken finger at a teacher and saying 'Pow, pow.' School

officials claim the student's action violated the school's threatening speech policy. Kissinger's parents have decided not to pursue any further action." http://www.rutherford.org/articles_db/legal_features.asp?article_id=71.

6. Ibid.

7. A 1999 article in *U.S. News & World Report* includes a warning about Mosaic 2000 from Kevin Dwyer, president of the National Association of School Psychologists. In the article Dwyer is quoted as saying it is impossible to create "an evaluation tool that will identify a mass murderer." He goes on to suggest such a program could do irreparable harm. http://www.usnews.com/usnews/edu/articles/991011/archive_002072.htm.

8. Panel Report, H-4.

9. Ibid., 18.

10. "Cities in Crisis: A Special Analytic Report on High School Graduation," EPE Research Center, Christopher B. Swanson, director. A report prepared for America's Promise Alliance, April 1, 2008, http://www .americaspromise.org/APAPage.aspx?id=10354.

11. The Treatment Advocacy Center released a report on the nationwide shortage of beds on March 17, 2008. "The Shortage of Public Hospital Beds for Mentally Ill Persons" revealed a deficit of almost 100,000 beds across the country.

Chapter 9

1. Newman et al., *Rampage*, 252.

2. Stephen King, "On Predicting Violence," April 20, 2007, http://www .ew.com/ew/article/0,,20036014,00.html. For an interesting and thoughtful response to issues relating to school violence, see Stephen King's keynote address, the Vermont Library Conference, May 1999. Entitled "The Bogeyboys," and written soon after the attacks on Columbine, it addresses issues such as censorship and gun control. It is available at http://www .horrorking.com/interview7.html.

3. Monica Barron, "Creative Writing Class as Crucible," *Academe* (November–December 2007), http://www.aaup.org/AAUP/pubsres/ academe/2007/ND/Feat/barr.htm.

4. Chris M. Anson, "What's Writing Got to Do with Campus Terrorism?" *Academe* (November–December 2007), http://www.aaup.org/AAUP/ pubsres/academe/2007/ND/Feat/anso.htm.

5. David Fenza, "About AWP: The Growth of Creative Writing Programs," http://www.awpwriter.org/aboutawp/index.htm.

6. Mike Allen, "College paper has bad ending," *Roanoke Times*, March 8, 2008, http://www.roanoke.com/news/roanoke/wb/153661.

7. According to an article by Mike Allen in the *Roanoke Times:* "Barber also
has angrily challenged claims made in Scott County court documents that
he was involuntarily committed to a mental institution after the guns were
found. It was the assertion by campus police that he had been committed
that led a judge to suspend his concealed-carry permit. Barber has shown
the *Roanoke Times* copies of a temporary detention order signed Feb. 29
and a release paper dated March 3. Together, they appear to indicate that
he was held in a mental institution for several days but that his evaluators
found nothing wrong with him." "Expelled UVa-wise student to continue
legal battle," March 17, 2008, http://www.roanoke.com/news/roanoke/
wb/154908.

Chapter 10

1. "The Killer at Thurston High: Kip's Writings & Statements," *Frontline,*
http://www.pbs.org/wgbh/pages/frontline/shows/kinkel/kip/writings
.html.
2. Panel Report, 75.
3. See Michael Janofsky's summary of the May 2000 report issued by investigators of Columbine: "Columbine Victims Were Killed Minutes into
Siege at Colorado School," May 16, 2000, http://query.nytimes.com/
gst/fullpage.html?res=9B06E7D8113BF935A25756C0A9669C8B63&
sec=&spon=&pagewanted=2/.
4. Jennifer Epstein, "Beer, Brotherhood and Guns," published by
insidehighered.com, reproduced in the Panel Report, Appendix K,
"Mixture of Guns and Alcohol on Campus," K–4.
5. Sharon Begley, "The Anatomy of Violence," *Newsweek,* April 30, 2007, 45.
6. According to the Violence Policy Center, Andrew Golden took seven
weapons belonging to his grandfather and three from his father. See
http://www.vpc.org/studies/wgun980324.htm.
7. Jeffrey Kluger, "Why They Kill," *Time,* April 30, 2007, 54–59.
8. Eve Kupersanin, "FBI Expert Says School Shooters Always Give Hints
About Plan," *Psychiatric News* 37, no. 12 (June 21, 2002), 2, http://
pn.psychiatryonline.org/cgi/content/full/37/12/2/.
9. The Department of Education's listing "Teacher Shortage Areas: Nationwide Listing" demonstrates how widespread this problem is in the United
States. In addition to a lack of science and math educators, schools in many
states have a chronic shortage of special education teachers and counselors.
The risk this poses to student welfare and school safety is considerable.
See http://www.ed.gov/about/offices/list/ope/pol/tsa.doc.
10. Schools and universities are seeing increasing demands placed on mental

health services by students, but many do not have enough mental health professionals on staff. Experts have recommended that the ratio of counselors to students should be about 1 to 1,500. At Virginia Tech before the shootings, the ratio was 1 to 2,700. In October 2008, well over a year after the shootings, Virginia Tech received $2.65 million in federal funds to hire six new counselors at the Cook Counseling Center and case manager positions in Student Affairs. There are now 1,750 students to every counselor. The CCC handled 11,065 student visits in academic year 2007–8. This is up sharply from academic year 2005–6 when the center had approximately 7,145 student visits. See Greg Esposito, "Tech gets funds to keep healing going," *Roanoke Times,* October 10, 2008.

11. The prevalence of depression on college campuses is cause for concern. Anecdotally, over the past twenty-five years, I have witnessed a steady growth in the numbers of students who are suffering from depression. The statistics bear this out. According to an article by Jennifer Sisk in *Social Work Today,* the statistics are "staggering": "College-aged students are more likely to experience depression than other age groups, according to published studies, statistics from mental health organizations, and observations by social workers and other professionals working with the college population. The 2005 National College Health Assessment (NCHA), a survey of nearly 17,000 college students conducted by the American College Health Association, revealed that 25% reported they 'felt so depressed it was difficult to function' three to eight times during the past year and 21% reported they 'seriously considered suicide' one or more times during the past year. In the NCHA survey, students also ranked depression as one of the top 10 impediments to academic performance." Jennifer Sisk, "Depression on College Campuses—the Downside of Higher Education," *Social Work Today* 6, no. 5, 17, http://www.social worktoday.com/archive/swsept2006p17.shtml.

12. For a discussion of some of culture's role in school shootings, see Mark H. Moore, Carol V. Petrie, Anthony A. Braga, and Brenda L. McLaughlin, eds., *Deadly Lessons: Understanding Lethal School Violence,* National Research Council and Institute of Medicine, Case Studies of School Violence Committee (Washington, D.C.: The National Academies Press, 2003), 253–56.

13. Some studies have shown that bullying is a significant factor in school shootings, though others point to the discrepancy between perceived injustice and actual bullying in the minds of some shooters. See *Deadly Lessons,* 146.

14. Recent studies suggest that, when carefully monitored, the benefits of antidepressants outweigh the risks. But the abuse of prescription medication

is on the rise, according to the Office of National Drug Control Policy, which shows alarming trends in teen abuse of prescription drugs. See http://www.whitehousedrugpolicy.gov/news/press07/021407.html.

15. See Jeffrey A. Bridge, Joel B. Greenhouse, and Arielle H. Weldon, "Suicide Trends Among Youths Aged 10–19 Years in the United States, 1996–2005," *JAMA, The Journal of the American Medical Association* 300, no. 9 (September 3, 2008): "Following a decade of steady decline, the suicide rate among US youth younger than 20 years increased by 18% from 2003 to 2004, the largest single-year change in the pediatric suicide rate over the past 15 years." Although there was a 5 percent decline from 2004 to 2005, the rate of 4.5 suicides per 100,000 in 2005 is still high, and translates to 1,883 teen suicides in 2005. According to the National Institute of Mental Health (NIMH), suicide was the third leading cause of death in 2004 among children and young people. http://www.nimh.nih.gov/health/publications/suicide-in-the-us-statistics-and-prevention.shtml#children.

16. Shawna Morrison, "Charges lessened against teens inspired by Joker," *Roanoke Times*, September 17, 2008.

17. Lines reproduced as they appear in the Panel Report, 46. From Shakespeare's *Romeo and Juliet*, act 2, scene ii.

18. According to an article in *USA Today*, "For the first time in 2001, Brenda Spencer claimed her violence grew out of an abusive home life in which her father beat and sexually abused her. Her father, Wallace Spencer, has never spoken publicly about the case. He did not answer a reporter's knock on his door last week and his phone number is not listed. [Parole board chairman Brett] Granlund expressed doubt about the sexual abuse allegations, saying Spencer had never discussed them with counselors." http://www.usatoday.com/news/nation/2001-04-18-spencer.htm.

19. Steven Pinker, *How the Mind Works* (New York: W. W. Norton, 1997), 364.

20. American Psychiatric Association, *Diagnostic and Statistical Manual of Mental Disorders,* 4th ed., Text Revision (DSM-IV-TR) (Washington, D.C.: APA, 2000).

21. Newman et al., *Rampage,* 264–66.

22. Ibid., 266.

23. Dave Grossman, *On Killing: The Psychological Cost of Learning to Kill in War and Society* (New York: Little, Brown, 2006), 250.

Chapter 11

1. Dominic Cavendish, "Edinburgh Festival 2008: When an interviewer strikes deeper than a sledgehammer," *Telegraph,* August 15, 2008.

2. Seung-Hui Cho: "You have vandalized my heart, raped my soul and torched my conscience. You thought it was one pathetic boy's life you were extinguishing. Thanks to you, I die like Jesus Christ, to inspire generations of the weak and the defenseless people." http://news.bbc.co.uk/1/hi/world/americas/6570369.stm.

Chapter 12

1. AAJA.org, "Media Advisory: Coverage on the Virginia Tech Shooting," April 16, 2007, http://www.aaja.org/news/aajanews/2007_04_16_01/.

2. SuChin Pak, "Why Is Cho's Foreign Status an Issue?" MTV.com, April 20, 2007, http://www.mtv.com/news/articles/1557728/20070420/story.jhtml.

3. For a discussion of the religious connotations of the term "Ismail Ax," see Eric Benderoff, "Many Theories for 'Ismail Ax,'" *Chicago Tribune,* April 17, 2007, http://www.chicagotribune.com/news/nationworld/chi-0704170800apr18,0,6351168.story.

4. See Panel Report, 85. The apparent conflict between Cho's desire for anonymity and his desire for fame is explained briefly in the report: "Mentally disturbed killers often make one plan and then change it for some reason."

5. For an analysis of the handling of the investigation and trial of those who were identified as being part of the Virginia jihad network, particularly Ali Al-Timimi, see Milton Viorst, "The Education of Ali Al-Timimi," *Atlantic Monthly,* June 2006, http://www.theatlantic.com/doc/200606/viorst-terrorist.

6. The discussion of the term, though it was one of the few clues Seung-Hui Cho left, was only referenced once in the Panel Report: "The panel was allowed to view material Cho sent to NBC. The package was signed 'A. Ishmael,' similar to the 'Ax Ishamel' name he had written on his arm in ink at the time he committed suicide and also the name he used to sign some e-mails. The significance of the name remains to be explained but it may be tie [*sic*] to his self-view as a member of the oppressed" (85).

7. Lobbying and advocacy groups such as Equitas, a Canada-based think tank, are among those suggesting that connections between Cho and Virginia-based jihadists have been overlooked. Their September 2008 report, referenced by security consultant Vincent J. Bove on his website, points to circumstantial connections between Virginia Tech students Seung-Hui Cho and Yong Ki Kwon. These include their ethnicity (a tenuous link at best, particularly as the group was multiracial), the fact that both men attended Virginia Tech, and the fact that they both came from Fairfax, Virginia (a large area of more than a million inhabitants). In June 2003, CNN correspondent Kelli Arena detailed the extent of the Virginia jihad network (http://www.cnn.com/2003/US/06/27/terror.arrests/). The

effort to locate Cho's computer files and cell phone records was unsuccessful, though law enforcement devoted a significant amount of time to this, dredging the duck pond on campus because Cho was spotted near this location on the morning of the murder. The void created by the lack of information provided by the administration has helped fuel speculation. Following an October 2008 meeting between victims' families and the members of the Virginia Tech Policy Group, the *Richmond Times-Dispatch* reported on October 19, 2008, that among the things frustrating victims' families was the fact that police never searched the rental van Cho had driven for almost a month prior to the attack; see David Ress, "New timeline for April 16 raises questions for Tech," *Richmond Times-Dispatch,* October 19, 2008.

8. There have been other nonwhite male school shooters, such as Taiwanese student Wayne Lo, who attacked Simon's Rock College in 1992, killing two people and injuring four others, and there are rare examples of female shooters such as Brenda Spencer who killed two adults and wounded nine children in 1979. In general, however, most school shooters have been young white males.

9. "cho seung-hui: stereotyped to death," April 19, 2007, http://skeptical brotha.wordpress.com/2007/04/19/cho-seung-hui-stereotyped-to-death/.

10. See Panel Report, 24.

Chapter 13

1. Dorothy H. Cohen, "What Changes Do We Need?" in *The Learning Child: Guidelines for Parents and Teacher* (New York: Schocken Books, 1988), 28.

2. Peter Wallenstein, *Virginia Tech, Land-Grant University, 1872-1997: History of a School, a State, a Nation* (Blacksburg, VA: Pocahontas Press, 1997), 86.

3. Cho was advised by his high school guidance counselor and his parents to attend a smaller institution: "When his guidance counselor talked to Cho and his family about college, she strongly recommended they send him to a small school close to home where he could more easily make the transition to college life. She cautioned that Virginia Tech was too large. However, Cho appeared very self-directed and independent in his decision." Panel Report, 37.

4. Judy Fortin, "Hovering parents need to step back at college time," CNN.com, February 4, 2008, http://www.cnn.com/2008/HEALTH/family/02/04/hm.helicopter.parents/index.html.

5. Lucinda Roy, "The Perils and Rewards of Creating a Custom Text," in *Composition: Writing, Revising, and Speaking,* by Virginia Tech

Department of English faculty and students (Boston: Pearson Custom Publishing; Virginia Tech, 2004), xvi.

Epilogue

1. "Governor Kaine Signs Legislation in Response to Virginia Tech Shootings," press release, http://www.governor.virginia.gov/mediarelations/NewsReleases/viewRelease.cfm?id=637.
2. Laurence Hammack, "Suicide shows facility crunch," *Roanoke Times*, September 23, 2008. The article cites the severe shortage of beds at psychiatric hospitals in the region: "When there is a need for secure treatment but no bed space available, as is often the case, patients sometimes spend hours even days waiting in the emergency room."
3. Anita Kumar, "Judge Agrees to Va. Tech Payout," *Washington Post*, June 18, 2008, http://www.washingtonpost.com/wp-dyn/content/article/2008/06/17/AR2008061701086.html.
4. David Ress, "New timeline for April 16 raises questions for Tech," *Richmond Times-Dispatch*, October 19, 2008.
5. Ibid.
6. David Ress, "Tech families press Kaine," *Richmond Times-Dispatch*, November 23, 2008, http://www.timesdispatch.com/rtd/news/state_regional/article/TECH23_20081122-232016/119492/.

Index

"a boy named LOSER" (Cho),
  56–58
abuse, 176, 232
Academy of Teaching Excellence, 178
advising students, 189–90
Alexander, Catherine, 243, 244–45
American Psychological Association,
  200
Americans with Disabilities Act
  (ADA), 170
America's Promise Alliance, 184–85
Amish community, 252–53
amok state, 232–34
Anarchist's Cookbook, The, 216
Anson, Chris M., 203
Appalachian School of Law, 218
Asian American Journalists Associa-
  tion (AAJA), 260–61
Association of Writers and Writing
  Programs (AWP), 205, 209
at risk, meaning of term, 35
autism, 250, 265, 309n.4
Auvinen, Pekka-Eric, 268

Barber, Stephen Daniel, 206–7
Barnett, Paul M., 65, 143
Barron, Monica, 203, 206
Bath, Mich., school attack (1927), 22
Beamer, Frank, 139
Bean, Carl, 67, 79, 80–84, 85
Bethel, Alaska, shootings (1997),
  227–28
Betzel, Cathy, 63
Blacksburg, Va., 120–29; as "com-
  pany" town, 122–26; football games
  in, 126–29; previous double homi-
  cide in (Morva incident), 18–19,
  105–6; racial diversity lacking in,
  120–21, 272; Roy's first years in,
  122–23; tolerance of differences
  in, 119, 120
Bloomberg, Michael, 223
Board of Visitors, 137, 138
bombs, in school attacks, 216, 235
Bove, Vincent J., 132
Bowling for Columbine, 216
Bowman, Amylee, 235, 236

Bowman, Rex, 103
Boy from Centreville, The, 243–46
Breen, Tom, 93
Brockley County School for Boys, London, 179–83
Brooks, Gwendolyn, 54, 211
Brown, James Thomas "Tom," 130, 131, 159, 165
Browning, Joan, 273
Buell Elementary, Flint, Mich., shooting (2000), 221–22
bullying, 216, 227
Bureau of Alcohol, Tobacco, Firearms and Explosives (ATF), 27, 80, 83, 174
Bush, George W., 78
Business Information Systems, 150–51, 233
Byers, Ralph, 103–4

"Cain Rose Up" (King), 198
Capus, Steve, 88
Care Team, 131, 159, 162–63
Carilion St. Albans Psychiatric Hospital, 64–65
Carlisle, Fred, 137
Carneal, Michael, 264
censorship, 155, 194, 199
Center for Peace Studies and Violence Prevention, 293
Center for Student Engagement and Community Partnerships, 293
Central School of Speech and Drama, 243, 244
Chicago Sun-Times, 227
Cho, Seung-Hui: advised not to attend Virginia Tech, 64, 279; ammunition carried by, 235; autism ascribed to, 265, 309n.4; autopsy findings on, 233; backpack carried by, 52; "a boy named LOSER" by, 56–58; classmates photographed, 32, 37, 41; Columbine as inspiration for, 66, 170, 172, 198, 214; Cook Counseling Center contacted by, 3, 62–64, 65–66, 70–71, 143–44, 147; counseling recommended for, 39, 40, 41, 43–44, 45, 49, 50, 52, 54–55, 59, 62, 65–66; demeanor of, 39, 229–30; depression of, 169–70, 172, 234; disappearance of counseling records of, 71, 110, 143, 148, 298; disturbing behavior of, 31, 32, 37, 38; disturbing writings of, 24, 28, 29, 30–32, 37–38, 39, 40, 42, 117, 118, 143, 163, 175; evaluated at Carilion St. Albans, 64–65; extreme shyness of, 67, 169, 175; fiction writing of, 34–35, 38–39, 46, 56, 57, 58–59, 116, 119, 201, 206, 230, 233, 267; form of address preferred by, 45; gun as weapon of choice for, 214, 216–17; gun purchases of, 220, 224–25; handwriting of, 33; in high school, 116–18; identified as Asian male, 260–62, 264–65, 266; identified as shooter, 23–24; indifference of, 118; intelligence of, 233; isolation cultivated by, 118–20, 169, 261, 267; left off memorials, 252; letter sent to English department by, on day of shootings, 79–80, 81, 83–85, 107, 150; names "Ismail Ax" and "A. Ishmael" used by, 262–63; neatness of, 51; other school shooters compared to, 214–15; performance aspect of rampage of, 231–32; photograph and video images of, 213–14, 244, 245; poem cowritten by Roy and, 50–51, 52–53, 56; possible collaborator of, 80–81, 99; roommates' concerns about, 64, 119; Roy's conclusions about, 292; Roy's e-mails and phone calls about, 31–32, 40–41, 42–43; Roy's initial interview with, 29, 33, 35, 36–40, 52, 60; Roy's one-on-one meetings with, 2–3, 25–26, 42, 43, 45–56, 66–67, 184, 210, 245, 247; sadness of, 51; selective mutism of, 4, 36–37, 63, 169, 170, 175, 234, 279; speaking

voice and manner of, 40, 45, 49–50, 51; speculation about Muslim and terrorist connections of, 262–64; Student A's identification with, 163–64; as student in Roy's Intro to Poetry class, 33–35, 46, 50, 51, 57; studied silence of, 47–48; suicide of, 119, 213–14, 231; sunglasses worn indoors by, 31, 36, 38, 40, 45, 47, 48, 51, 230, 233; "verbatim play" based on rampage of, 243–46; video package sent to NBC by, 79, 85, 86, 87–88, 89, 107, 115, 262; Virginia Tech administration's obsession with privacy rights of, 70–71, 72, 98–99, 141–43, 152; worldview of, 267–68; young women stalked and harassed by, 64, 119, 120, 230–31

Cho, Sun-Kyung (sister), 28–29, 39, 299–300

Cho family, information shared by, 72–73

Christiansburg Institute, 277

Christmas Carol, A (Dickens), 190

"class of '69," 139–40

CNN, 13–14, 17, 18, 19, 22, 88–89, 280, 288

Coetzee, J. M., 204–5

Cohen, Dorothy H., 277

Collective Soul, 230

College of Education, 137

College of Liberal Arts and Human Sciences (CLAHS), 27, 32, 67, 155, 293

colleges and universities: class size at, 133–34, 193, 196–97; community structures of, 140; fiscal challenges of, 129, 133, 134, 135, 177, 178; graduates with leadership roles at, 139–40; lack of communication between high schools and, 177–78; large campus environment and, 278–79; safety concerns of, 131–32; teaching vs. research as focus in, 178; tuition increases at, 133

Collegiate Times, 156

Columbine, Colo., shootings (1999), 66, 90, 144, 170, 172, 173, 175, 198, 216, 218, 229, 235, 251–52, 294

Cook Counseling Center (CCC), 24, 27, 32, 41, 42–44, 65, 94, 142, 155, 159; Cho's contacts with, 3, 62–64, 65–66, 70–71, 143–44, 147; disappearance of records of Cho's interactions with, 71, 110, 143, 148, 298; refusal of, to intercede with Cho, 43–44; safety assessments and, 143; staffing inadequacies at, 130

Cornell, Dewey G., 170

Corps of Cadets, 136

Couture-Nowak, Jocelyne, 293

creative writing, 191–212; as cathartic exercise, 198, 200, 201; class size and, 193, 196–97; damaged or disturbed people and, 201–3; discipline required in, 192, 200–201, 202; relationship between fiction and truth in, 205–6; relationship between writer's character and his or her art in, 204–5; teaching of, 192–97, 201–7, 209; violence as dominant theme in, 197–200; and violence in students' writings, 203–4, 206–8; "writerly" way of life and, 202

"Creative Writing Class as Crucible" (Barron), 203

"Crisis of Leadership" (Bove), 132

Crouse, Roy, 65

D'Aguiar, Fred, 31, 32, 38, 41, 42, 45, 268

Dark Knight, The, 228, 229

Davids, Chris, 116–17

Davies, Gordon, 101–2, 146

Dawson, Tawana, 174

Deadly Lessons, 216

de Becker, Gavin, and Associates, 173–74

Dedman, Bill, 227

deeply disturbed, meaning of term, 35

depression, 248; increase in number of students suffering from, 35, 312n.11

Derbyshire, John, 237–38

Dickens, Charles, 190

DiIulio, John J., Jr., 170

disabilities, disclosure of, 36–37

Discovery of Poetry, The (Mayes), 57

Disgrace (Coetzee), 204–5

Division of Student Affairs, 144

Edinburgh Festival, 243–44

education theories, 167–69, 178–79

Edwards, John (Virginia legislator), 224

Elephant, 229

Eliot, T. S., 29, 288–89

Elkins, Ron, 207

Emergency Plan 2005 (ERP-2005), 101, 135

English department, 77, 142; Cho's letter to, on day of shootings, 79–80, 81, 83–85, 107, 150; code of, for dealing with angry students, 41–42, 146; documents handed over to police by, 149–50; e-mail sent to, after shootings, 80, 83–84; legal advice from university attorneys sought for, 145–46; ordered to hand over all computer files for imaging, 150–54; panelists' interviews with, 145, 146–47; Roy's stepping down from chair of, 59–60, 80; Student A and, 155–64, 165, 269–70

Epstein, Jennifer, 219

Esposito, Greg, 96–97

Falco, Ed, 67

Family Educational Rights and Privacy Act (FERPA), 98–99, 141–42, 171, 281

Farmer Hokie incident, 124–25

FBI, 27, 73, 80, 82, 83, 215–16

"Firearms Education Week," 220

First Amendment, 141, 199–200. *See also* free speech

first-person-shooter games, 236, 237

Fisher, Marc, 70–71

Flanagan, Elizabeth A., 140

Flinchum, Wendell, 14, 20–21, 78, 83, 84, 85, 103–5, 297

Flynn, Christopher, 143

football, 126–29, 139

Ford, David, 99–101, 104–5, 106, 108–9, 298

Forehand, Ronald C., 152–53

"For the Anniversary of My Death" (Merwin), 289

free speech, 155, 158, 194; students' right to, 156–57, 165, 166

Freire, Paolo, 168, 169

Frost, Robert, 255–57, 258

generational divide, 277–78, 279–84

Gillies, Blacksburg, Va., 123

Giovanni, Nikki, 2, 28, 30, 31, 32, 36, 39, 41, 42, 51, 64, 163, 206, 268–69

Gobble de Art, 124

Golden, Andrew, 222, 235

Gordimer, Nadine, 205

grief: five stages of, 247–48; Frost's "Home Burial" and, 255–57

Grossman, Dave, 225, 236–37

gun rights advocates, 142, 199, 217, 222–24, 238

guns, 216–25; availability of, 216, 220–25, 238; buying ammunition for, 225; campus regulations on, 52, 217–20; in Cho's iconic images, 213–14; as weapon of choice in school attacks, 216–17

gun show purchases, 223–24, 294

Guys and Guns Amok (Kellner), 232

Hardcastle, Valerie, 146

Harris, Eric, 170, 214–15, 226, 229, 235

Harrold, Tex., teachers allowed to carry guns in, 218–19

Haugh, Heather, 297

Head, Bessie, 13, 16, 29

health insurance, 144
Heard, Georgia, 192
Heidbreder, Kay, 98–99, 101
helicopter parents, 280–81
Heston, Charlton, 222–23
Hicok, Robert, 66–67
Hikes, Zenobia L., 140
Hilscher, Emily, 104, 107–8, 297
Hincker, Larry, 25–26, 52, 101, 103, 110, 138, 217
HIPAA, 98, 141–42
Hokie bird, 123–25
Hokie Spirit Memorial Fund, 92
Holmes, John Clellon, 286–87
Holocaust, 262
"Home Burial" (Frost), 255–57, 258
Houston, Vince, 20
Houston Chronicle, 218
How the Mind Works (Pinker), 232–33
Hyatt, James A., 103

Ideal Teacher, 167, 169, 178–79
Intermittent Explosive Disorder (IED), 234
Internet, 81, 142, 187–88, 295–96
Itzin, Catherine, 199

Jackson, Larry (husband), 14, 15, 17, 20, 21, 26–27, 161, 162, 247, 257–58, 271, 272, 290
Johnson, Mitchell, 222, 235
Judicial Affairs, 142, 155
Judicial System, 144

Kaine, Timothy M., 72, 78, 93–94, 148, 154, 223, 251, 289, 293–94, 297–98; Executive Order 53 of, 70, 73, 147; panel appointed by (*see* Panel Report; Panel Review)
Kazmierczak, Steve, 220
Kellner, Douglas, 232
King, Stephen, 197–98
King Lear (Shakespeare), 245, 254, 257

Kinkel, Kip, 214–15, 216, 264
Klebold, Dylan, 170, 214–15, 226, 229, 235
Kübler-Ross, Elisabeth, 247
Kurz, Hank, Jr., 94
Kwon, Yong Ki, 263–64

Lancaster County, Pa., shootings (2006), 252–53
Lavery, William E., 136–37
Librescu, Liviu, 2, 262
Lorde, Audre, 110
Lord of the Rings (Tolkien), 275–76
Loukaitis, Barry, 197

Marotta, Daniel, 90
Martin, Marcus L., 101–2
Massengill, Gerald, 104, 297
Mayes, Frances, 57
McBryde, John McLaren, 278, 279
McComas, James "Jim," 137
McCoy, Lenwood, 97–98, 145, 148
McDonnell, Robert F., 153–54
McFarland, Derrick, 18, 106
McNamee, Mark, 27, 69, 79, 82, 84, 130, 138, 142, 150, 152
media, 25–26, 85, 86–95, 111, 288; backlash against, 87, 90–91; positive aspects of, 89, 91–92; Roy's comments to, 25–26, 74–75, 146, 246, 248; school shootings sensationalized by, 87–90; talking points for university employees and, 91, 141; Virginia Tech's culture of silence and, 68–73, 90–95, 141–43
memorials, inclusion of shooters in, 251–52
mental health services, 250–51, 293–94, 295, 311–12n.10. *See also* Cook Counseling Center
Meredith, Joe W., Jr., 139
Merwin, W. S., 289
Metz, Nancy, 31
military training, 136, 236–37
Miller, Robert, 41, 44, 143

Mill High School, Millbrae, Calif., 236

"Modest Proposal, A" (Swift), 42, 164, 206

Moore, Michael, 216

Morva, William, 18–19, 105–6

Mosaic Assessment of Student Threats (MAST), 173–74

Moses Lake, Wash., shootings (1996), 197

Myrick, Joel, 218

Narcissistic Personality Disorder (NPD), 234

Nash, Mary Beth, 147

National Collegiate Athletic Association (NCAA), 136–37

National Research Council and Institute of Medicine, 216

National Rifle Association (NRA), 142, 199, 219, 222–23

National Science Foundation (NSF), 132

NBC, video package sent by Cho to, 79, 85, 86, 87–88, 89, 107, 115, 262

New Bedford High School, attack planned on, 235, 236

Newman, Katherine, 69, 115–16, 197, 235, 236, 280

New River Valley Community Services (NRVCS), 64–65

Newson, Elizabeth, 200

New York Times, 23, 136–37, 143

New York Times Magazine, 287

New York Yankees, 92

Nickel, Patricia Mooney, 106

Niles, Jerome A., 131, 142, 144, 152

Norris, Lisa, 67, 269

Norris Hall, after shootings, 285–86, 293

Nowak, Jerzy, 293

O'Brien, Soledad, 75

Odighizuwa, Peter, 218

Office for Student Life and Advocacy (OSLA), 130

Office of the Attorney General of the Commonwealth of Virginia, 152–54

Office of the Dean of Students (ODS), 130–31, 142

Office of University Legal Counsel, 79, 82, 84

older generation, interaction of young people with, 277–78

On Killing (Grossman), 225, 236–37

Oregon State, 219

O'Rourke, Kimberly, 77

O'Toole, Mary Ellen, 226

Pak, SuChin, 261

Panel Report, 3, 67, 93, 94, 101, 119, 130–31, 264, 267, 279, 281; on Cho's childhood and mental health, 73; on Cho's contacts with Cook Counseling Center, 3, 62–64; on Cho's handling at Carilion St. Albans, 64–65; on Cho's harassment of female students, 64; on Cho's letter to English department, 81; on Cho's medical history, 169–70; on Cho's roommates' concerns, 64; on contacting of parents, 176; on inadequate information sharing, 142–43, 170, 171; on regulation of guns on campus, 217–18, 219; security recommendations in, 131, 293; "Summary of Key Findings" in, 63, 66; threat assessment teams recommended by, 144–45, 175–76; timeline in, 102, 108; "University Setting and Campus Security" in, 154–55; "Virginia Tech Cooperation" in, 148–49; on Virginia Tech Judicial System, 144

Panel Review, 5, 92, 96–111, 149; Cho's academic and mental health records kept from, 70–71; interviews with, monitored by university attorneys, 147, 148; McCoy as official liaison with, 97–98, 145, 148; Roy's interview with,

62, 145, 146–47, 149; subpoena
power lacked by, 149
parent-child relationships, 277–78,
279–84
passive voice constructions, 105
Pearl, Miss., shooting (1997), 218
Pedagogy of the Oppressed, The
(Freire), 168
Pendergrass, Barbara, 130
Penn State, 133
Perfect Student, 167, 169, 178–79
permanent records, 171–72, 174–75
Peterson, Celeste, 93
Pinker, Steven, 232–33, 234
Policy Group, 68, 97, 99–102, 104–11,
149, 296, 297, 298
Pornography (Itzin), 199
Powell, Alma and Colin, 184–85
privacy of students and student rec-
ords: federal and state laws on, 98–
99, 141–43, 170–71; permanent
records and, 171–72, 174; Virginia
Tech's obsession with, 70–71, 72,
98–99, 110, 141–43, 152, 281

racial prejudice, 259–74; access to
higher education and, 272; ascribed
to Virginia Tech, 268–69; in Cho's
worldview, 267–68; identification
of Cho as Asian male and, 260–62,
264–65, 266; racial diversity of
Cho's victims and, 266–67; reluctance to give feedback to people of
color and, 265–66; Roy accused of,
270–71; Roy's experiences of, 259–
60, 271–72; in small rural towns,
271–72
Rage (King), 197–98
Rampage (Newman), 69, 115–16, 197,
235, 236, 280
Ramsey, Evan, 227–28
RateVTTeachers.com, 81, 187–88
"Raw Fisher," 70–71
Ress, David, 103, 104, 296–98
"Reuben Bright" (Robinson), 285–86

Reynolds, Roscoe, 224
Richardson, Robert, 172–73
Richmond Times-Dispatch, 103, 110,
296–98
Ridge, Tom, 102
Roanoke Times, 20, 72, 92, 96–97, 207
*Robert Richardson vs. Concord School
District (IN)*, 172–73
Robinson, E. A., 285–86
Rolland, Kayla, 221
Romeo and Juliet (Shakespeare), 230,
231
ROTC, 136, 220
Royer, Randall Todd, 263
Rude, Carolyn, 19, 25, 67, 79, 84–85,
149
Ruemmler, Kathryn, 74
Ruggiero, Cheryl, 31, 33, 36, 37, 38,
39, 40, 41, 52
Rutherford Institute, 172–73

Santos, Carlos, 102
Scalia, Christopher, 207, 208
school shootings, 6–7, 213–39,
294–95; amok state and, 232–34;
attention-getting in, 116; availability of guns and, 216, 220–25, 238;
averting of, 234–36, 295; common
characteristics of, 214–15; by girls
and women, 232; girls often targeted in, 232; gun as weapon of
choice in, 216–17; highest death
tolls in, 22; inner-city violence vs.,
115–16; media coverage of, 89–90;
planning of, 216; predictive factors
and, 216; regulation of guns on
campus and, 217–20; risk factors
for, 226–27; statistics on risk of,
225–26; vulnerability of classrooms
to, 219–20, 238
Second Amendment, 199–200,
222–23
"Second Coming, The" (Yeats), 48
sestinas, 56–58, 60–61, 300
"Seung" (poem), 50–51, 52–53, 56

Shakespeare, William, 230, 231, 245, 254, 257

Shepherd, Tammy, 14–15, 19–20, 41, 55

"Shine" (song), 230

Shrader, Jeffrey, 147

Sierra Leone, 15–17, 23, 43, 53, 60, 89, 123, 181, 234, 253

Skadden, Arps, 281

Sluss, Michael, 96–97

Smith, Ed, 17

Smith, Vicki, 94

Smoot, Raymond D., Jr., 139

Sood, Aradhana A. "Bela," 101–2

Spencer, Brenda, 232

Squires Student Center, 106

Steger, Charles W., 21, 52, 74, 76, 79, 81, 82, 84, 96–98, 132, 139–40, 145, 146, 147, 150, 289; ban on communication between Roy and, 73–77; delay in responding to double homicide and, 96–97, 99–109; Kaine's support for, 93–94; personality and demeanor of, 103, 138; petition in support of, 78; silence of, with regard to Cho shootings, 5, 68, 69, 71, 72, 91, 92, 111, 298

Stevens, Siaka, 89

Strickland, Diane, 146

Student A (troubled student in English department), 155–64, 165, 269–70

Student Affairs, 27, 32, 130, 155, 159

student evaluations, 81, 187–88

Students for Concealed Carry on Campus (SCCC), 219, 220

superpredators, 170

Supreme Court, U.S., 221, 222

Sutphin, Eric, 18, 106

Swift, Jonathan, 42, 164, 206

"Tech Way," 135–36

terrorism, 262–64

"There Is an Unknown on Campus" (Nickel), 106

"This Is the Beat Generation" (Holmes), 287

Thompson, Eric, 220

threat assessment, Mosaic approach to, 173–74

threat assessment teams, 144–45, 159, 175–77

Three Musketeers, The, 80

Thurston High School, Oreg., shootings (1998), 215

Tillar, Thomas C., Jr., 139

Time, 213, 225

Timimi, Ali Al-, 264

Tolkien, J. R. R., 275–76

Torgersen, Paul E., 137–38

"To the Young Who Want do Die" (Brooks), 54

Treatment Advocacy Center, 189

Trench Coat Mafia, 235, 236

troubled, meaning of term, 35

troubled students: advising, 189–90; contacting family of, 176; English department's code for handling of, 41–42, 146; identified as potential threat, 176–77; increase in number of, 35, 163; permanent records and, 171–72, 174–75; personal risk taken on by those who deal with, 165; scarcity of treatment facilities for, 189; Student A, 155–64, 165, 269–70; teachers asked to take on too much responsibility for, 185–87; threat assessment teams and, 144–45, 159, 175–77; training teachers to deal with, 189; Virginia Tech guidelines and, 165–66

Tuusula, Finland, shootings (2007), 268

universities. See colleges and universities

University of Arkansas' Creative Writing program, 37, 194–96, 286–87

University of Texas-Austin Tower sniper (1966), 233
University of Virginia, Wise, 207–8
University Relations, 25–26, 91, 102
University Studies, 134–35
USA Today, 93, 94, 221

Van Sant, Gus, 229
Vietnam War, 237
violence, 250; among school-age children, 185–87; in popular culture, 197–200, 203, 209, 228–29, 236–37; statistics on, 225–26; in students' writings, 203–4, 206–8
Viorst, Milton, 263
Virginia State police, 80
Virginia Tech: athletics at, 126–29, 136–37, 139; ban on communication between Roy and central administration of, 73–77, 154; bomb threats at (April 13, 2007), 106; campus security at, 70, 131, 154–55, 293; class registration problematic at, 134; declaration of majors at, 134–35; delay in response to double homicide at, 5, 68, 75, 93, 96–97, 99–109, 296–97; difficulties in getting help for troubled student at, 30, 32, 35–36, 41, 43–44, 63, 67; expansion of student body at, 134; graduation at (2007), 92; guns banned at, 52, 217; handling of troubled students at, 131; hierarchical system at, 104, 135–36; international students and faculty at, 119, 120, 121; litigation concerns and, 4, 150, 153; mascot of (Hokie bird), 123–25; memorial service at, 78, 126, 129; memorial stone at, 252; military heritage of, 136; obsessed with student privacy, 70–71, 72, 98–99, 110, 141–43, 152, 281; one-year anniversary of shootings at, 285–91; public outrage at administration of, 67–68, 92, 93; restrictions on legal advice

for employees of, 145–46; resumption of classes at, 78–84, 85; Roy's career at, 122–23; settlement of victims' families and, 296; silence of, with regard to Cho shootings, 5, 68–73, 90–95, 111, 141–43, 264; "Top 30" goal of, 132–33; Town-Gown fusion and, 122–26
Virginia Tech (Wallenstein), 278
Virginia Tech Police Department (VTPD), 20–22, 27, 32, 64, 70, 74, 79–80, 84, 102, 103–5, 106, 108, 120, 135, 142, 155, 219, 293; given information by Roy, 26–27, 74, 75, 149–50; Student A and, 159–61, 162, 165. *See also* Flinchum, Wendell

Wallenstein, Peter, 278
Washington Post, 70–71
Watford, Bevlee, 130
Westfield High School, Chantilly, Va., 116–18
Westside Middle School shootings (1998), 222, 235
"What's Writing Got to Do with Campus Terrorism?" (Anson), 203
Whitehead, James T., 194, 287
Whitman, Charles, 233
Women's Center, 155
Woodham, Luke, 218, 264
World War II, 237
Writers in the Schools, 205
writing, 191–212; crossing generational divide in, 282–84; speech vs., 191–92. *See also* creative writing
Wyatt, Randy, 207

Yeats, William Butler, 48

zero tolerance policies, 172–73, 174, 177

About
the
Author

LUCINDA ROY is an Alumni Distinguished Professor at Virginia Tech, where she has taught since 1985. Author of the novels *Lady Moses* and *The Hotel Alleluia* and two poetry collections, she is the recipient of numerous writing and teaching awards, including a statewide Outstanding Faculty Award in 2005. From 2002 to 2006, she served as chair of Virginia Tech's Department of English. She was named as 2009 Newsmaker of the Year by Virginia Press Women.